Capitalism, Inequality and Labour in India

AF172916

Jan Breman takes dispossession as his central theme in this ambitious analysis of labour bondage in India's changing political economy from 1962 to 2017. When, in the remote past, tribal and low-caste communities were attached to landowning households, their lack of freedom was framed as subsistence-oriented dependency. Breman argues that with colonial rule came the intrusion of capitalism into India's agrarian economy, leading to a decline in the idea of patronage in the relationship between bonded labour and landowner. Instead, servitude was reshaped as indebtedness. As labour was transformed into a commodity, peasant workers were increasingly pushed out of agriculture and the village, but remained adrift in the wider economy. The cohorts of this footloose workforce are exploited when their labour power is required and excluded when they are surplus to demand. The outcome is progressive inequality that is thoroughly capitalist in nature.

JAN BREMAN is Honorary Fellow of the Institute of Social History, Amsterdam, and Emeritus Professor at the University of Amsterdam. He is the author of many publications, including *Footloose Labour: Working in India's Informal Economy*, for which he was awarded the Edgar Graham Book prize by SOAS.

Capitalism, Inequality and Labour in India

Jan Breman

University of Amsterdam

CAMBRIDGE
UNIVERSITY PRESS

University Printing House, Cambridge CB2 8BS, United Kingdom

One Liberty Plaza, 20th Floor, New York, NY 10006, USA

477 Williamstown Road, Port Melbourne, VIC 3207, Australia

314-321, 3rd Floor, Plot 3, Splendor Forum, Jasola District Centre, New Delhi - 110025, India

103 Penang Road, #05-06/07, Visioncrest Commercial, Singapore 238467

Cambridge University Press is part of the University of Cambridge.

It furthers the University's mission by disseminating knowledge in the pursuit of education, learning and research at the highest international levels of excellence.

www.cambridge.org
Information on this title: www.cambridge.org/9781108712279
DOI: 10.1017/9781108687485

First published 2019
First paperback edition 2022

A catalogue record for this publication is available from the British Library

ISBN 978-1-108-48241-7 Hardback
ISBN 978-1-108-71227-9 Paperback

Contents

vi   Contents

Figures

The photographs were taken by Ravi Agarwal in Surat city and its rural hinterland, and are reproduced with his permission. Together with 100 more, they illustrate the text of *Down and Out: Labouring under Global Capitalism,* a colour photobook edited by Jan Breman & Arvind Das (text); Ravi Agarwal (photographs); Brinda Datta (design). New Delhi: Oxford University Press/Amsterdam: Amsterdam University Press, 2000.

Preface

This study is a synthesis of my research on labour bondage in India between 1962 and 2017. The focus is on what has happened since the country became a sovereign state in the middle of the twentieth century. To find out how labour entrapped under duress fared and how it was conceived, classified and treated over several decades it is imperative to trace the imprint left by colonial rule and the anti-colonial fight on the working classes in the lower realms of what was essentially a peasant economy and society. Moreover it is impossible to understand the phenomenon of human bondage in the twenty-first century without contextualizing the problem as part of a globalized economy dictated by the interests of capital at the expense of labour.

In the first part I relate how politics and governance have dealt with the issue of bondage. Most official committees or panels set up to document the labour regime recommended solutions to the problems they identified. However, first the colonial state and then the post-colonial government by and large soft-pedalled, ignored or squarely denied that bondage was practised – and now, with equal subterfuge, that it continues to exist. I rejected this as a blatant misapprehension and backed my comments up with empirical investigations I conducted in Gujarat; what's more, I argued, bondage had a much wider prevalence. For more than half a century my reports on the plight of the working poor remained at odds with the acknowledged wisdom as recorded in the annals of the state.

The second part examines the history of labour bondage in West India. The tribal peasants who tilled plots in a rudimentary fashion and shifting cultivation on the central plain were dispossessed by bands of settlers in the unknown past. The colonists established themselves on the caste-tribe frontier – the site of a clash of civilizations throughout the subcontinent of South Asia – as owners of the land. They opened the land for regular and sedentary cultivation and upgraded themselves in the evolving Hinduized hierarchy by attaching displaced members from tribal communities in servitude to their agrarian property. This was the origin of the *hali* system that officials of the East India Company found widely

practised in the southern districts of Gujarat when they set up administration in the early nineteenth century. With the abolition of slavery a few
decades later bondage was legally construed in the imperialized domains
as a labour contract, voluntarily engaged into on receipt of an advance,
with the obligation to repay the debt incurred or – if that turned out to be
impossible (as it always was) – to work it off. Debt bondage was thus the
operational device that enabled a dominating caste-class of landowners
to secure a workforce at the lowest possible price – the provision of bare
livelihood – and spare themselves the demeaning task of tilling the fields.

I have analyzed agrestic servitude as it operated in the precolonial and
colonial past in terms of patronage and exploitation. The intrusion of
capitalism into the rural economy towards the end of the nineteenth
century changed the nature of the master-servant relationship. A process
of commodification eroded the features of patronage but intensified the
exploitation of the workforce, which now took the shape of an agrarian
proletariat still locked in bondage. In the growing resistance to colonial
rule the leadership of the Congress movement decided to condone the
practice and prioritize the interests of the peasant elite. Rather than
blaming the main landowners for the continued imposition of unfree
labour, they accused the landless of seeking security in attachment. The
mission launched by the disciples of Mahatma Gandhi in south Gujarat
to civilize the tribal castes subordinated instead of emancipated them.
The struggle for national freedom was waged with the promise to return
land to the tiller, but the landless remained as dispossessed as before.
The state of pauperism in which I found them in the early 1960s was
not the cause but the consequence of labour bondage.

The third part describes and analyzes events in the last half century,
roughly from 1970 onwards, on the basis of fieldwork carried out in my
old as well as new rural and urban research locales in Gujarat. The *hali*
system as it used to operate in the past had disintegrated, but its disappearance was not due to any action taken by the government. It was the
outcome of the casualization of employment, the replacement of farm
servants with daily wage labour, which was available throughout the year
in ample supply. The landowning and landless households had distanced
themselves from each other and a noticeable feature of their falling apart
was that the farmers did not allow the labourers they engaged to live on
their premises. The majority of landless households were resettled in
colonies on the outskirts of the village. Driving them out emphasized
and visibly demarcated the social marginality of the bottom class-caste in
the countryside.

Of great significance next was the increasing mobility of rural labour.
The land-poor and landless, a very high proportion of the agrarian

workforce without viable means of production, were pushed out of their habitat for lack of regular employment. The off-and-on search for work elsewhere was caused to no less extent by the influx during the peak season of the annual cycle of migrants willing to work for lower wages who proved also to be more pliable than local labourers. Better connectivity widened the scale of the labour market but the migration, both intra-rural and rural-urban, has remained circular in nature: workers depart, only to return after a season or at the end of a short working life. By now it was clear that the long-awaited transformation from a rural-agrarian to an urban-industrial economy and society would not take place. The planned transition to a welfare state with formal conditions of employment for the country's swelling workforce made redundant in agriculture was aborted. Instead of coming to enjoy the comfort of regularity, security and protection of a standard labour contract backed up by state-provided benefits of social welfarism, India's working masses were downgraded and subjected to exploitation as well as exclusion.

Labour is made mobile but exists in a state of immobility. Short of financial means for livelihood in the slack season, as well as for marking life-cycle events, such as weddings and deaths, the castes-classes at the bottom of the economy are forced to sell their labour value in advance to contractors or jobbers who, as agents of rural and urban employers, recruit them for a price lower than the going market rate. The workers leave home in debt and are supposed to work off the cash received while the wage balance they have earned is settled only on termination of their engagement. I have labelled this modality of employment neo-bondage, a form of unfree labour that thrives on the accumulation-dispossession syndrome made manifest in a mercantile-financialized type of capitalism. Indebtedness is the operational device of a political economy that has assumed hegemonic power in a globalized setting.

In the wake of Independence a civilizational heritage of engrained inequality did not dissolve but continued to exist in what was shaped as a growth strategy. Planners and politicians promised redistribution of the gains and an end to exclusion from mainstream society, but abysmally failed to deliver. Dispossession turned out to be a stretch on the road leading to disenfranchisement. Loss of property rights led to displacement, footlooseness and of late also to increasing disuse. Driven by neoliberal doctrine, informalization and circulation of labour have led to progressive inequality. A new class of nowhere people has emerged, forced to drift between what passes for 'home' and a place of 'work'. Putting the urban economy at the top of the agenda has greatly aggravated agrarian distress. The labouring poor are pushed out of their rural habitat because they lack regular employment but are not allowed to settle down in the places they go to find work. Locked away in difficult-to-access, jerry-built and unregulated shelters, they are well-nigh invisible in the countryside or on the city's outskirts. In their marginality they seem to pose no threat to the vested interests of capital and its agents. Dispossession has reached such a stage that for a substantial segment of the labouring poor self-employment, the remedy propagated in neoliberal doctrine as the way out of fast-growing worklessness, is made impossible. Driven by politics and governance 'the Gujarat model of growth and development' is a frightful one. Under the Hindutva banner this scenario has in the last few years been scaled up as a recipe for the country at large. Both in design and practice its policies discriminate against the people written about in this treatise and keep them beyond the pale of inclusion.

Acknowledgements

For Ilse, who shared my moments of sorrow and grief while I was engaged in the work that led to this book. The people who allowed me to get close to the work they do and the life they lead, while being denied the decency, respectability and dignity which should qualify their human existence, remain anonymous. I also owe a debt of gratitude to colleagues, companions and comrades – too many to name over more than half a century – who enabled me to write the story as it is.

Part I

Labour as Codified in the Annals of the State

1 The Country Liberated

In the Wake of Independence

Bonded labour has been a recurrent theme of research in my academic career. It was the focus of the anthropological fieldwork I conducted in 1961–2 as a Ph.D. student at the University of Amsterdam. My village-level investigations in south Gujarat concentrated on the changing relationship between the two classes/castes found at polar ends of the agrarian hierarchy: landless labourers who were members of a tribal community and their employers, big farmers whom I identified as a dominant caste of local landlords. To take stock of what was going on led me to find out how it had come about: I followed up my fieldwork by exploring colonial archives that shed light on the past. It was clear that the servitude of the agrarian underclass, framed in debt bondage, had over time lost its former character. A new generation's labour power, instead of being permanently appropriated in a beck-and-call relationship, was casualized as labourers took work as daily wage earners. The decisive features of agrarian bondage as it used to exist were, in my analysis, exploitation and patronage. I emphasized that the master-servant relationship or *halipratha* had its origin in an era when systematic market production was not yet of major importance and money played a minor role in the local exchange of goods and services. The pre-capitalist nature of the subsistence-oriented economy implied that engaging servants not only liberated the master and his family from the physical labour of cultivating the land but was also driven by his ambition to subordinate clients who became assets in gaining political power and social status (Breman 1974a). Being attached to a landlord willing to provide a livelihood was an attractive option for an agrarian underclass deprived of the chance to own land in their own right. As viewed from above, to become a *hali* was to access a secure and safe existence. Gandhian constructive workers concurred, and wrote up the relationship as compliance, an opinion I shall challenge later on:

It has become a matter of prestige in the Dubla community to be a Hali, to work for a Dhaniamo.[1] As a woman has no prestige in society without having a husband, similarly a Halpati without a Dhaniamo as his master has no prestige in his community. (Dave 1946: 18)

Mahatma Gandhi toured the countryside of south Gujarat in 1921 to inform himself on the problems of the peasantry. When he came to know of the condition in which the tribal Dubla community lived and worked he decided to call off the disobedience movement he had hoped to launch in Bardoli. How can we fight against colonial rule, the leader of the freedom movement exclaimed, when it implies tolerating a state of bondage in our own midst? Gandhi changed the name of this tribal community as a mark of their emancipation. Instead of being Dublas (their habitual name, which has the derogatory meaning of 'weaklings'), they would henceforth be labelled Halpatis or 'lords of the plough'. Sardar Patel fought and won the no-tax struggle of 1928 that stood to benefit the dominant landowning caste in Bardoli, wilfully ignoring the widespread system of bondage in the bottom ranks of the peasantry. However, the Congress leadership could not any longer avoid taking a firm stand on this issue. It was forced to respond to the mobilization of the land-poor and landless classes by an agrarian trade union in the 1930s. Agitating for tenancy reforms and abolition of *halipratha*, the participants of a mass rally called by the Gujarat branch of Kisan Sabha[2] dared to invade the 1938 meeting of the All India Congress Committee in a village close to Bardoli. In a subsequent meeting, Sardar Patel berated the underclass for lacking the drive to change their uncivilized way of life. He implored them to accept prohibition and abstain from drinking, to forgo borrowing from landowners and instead to save up and pay for the cost of their marriage and other life-cycle events themselves. In lengthy consultations between leading landowners and Gandhian spokesmen on behalf of the landless, an agreement was reached to end *halipratha*. The terms of the settlement included: debt cancellation beyond twelve years of service; a daily wage to be paid in cash (four-and-half *annas* for men and three for women); no ready-made food from the master's house or other perquisites, which had previously been given incidentally; and, finally, a workday lasting eight hours, possibly rising to ten hours in the peak season. In the presence of Mahatma Gandhi, who criticized landowners for their stinginess and urged the landless to live within their means, Bonded Labour Liberation Day was proclaimed on

[1] Dhaniamo was an honorific name for the benevolent landlord who saw to the well-being of his servants.
[2] Kisan Sabha was a radical union of land-poor and landless peasants.

26 January 1939. However, as I shall elaborate later on in this study, the deal was not enacted because employers proved to be unwilling to abide by the meagre terms of this compromise.

The process of agrarian growth described and analyzed in my dissertation indicated that the transition of agriculture to capitalism started in the final decades of the nineteenth century. A main yardstick was the switch from food grains to cash crops. Commercialization and monetization of the rural economy were benchmarks for the gradual transformation taking place. The new mode of production had major consequences for the pattern of employment. Commodification of labour found expression in the replacement of attached farm servants with daily wage earners hired whenever required. Their wage was somewhat higher in the peak season but very low in slack periods, which could last for three months – during which they were only employed off and on. The more sizeable landowners did not bother much about the sharp fluctuations in demand and continued to make use of farm servants to till their land, to take care of the cattle and to perform a variety of chores in the master's courtyard and house. But the features of patronage, which had earlier been inherent to their servitude, disappeared. Permission to build a hut on the master's land at a site close to his residence, which actually followed from the beck-and-call character of the relationship, was haltingly or no longer given. The same happened to the use of a small plot on which the *hali* was allowed to grow some grain to fall back on when out of work. Perquisites in addition to the daily grain ration, which also in the past had been favours arbitrarily given or withheld – such as some clothes at the change of season, a meal, tea or tobacco on busy days – also became rare or non-existent. What remained was naked exploitation in a thoroughly commodified relationship. This deterioration found expression in a lengthening of the workday and a marked reluctance to add further advances to the initial engagement 'loan', although such credit was badly needed because of the wage deficit. Employers were increasingly unwilling to take care of those among their *halis* who had fallen ill or grown old. Tales of a mutual trust in the pre-capitalist past, which evokes the image of a benevolent master and a loyal servant related to each other in a pseudo-familial and harmonious bond, have to be viewed with scepticism – if only because these narratives, put on record in colonial documents, were told by the landlords, while their serfs had neither voice nor visibility. But this repudiation should not lead us to deny that the ethos of capitalism resulted in a thorough restructuring in the mode of employment that connected bottom and top of the rural economy.

Gandhian social workers were horrified to see the misery among the landless when they started to move around among the down and out in the rural landscape. In an encounter in the mid-1920s, which was brought to the notice of Mahatma Gandhi, two of his disciples had a conversation with a Dubla woman sitting in front of a hut with her seven children. In a column entitled 'Face to Face with the Pauper', Gandhi wrote up the answers they got to their questions:

'Where is your man? Gone out?' 'The master has summoned him and he has gone there.' The master happened to be known to one of us. The family were servants (or slaves?) of this master who ill-treated them and the poor man had fled from his clutches. But the master had traced him out and one might well imagine what had happened to the wretch. As though this was not enough, we asked one more question before we left her in peace. 'Did you go to work today?' 'How could I go? Who would take care of these children?' We were silenced, but in a moment we mustered courage to say to her: 'If you have a wheel, the children can playfully spin on it, and you can earn a few coppers.' (Gandhi 1927a)

After Independence the government of the Bombay state, which also incorporated Gujarat, set up a panel for 'suggesting measures necessary for rehabilitating this class of agricultural labourers and for enabling them to live a life consistent with human dignity and self-respect'. The two economists commissioned for the job reported that the initial loan that attached the worker was not paid off but steadily increased to a much higher amount because the low wage received did not permit debt redemption. They found it impossible to gather information on indebtedness since the illiterate *halis* had no clue when, what and how much they had 'borrowed'. Even the masters did not always keep account and on being asked were apt to mention a fictitious amount, arrived at by inflating and converting in cash what they had given in kind. The tribal identity of the land-poor and landless underclasses – estimated conservatively at one-fifth of the rural population – confirmed their backward condition and lack of bargaining power. In order to defuse rising class conflict and to prevent the political radicalism that had begun to gain ground from spreading, the report argued that abolition of the *hali* system was urgently required. The deep misery in which these rural poor lived required many further measures, including a wage hike. But all reforms would turn out to be ineffective, the authors argued, as long as agricultural labour remained stuck in a mindset that prevented progress:

The Hali and his children take for granted the mould of life in which they are born. Long years of suppression have so devitalised them that they have not even the strength of dreaming of a better life. Custom and tradition have stultified not only their living but also their aspirations. Their tallest prayer is, to be blessed with a *dhaniyamo* who is kind and considerate. No wonder, there are many Halis who in their heart of heart dread the abolition of the Hali system. (Report of the Hali Labour Enquiry Committee 1948: 36)

This assessment put the onus for ending labour bondage on its victims, who were blamed for their pauperized mindset, rather than on the master who forced the farm servant to live in his shadow in order to restrain subordinate manoeuvrability. The report was not made public by the Government of Bombay but in a press note the minister in charge (Morarji Desai – who had ordered the enquiry and hailed from the heartland of *halipratha* himself) and the labour minister (Gulzarilal Nanda) jointly went on record as stating that since the system had never been legally sanctioned there was no need to declare it illegal. A press note was issued informing the public that an amicable settlement had been arrived at between Kheduts (farmers) and Halpatis (landless labourers) of the Surat District in a meeting held in Bardoli. Representatives from both sides had agreed that abolition of the *hali* system of forced labour was in their mutual interest. The terms of the settlement stipulated wages for casually or yearly employed male and female labourers as well as for females and children hired for domestic purposes. The Bardoli agreement, which came into force on 17 June 1948, declared the *hali* system abolished and secured for the landless labourers decent working and living conditions (Government of India, Ministry of Labour 1952: 92; Shah 1958: 209–11). However, the Congress Agrarian Reforms Committee in 1951 reported that labour bondage continued to be practised in Gujarat and sharply criticized the party leadership for not having addressed the problem of landless labour in the agrarian reforms after Independence. Central government's 1948 appeal that a minimum wage be fixed for agricultural labour was in vain and Bombay was one of the many states that failed to act upon it. The Scheduled Areas and Scheduled Tribes Commission wrote in its annual report of 1960–1 that, despite the claim of the by now separate state of Gujarat, the system of bonded labour had still not been eradicated. The leadership of the ruling party insisted, as before, that this was because the victims did not want to terminate their bondage. In 1963 I heard Morarji Desai – by now minister of finance in the central government – again arguing along these lines. In a meeting held in an orchard close to the location of my fieldwork this prominent senior politician of the Congress Party maintained that the end of rural poverty was high on his party's agenda. He called on the Halpatis drummed up for the occasion to escape their bondage by not taking loans for marriage and abandoning sinful habits such as drinking liquor (Breman 1985: 146–7).

Phasing out Bondage?

Acknowledging the massive number and importance of workers at the bottom in the prime sector of the economy, the Indian government conducted a large-scale Agricultural Labour Enquiry (ALE) in 1950–1 to monitor their condition in 800 villages spread throughout the country. In a survey covering 100,000 families data was compiled on land-holding, employment, wage rates and means of payment, household income and expenditure. Agricultural labourers were defined as 'all those who work in the fields for wages'. The scope for non-agrarian work was found to be quite limited. There was a bewildering variety of engagement contracts and means of remuneration. Average waged employment amounted to about 200 days a year for males in West India. This figure was much lower for daily wage earners, while farm servants classified as attached had the highest number of workdays. Women and children were hired less frequently, particularly in the slack season. Male casual workers were found to be paid less than R. 1 a day, while labourers permanently contracted received at least 30 per cent less. Of course, the rates for women and children at work were fixed at a much lower level. The national average annual income of an agricultural labour family stood at Rs. 447 or Rs. 104 per capita, going down to respectively Rs. 391 and Rs. 91 in West India, which had the highest proportion of landless households. Average expenditure reached Rs. 468 for a family or Rs. 107 per capita in the country at large, an amount that nearly every-where was higher than earned income. Of the family budget 85 per cent had to be spent on food, almost exclusively consisting of grain, leaving next to nothing for other bare necessities. The deficit underscores the hardly surprising finding that about half of these families were indebted, confirming the indigence in which this underclass was sunk. In a review of the findings – laid down in eleven volumes and 3,000 pages – Alice and Daniel Thorner wrote that this was how *not* to conduct a large-scale agrarian survey. Their main critical query concerned the way in which agricultural labour had been divided in 'attached' as against 'casual'. Although this was the most fundamental distinction made, the size of the first category had not been defined properly and was therefore highly underestimated in the investigations (Thorner, A. & D. 1962: 173–89). A second round of the same enquiry a few years later, of a much better quality, reported no improvement. Poverty was as rampant, as before, if not more so due to stagnating or even falling wages. The proportion of agricultural labour households in debt at the all-India level had increased from 45 per cent in 1950–1 to 64 per cent in 1956–7 and the average amount of debt had nearly doubled (Government of India, Labour

Bureau, Ministry of Labour and Employment, Agricultural Labour in India, 1960, vol. I: 225). One out of four landless households were listed as attached, a much higher figure than found in the first enquiry. To say that labour bondage had gone up would be a debatable conclusion because of methodological inconsistency between the two rounds. While in the first enquiry wages earned by members of the household was the criterion, in the second enquiry days of employment was the measure for classification. The finding now reported that one-quarter of agricultural labourers were not free to decide for whom to work must have been quite embarrassing politically and in terms of policy. After all, social justice and the making of a welfare state were codified in India's Constitution, objectives fundamental to formulating the ambitious body of labour regulations that were enacted.

The Indian government was fully cognizant that systems of agrarian bondage continued to exist. In 1948 P. S. Dhamne was appointed as officer on special duty, forced labour in the Ministry of Labour with the instruction to study the various legal enactments – central, provincial and Indian states – and all available literature relating to forced labour. He was asked to submit a report 'indicating the extent to which the existing legislation was inadequate for stopping forced labour, what further legislation was required and which of the defects could be cured by administrative action commenting generally on matters connected with the subject' (Government of India, Ministry of Labour 1956). The official found himself in a conundrum as to whether or not to include debt bondage as forced or compulsory labour. He defined the still-existent practice as all work or service exacted from any person under the menace of any penalty and for which the said person had not offered himself voluntarily. His initial argument was that the peasant worker was not coerced because he did not attach himself involuntarily. Besides, repayment of the loan that marked the beginning of the relationship would set him free again. But then Dhamne conceded that this option did not materialize since the low wages paid meant the worker was unable to settle his debt by working it off. Having made up his mind that debt bondage was indeed a form of forced labour, Dhamne backed up his conclusion by pointing out that it was not countenanced by law, which inflicted the punishment of a fine or imprisonment for unlawful compulsion to labour against the will of a person:

On the contrary all Provincial Governments and some State Governments have enacted legislation to check this practice and relieve the debtors from the clutches of the creditors; yet it has not been completely uprooted. Many a time the whole family of the debtor has to work for such creditor. Though the debt is usually meant to be repaid, it is never repaid and the obligation to render service becomes perpetual. (Government of India, Ministry of Labour 1956: 40).

Elaborating on the prevalence of debt bondage in different parts of the country, Dhamne also highlighted the *hali* system of south Gujarat with details extracted from the Report of the Hali Labour Enquiry Committee already discussed. Clearly taken aback by the findings, the authorities claimed in a loose, one-page note inserted in the official publication that 'the report relates to the period 1949–51 and nothing therein should be taken to indicate that forced labour is still prevalent in the country'.

In the first round of the ALE the meaning of 'attached' had not been specified, but the official in charge of the investigations in the second round was not shy of clarifying the label as servitude. This was A. M. Lorenzo, director of the Government Labour Bureau, who in his earlier job as an academic at the University of Lucknow had published a monograph in which he elaborated on systems of labour bondage or agrestic serfdom practised in Northern India (Lorenzo 1943; see also Desai 1942). In a few states special measures had been taken to resettle the landless on waste land or vacant holdings when extradited from their hut on the master's land. Their shelter was as wretched as it had always been and its inventory was best described by the lack of it (Breman 2007b: 36). The Hali Labour Enquiry Committee's recommendation that liberated farm servants be given revenue-free land grants (*gamtals*) had been sanctioned for only a few villages. The scheme was urgently required in view of the subhuman standard of the huts in which the landless were made to live:

Almost invariably, they are improvised out of inadequate and inferior material, with the consequences that they do not provide adequate protection against rain water for some time and water percolates into the hut from many spots. There is no arrangement for proper ventilation. Practically none of the huts inspected by us were divided or partitioned in some sort of apartments to ensure privacy. [It is] Only when the inside space has to be shared with domesticated animals that some kind of provisional demarcation is made with a few bamboos attached to the wooden pillars supporting the structure. The inside of the hut, therefore, is in perpetual darkness lit up occasionally by the fire place during the day and by a crude kerosene lamp for some time at night. The provision of the kitchen inside the hut, made of lightly ignitable material, no wonder, leads to frequent fires, reduces the hut to ashes and destroying the small belongings of the Halis ... For the size of the Hali family the space inside the hut is inadequate. Investigation into this aspect indicated 20 square feet of living space on average per individual. This space is further reduced when animals share the hut in common with the Hali. (Report of the Hali Labour Enquiry Committee 1948: 18)

The investigators specified the *halis'* meagre belongings. Their estimated value was Rs. 11 and 6 *annas* per household, hardly more than the the the head of the household's monthly income could amount to. The second ALE concluded that a combination of liabilities – immense poverty, ignorance, underemployment, lack of occupational diversity and the closed character of the rural economy – meant that agricultural labourers were prone to live in perpetual debt.

The Government of Gujarat, prompted by a series of clashes between landowners and landless labourers, appointed a committee in 1962 to propose a minimum wage rate for employment in agriculture. The chairman was one of the two panellists who had drafted the report fourteen years before. He had then added a minute of dissent, arguing that the recommended pay of R. 1 a day, scorned by Mahatma Gandhi as much too low, was in his opinion unduly high and not affordable for the farmers; according to him, 12 *annas* for men and 9 for women would have been good enough. In his role as chairman of the state committee set up to advise at which level to fix a minimum wage for agricultural labour, M. B. Desai remained as biased as before. Respected for his intimate knowledge of Gujarat's rural economy and hailing from the class of landlords himself, he stood out as the committee's key member and main author of the new report, which was submitted in 1966. Although less prevalent than earlier, *halipratha* had not yet ended – as I also concluded in my fieldwork-based study pertaining to the early 1960s. Over time the percentage of the tribal land-poor and landless casualized as daily wage earners had increased. But attached servants working throughout the year for the same master were still a sizeable category. Supervisory cultivation had also spread to a middle tier of landowners: growing cash crops, initially cotton, these well-to-do farmers had replaced their own labour with that of permanent servants attached to their household. Kanbi Patels in particular were keen to convert their upward mobility to dominant caste status and used the acquired prosperity to opt for conspicuous leisure. However, in their newly adopted lifestyle they abandoned the custom of acting as – or at least pretending to act as – benevolent masters for their debt-bonded subordinates. From the very beginning their treatment, in proper capitalist fashion, was more exploitative than the patron-like behaviour of the Anavil Brahmin landlords in the past had been (Breman 1985). The ranks of the Kanbi Patels also vehemently opposed social work activity aimed at uplifting tribal communities. When Gandhian disciples opened a night school to teach children of the local landless the basics of reading and writing in a village near Bardoli they were forced to close down when confronted by the hostility of the local notables. In his fight for national freedom Gandhi insisted on the emancipation of the landless underclass and campaigned in vain for their inclusion in mainstream society. Disdain among the rural powerful for the Mahatma and his morality grew when he baptized them as Halpatis, urging them to abandon their derogated Dubla identity and rise up from subordination.

As the Hali Labour Enquiry had done in 1948, the report of the Minimum Wages Advisory Committee was prone to attribute the tenacious hold of labour bondage one-sidedly to the defective behaviour of the landless. The landless were blamed for lack of efficiency, accused of being being work-shy and too apathetic to search for other employment and criticized for their addiction to energy-sapping vices such as drinking liquor and eating meat:

Visits to *halpati* colonies presented a picture of unhealthy and unhygienic conditions of accommodation with meagre household effects for less than a bare living. The surroundings were filthy and neglected. Vices, particularly of illicit drinking were the rule. The *halis* and their families were under-nourished and in poor health. Large families with many children doing nothing or little and living a purposeless or directionless life were other tragic features. Some *dhaniamas* claimed to provide medical aid to the *halis*. In quite a few cases *halis* conveyed that medical expenses on them were adjusted against the wage they earned later. The borrowings and indebtedness ordinarily against future wages and default in repayment of loans were rampant. Even earnings were insufficient for living. Increased debts could thus be the inevitable phenomenon. (Government of Gujarat 1966: 39.)

But the former mood of acquiescence had made way to a disgruntled demeanour among the landless, who began to be obstinate and assertive in the face of oppression. It made farmers wary of engaging new *halis* since many in the younger generation resisted the harsh treatment meted out to them and deserted their master. The landowners were unable to resort to legal action to recoup the credit invested in the labourer's permanent availability. The accumulated debt was a mixture of cash payment and a wide variety of allowances in kind. Many of these perks did not involve any extra outlay but were in the character of leftovers, as in the case of hand-me-down clothes given a new lease of life after having been worn by members of the master's household. On days of unemployment, which amounted to more than 100 a year, the provision of a grain ration (*khavathi,* meaning to eat), was of crucial importance for feeding the labouring household. The report commented that when all these wage items, which also fluctuated seasonally, were computed in monetary terms, the total amount would probably add up to a cash payment even higher than the rate the committee was willing to contemplate. Moreover, the pivotal question was whether remuneration should be based on what the worker minimally needed to survive or on what his employer could afford to spend. The committee took a principled stand and decided that the recommended wage would have to be settled in cash only, since allowances in kind were considered to be degrading. Whimsically given or withheld, they undermined the dignity of the master's subordinates. The report signalled loud and clear that attachment in debt, while still practised, was obsolete and had to be wiped out:

The detestable *hali* system seems to have considerably loosened. There are now no restrictions on the Dubla halis to change their employers. Even then the methods of wage payment under the old system stick. It is not only exploitative but soul killing. The employer under the system is deprived of his emotional upsurge. He is not moved by the misery of the labourer. The compassion that he shows towards his Dubla worker is discretionary and *ad hoc*. The labourer under the system has lost all initiative and is an embodiment of frustration. (Government of Gujarat 1966: 64.)

Discussing a range of ameliorative measures, the onus was not on what the employers should do – pay a significantly higher wage – but on action the Minimum Wages Advisory Committee (MWAC) urged the government to take – for instance, to provide health care, education, housing and public food distribution and even to arrange subsidized utility clothing for the landless. Paying for these badly needed improvements out of an increased wage packet had to wait until the business of farming became more productive and profitable. Until then the state had to step in and be held accountable for raising the appallingly low living standards of the labouring poor. The recommended remedy was of vital importance since widespread evidence of a looming class conflict threatened to upset the spirit of togetherness that still existed:

The implication of a lack of policy for agrarian labour to the political and social stability would be easily appreciated. The developments in Asia and Africa are an eye-opener. The working class in general and the agrarian labourer in particular has retained their moorings to our basic philosophy of life and living. They might have grown restless and frustrated now and again, but by and large they have shown great patience in the otherwise discouraging situation around them. This is extremely healthy for the country and for all its citizens. This, however, should not make us complacent. It should be treated as a favourable factor to do something quickly to improve the lot of those on whose faces we see signs of discontent and disparagement. (Government of Gujarat 1966: 78–9)

The ominous harangue ended with the warning that the forces of extremism were waiting to take over should these flashes of turmoil intensify and an appeal to all stakeholders to contribute to the realization of a society and socio-economic relationships acceptable to all. However, the wage proposed – a minor hike from the going rate of R. 1 for men to R. 1.5–2 rupees for men and 30 per cent less for women, notwithstanding an earlier statement in favour of equal pay for equal work – did not match the bare minimum an agricultural labour household needed to live on. One of the committee members, the leader of the Gandhian movement in South Gujarat, objected saying that the proposed rate would perpetuate immense poverty. He insisted that farmers in irrigated tracts, in particular, were able to pay much more. His plea to reconsider was to no avail and in the end he was persuaded to line up with the majority. Also, as the chairman pointed out, several factors tended to depress wages: the high pressure on land, together with the abundant supply of landless labour; the lack of employment in other sectors of the rural economy; the inclination of the underclass to stay put rather than move on in search of better employment; and the social and political leverage of the dominant castes in the countryside. Having received the recommendations of the MWAC, the government of Gujarat took six more years to prescribe a minimum wage. When finally enacted in 1972, it was set at such a low level that in order to survive the land-poor and landless had to incur debts to cover their budgetary deficit. Even the excessively low rate that had been fixed was not enforced. Was the committee's chairman justified when he strongly rejected the criticism that blamed the farmer-employers for their antisocial attitude? He explicitly stated that 'there is no need to single them out for a reactionary categorization. Like all social strata, the large bulk of them would be socially enlightened.' His postulate turned out to have been all too rosy in the light of later events. On a tour around his constituency, in the vicinity of my fieldwork locale, the minister in charge of minimum wage enactment was heckled by angry farmers. He pacified them with the curt comment that some laws such as the one they disputed were not meant to be implemented.

Waiting for the Welfare State

The report of the first National Commission on Labour (NCL), published in 1969, took for granted the long-awaited transition from an agrarian-rural to an industrial-urban economy. Progress was being made, although at a more sluggish pace than desired, but in line with the plans drawn up every five years. Reading through the pages one gets the impression that much had already been achieved. The checkpoints of the well-orchestrated transformation were itemized as self-sustained growth, rapid industrialization, development of agriculture, a meaningful rise in the people's standard of living, maximization of employment and equality of opportunity across all ranks. To top it all, the concentration of wealth and economic power had been successfully prevented. The wish list did not merely sum up the main objectives of India's economic and social policy but was also drafted with the belief that the designed blueprint was the roadmap politicians and policymakers felt bound by in what they promoted and managed to accomplish. The 'worker' was identified in the opening pages of the report as a man well adapted to the change going on. He was portrayed as a factory hand originally from the countryside but now firmly settled in the city with his family and far more urban in taste and outlook than his predecessor who still used to keep the connection with his village of origin intact:

The industrial worker of today has acquired a dignity not known to his predecessor. He is not any longer the unskilled coolie of the days gone by, engaged in an unending struggle to eke out his existence, neglected by society except for his labour, and with very limited aspirations. He has now a personality of his own. He shares the benefits, albeit meagre, which a welfare state with a vast population and inadequate resources can offer, and some more. He enjoys a measure of social security; he is secure in his employment once he enters it; he cannot be dismissed unjustly and has been given statutory protection against retrenchment and lay-off. (Government of India, Ministry of Labour, Employment and Rehabilitation 1969: 31–2)

I am intrigued by a footnote to this quoted passage that, evidently because of its derogatory meaning, 'the term coolie is now banned for official use' and shall come back to this official taboo later on. The account of labour conditions as they existed is equally phrased in hopeful terms. No doubt the progress made towards an urban-industrial way of life was much less noticeable in the countryside, still the abode of the large majority of the workforce, but we learn that over the years the profile of agricultural labour had also perceptibly changed for the better. He (yes, again the gendered idiom) is shown to have become politically conscious, eager to have his children educated, infused with higher aspirations than ever before and, among the younger generation in particular, not any longer focused on land and rurality. Anxious to move out, the labourers tend to be impatient about the slow growth of employment opportunities outside agriculture. In short, the report portrays a society set to develop fast and anxious to speed up the trajectory laid out to a much better future. The new labourer's prototype is a young male employed in modern industry, a literate and skilled factory hand committed to his regular and well-regulated job, being decently paid for his not unduly long workday, enjoying social security and protection and becoming well versed in an urban as well as a secular lifestyle.

The report takes for granted the institutional framework needed to bring about the emergence of industrial society and its socio-economic structure. Although a fully fledged industrial economy had not yet been established, its architecture was carefully designed in accordance with the directive principles of state policy summed up in the Constitution and prioritized in national objectives to establish a socialist society. In preparation, a legal and administrative infrastructure was needed. The report specified in great detail what all this entailed: a network of labour exchanges and training facilities; factory inspectors checking on working conditions, hours of work, protection against health hazards, availability of proper sanitation, canteens, etc.; mandatory regulations for fixing wages and paying bonuses; agencies to monitor the provision of social security benefits paid in case of sickness or on retirement; supervision of labour welfare and proper housing; the official facilitation of workers' associations and their promotion of collective action (see also Breman 1999a: 30–1). The number of trade unions had greatly increased, from 29 in 1927–8 to 13,023 in 1964–5. This sign of assertiveness becomes less impressive when we learn that their average membership had gone down from 3,594 initially to 592 in the previous year. Last but not least, a procedure for conciliation and arbitration had been instituted. A detailed set of arrangements for tripartite consultations in case of industrial disputes demonstrated the crucial presence of a government agency in the trajectory to industrialism. The framework for an urban-industrial society was in place but it certainly did not mean that all acts, ordinances and regulations were put into practice and had already enriched life and work for the targeted segment of the workforce. Public assistance in case of unemployment, disablement, old-age care and other instances of undeserved want also remained unaddressed until better times to come.

This is also where the good news dries up because many problems and obstacles are apparent on closer reading of the NCL report. To begin with, only a very small part of the workforce – in 1961, a mere 14 million out of a total of more than 189 million, or less than 8 per cent in the country at large – had been hired and paid for employment in what was called the organized or formal economy. This was the label applied to the waged workers who were supposed to benefit from the labour code outlined above. In addition to blue-collar manpower in registered industrial enterprises, they included a wide range of white-collar staff engaged in statal or parastatal trade and services – such as teachers, medical personnel, bank employees, clerks and other staff in corporate establishments, military and police of all ranks, government officials and, finally, all those at work in public utilities such as the electricity or water boards, bus and railway transport, post offices, ordnance undertakings, port authorities and other branches of state-run corporations. This public sector had come to play a leading role in the economy and had expanded to a much bigger size than before in order to stimulate and control the process of planned development. The amenities and facilities provided to its workforce indicated their privileged position. It did not mean, however, that they were always able to capitalize on their elevated status. Over the years wages as a proportion of total cost of production had declined and value added increased faster than workers' share in it. However, even if they were not always given their prescribed due according to the body of statutory rules and regulations, they could aspire to better facilities. Secondary terms of employment were also still inadequate, but a comprehensive system of social security was in the making. Once again, this trailblazing contingent of an urban-industrial economy accounted for only a very small portion of the working population. They were far outnumbered by the working masses in what now became labelled the unorganized sector.

The labour economist O. A. Ornati was among the first to classify the huge workforce not covered by what was supposed to become the standard labour contract as unorganized. Until the mid-twentieth century the Indian worker was defined as a figure of the modern economy and belonging to the tiny fraction who had found an industrial job. It was a fiction that reduced reality to wishful thinking, a pretension that could not be entertained any longer:

A very large group of workers finds employment in the myriad small manufacturing enterprises which produce a large variety of products for local consumption. Much of the production of shoes and leather products is conducted in factories which, because of their size, are not covered by the Factories Act. In addition, many workers are employed in small cereal-milling establishments, printing firms, bangle factories, and by mica processors. Working conditions in this sector vary considerably from region to region and from enterprise to enterprise. Little is known about the precise number of people employed or about the conditions under which they work. (Ornati 1955: 64–5)

The report of the NCL also adopted the term 'unorganized', although with a different meaning. It was now defined as 'those who have not been able to organize in pursuit of a common objective' (Government of India, Ministry of Labour, Employment and Rehabilitation 1969: 417). Moreover, the occupational range was widened to include engagement in waged work other than industry. The incapacity of this massive workforce to undertake collective action for getting higher wages and reasonable work conditions stemmed from their non-regulated employment in establishments marked by low capital intensity per worker. By way of example a few of these mainly urban-based vocations were flagged: the construction and building trade; operators of hand- and power-looms; tanneries; sweepers and scavengers; shops or commercial ventures next to a variety of artisanal workshops. Unskilled and without any bargaining strength due to ignorance and illiteracy, these workers were victims of the overbearing power of their employer. In the irregular operations that dominated in the lower echelons of the unorganized economy these workers were contracted as casual hands and hired for the moment to be instantly laid off when no longer required. The NCL recommended that the legislation promulgated for labour in the organized economy be extended to safeguard the welfare of the huge workforce so far unorganized. In addition to this class, estimated to include 10 million urban workers, another contingent found in larger towns and cities was designated as unprotected. With an implicit reference to what Ornati had concluded – 'very little is known about it and much less has been done to ameliorate its conditions of work' (Government of India, Ministry of Labour, Employment and Rehabilitation 1969: 434) – the number of workers in this category remained unlisted. A group of 11 million self-employed workers in the unorganized sector of the economy fell outside the orbit of the report. The National Commission justified this omission with the absurd argument that its terms of reference insisted on an employer-employee status.

A Redundant Workforce Stuck in an Agrarian-Rural Economy

The workforce count for the organized or unorganized sectors of the urban economy was not very reliable due to problems of definition and, to an even larger extent, lack of precision in the collection of statistical data. The demarcations made so far – protected and unprotected, which matches the contrast between organized and unorganized – were at best approximations. The grand total (14, 10 and 11 million) amounted to an estimated tally of 35 million workers. This figure constituted about one-fifth of the country's workforce, which in 1961 amounted to 189 million. However speculative the proportional share of each segment may have been (as well as understated, in the light of subsequent research), and irrespective of whether they worked in urban or rural locations, the label they had in common was their non-agrarian identity. It was clear that an urban-industrial way of life was still a far-off vision for the large majority of the people who had remained embedded in agriculture, which from generation to generation had been the prime sector of the economy.

The rural workforce included more than 162 million, of whom 20 million were not employed in agriculture. This, together with the 35 million in the urban economy with a non-agrarian identity already mentioned, leaves a total of 134 million still working in agriculture. Of this staggering multitude, 98 million (or seven out of ten) were classified as cultivators, variously as landowners, tenants or sharecroppers. Those with more land were non-cultivating owners who employed labour – in contrast to the much larger proportion of land-poor who were self-employed. Of the close to 37 million remaining, more than 6 million were engaged in forestry, fishing or working with livestock while a rough estimate of 31.5 million made up the largest class of waged workers in India, of inferior social status and at the lower end of the rural hierarchy: the largely landless agricultural labourers. The land reforms carried out in the wake of Independence had nearly everywhere bypassed people at the bottom of the agricultural economy who in the past had often been dispossessed from the fields they cultivated. Whatever land above the legal fixed ceiling was redistributed did not percolate back to them. Also the appeal made by the Gandhian movement nationwide to well-endowed landowners to donate parcels of land to those in the village who had none was a total washout. As the NCL report in 1969 observed, landless workers often did not even own the plot on which their hut stood. The conclusion reached is that the pattern of landholding had remained almost undisturbed. The problem faced by the rural under-class, as pointed out before, was the fluctuating demand for their labour power – leading to bouts of un- and underemployment, in particular for the majority of them who were casually engaged on a day-to-day basis. Seasonality, so stark a feature of the agrarian cycle, was aggravated by a very low wage rate. These vulnerabilities caused unmitigated poverty among the largest working class in the country, an outcome that was duly acknowledged:

... absence of any marked improvement in the condition of agricultural labour, an objective of planning in the context of the socialist pattern of society, viz., improvement in the levels of living of the lowest category of our working class commensurate with the total development, was far from being achieved. (Government of India, Ministry of Labour, Employment and Rehabilitation 1969: 397)

Female labour is only mentioned late in the first NCL report, although this segment constituted nearly one-third of the total workforce. The bulk were women engaged in agriculture. Those in the lower ranks had to cope without much or any protection when they belonged to the 'weaker section' of society. Similarly, there were 8 per cent workers less than 15 years of age in 1961, but the involvement of these children in the labour process was said to have gradually reduced with the ongoing spread of public education. Employment of children below the pre-scribed age was a persistent feature, however, of waged work in the unorganized sector. A reassuring note suggests that it happened more in far-off places and in rural areas where delivery of statutory provisions was more difficult to realize. Moreover, lack of enforcement was not always the critical issue since it had been brought to the notice of the commission that quite often the practice was inspired by feelings of sympathy rather than a desire to exploit. A study of the Labour Bureau showed that children were assigned comparatively light work wherever employed in plantations, factories and cottage- or small-scale industries. So what looked bad at first sight was on closer inspection said not to be so harmful.

The NCL report of 1969 created the image of a strong government at the helm of the economy and serving as the driving force of its growth. A well-intended architecture of implementation underpinned the proposed changes. Better conditions of employment and improvement in living standards for the working classes were major policy objectives. The envisaged development would follow the trajectory already taken by the world's leading nations – substitution of industry for agriculture as the main mode of production and transformation from a rural- to an urban-based society. Much had already been done to formulate an industrial labour code and operationalize it in an administrative frame to realize this ambitious set of objectives, with the government mediating between the conflicting interests of capital and labour. Sure, it would take time to execute necessary legal provisions and get them accepted by targeted stakeholders, but the transition to a welfare state was in the pipeline – to the promised benefit of all and sundry. Redeeming features included the contention that the debt bondage of an earlier era was now less practised. Although legislation had failed to end relations of agrarian dependency that arose from economic compulsion, bonded labour such as the *hali* system in Gujarat showed signs of disintegration. The report pointed out that where capitalist agriculture did improve, it resulted in more employment, reduction of underemployment, increase in wages above the minimum fixed rate and general improvement in the labouring existence. It was a hopeful conclusion backed up by the observation that a greater measure of social acceptability for the agricultural proletariat, irrespective of their inferior caste status, was evinced much more in developing areas than in areas where progress lagged behind. This was because in the former instance, the cultivator-employer in need of labour was prepared to offer concessions inspired by enlightened self-interest.

In Agonizing Reappraisal

Around this time, in the early 1970s, a shift began to occur in the way the labour problem was defined and dealt with. The development paradigm that had been laid out and adhered to in the planning process was in jeopardy because the long-awaited transition from an agrarian-rural to an industrial-urban economy and society had failed to materialize. This awareness brought to the fore a problem that in the subsequent decades would only escalate: generation of new employment opportunities proceeded at a much slower pace than expansion in the size of the working population. Despite a steady decline of the gross reproduction rate, this significant trend did not immediately lead to a substantial fall in net demographic growth because mortality had also gradually dropped to a lower level. The problem was particularly acute in the rural economy, which had lost occupational diversity in the colonial past. The rising pressure on scarce resources had to be mainly absorbed by agriculture, which intensified the quest for employment and means of livelihood. The heritage of colonial rule did not allow for a repeat of the transformative pathway out of stagnation that had contributed to the lead taken by the metropolitan powers. The politics and policies practised resulted in a pattern of static change or involution (Geertz 1963). When agrarian reforms were being drafted in the aftermath of decolonization, the Congress leadership had decided not to include the landless underclass in the redistribution, arguing that not enough land above the legal ceiling would become available to equip the vast masses stuck at the bottom with a viable holding. Amid a jubilant crowd of agricultural labourers assembled for the occasion, Sardar Patel had declared on Liberation Day in 1939 the abolition of the *halipratha* system. In his speech of congratulation he warned them, however, that the supply of labour in agriculture was far greater than the demand and he counselled his puzzled audience to seek other avenues of employment than the one in which they were stuck (Breman 2007b: 140).

The development paradigm as outlined and adhered to in the successive five-year plans (1951–6, 1956–61, 1961–6) had so far failed to unfold. In the urban economy modern industry had not made much headway, and the number of people settling in towns and cities had risen to a mere 18 per cent in 1961, a not very impressive shift away from residing in the countryside. The rural labour market showed hopeful signs of scale-enlargement and growing diversification as a consequence of the development of infrastructure, the spread of communication and better connectivity all around. However, the employment effects of these enabling features fell short of diminishing the pressure on an impoverished workforce in desperate search of sufficient income with which to make do. For the large majority of the land-poor and landless workforce agriculture was, as before, the mainstay – although terms and conditions of waged work had drastically changed. The capitalist mode of production had made increasing inroads in what remained the prime sector of the economy. Permanent labourers were replaced not only by daily hired casual workers but now also by gangs of migrants coming from outside at the peak periods of the agrarian cycle and going off again once their presence was no longer required. At the rural bottom a steadily growing number of wage hunters and gatherers were eager to move out, driven not so much by the prospect of finding a better deal elsewhere but in order to avoid distress at home. In the gradual and ongoing restructuring of the economy, agrarian bondage appeared to have become outdated. Daniel Thorner attested to its presumed disappearance in no uncertain terms:

There may be a few pockets or enclaves of India where some bond[ed] labour persists, but these are small. By and large the force of hired labourers in Indian agriculture is now made up of free men. One could not say this a generation ago. If we go back to the turn of the century, it is probable that the bulk of the agricultural labourers were unfree men, men who were in debt bondage or some other form of servitude. No one to my knowledge has yet traced the transition in Indian agriculture from a force of hired labourers who predominantly were unfree men (and women) who today are free. This is a change of immense significance, and is likely to have wide ramifications and repercussions in the next few decades. (Thorner, A. & D. 1962: 8)

The same conclusion is repeated in a subsequent paper, written in 1968, in which Thorner stated once more that this form of unfree labour, in the past rampant in many parts of India, had vanished except in backward areas (Thorner 1980: 246). The point of view Thorner expressed does not differ from the opinion of the National Commission on Labour in 1969 mentioned earlier, which also related agrarian servitude to backwardness. The implied suggestion is that systems such as *halipratha* in Gujarat had started to break down with the rising tide of capitalism.

I found no confirmation for such a fortunate turning of the tide in the region of my continued fieldwork in Gujarat between 1977 and 1982. Right through to today the pace of growth in this state is above the national average while wages for rural labour are among the lowest in the country. In my findings I emphasized how in the transition to a capitalist mode of production the dominant caste of landowners had not become more lenient but had rather hardened their stance towards agricultural labour, to the extent that they had replaced the local landless with migratory gangs coming from outside to work in their fields and to go off again when their presence was not required. These farmers, who had paved their way to prosperity and upward mobility, showed a strong antagonism to the labourers they used to attach as *halis*. These feelings indicated their unwillingness to employ their former servants any longer.

The utter disdain and aversion towards their subordinates I came across in my interaction with landowners of the dominant class was phrased in a social Darwinist language as in the passage quoted below:

... the Dublas are destined to remain poor and backward. The processes of civilization are strenuous and require hard labour and skill. We, Charotarias (Patidars) have created wealth wherever we have gone. Why? Because we are hardworking and our style of living is cultured. Whereas, these Dublas have none of these traits. They are the laziest in the world. They do not educate themselves. Their habits are bad and they live immoral living. They drink limitlessly and cause strife in their families. A (code of conduct) similar to our way of life and living does not exist among them. Gandhiji and his innumerable workers tried to improve their lot but they will simply not change. Civilization requires thinking about future and these Dublas, sometimes do not even think of the next meal, if they secure one for the present. No government, howsoever well intending, can improve a Dubla's lot.' (P. Patel, quoted in Breman 1985: 343)

Such statements happened to concur with my own assessment as to the mindset of the dominant famers in a new round of fieldwork. In addition, the much-reduced section of agricultural labourers employed throughout the year did not experience the same lack of freedom they had suffered in the past. Their exploitation had become commodified, which meant that the features of patronage-clientelism in the relationship had dwindled away on both sides. There was little doubt that farm servants' indebtedness to the big landowners who still needed them had survived, often to a much greater extent than before. But the beck-and-call relationship in which the *hali* used to be entrapped, together with his wife and children – working on the land but also doing chores in the master's house and courtyard – seemed to have changed. My perception of this alteration was shared by several other researchers commissioned by the Gujarat government to check on whether labour bondage still existed in the region of my own research (Breman 1985: 306–13).

The new spurt of interest in the issue was foreshadowed by the Bonded Labour Abolition Act promulgated in 1976. When Indira Gandhi claimed Congress leadership and distanced herself from the caucus of old party-hands she gained in popularity by declaring pro-poor policies. It was a shift in ambit that also found expression in the promise to wipe out labour bondage where it still existed in the agrarian economy. People found in that condition would be set free, liberated from their debt and protected against eviction from their homestead. But, as before, government both at the central and state level was reluctant to implement what had been enacted. A large number of non-government organizations in different parts of the country were more concerned and sent out search parties to identify victims of what was supposed to have been abolished.

A prominent example was the Gandhi Peace Foundation, which conducted a national survey on the incidence of bondage and reported that in the ten states investigated more than 2.5 million agrarian workers who belonged to Scheduled Castes or Tribes were found in that state of unfreedom. Among those investigated, three out of four confirmed that debt was the most important obligation that forced them into bondage. For Gujarat the estimated figure was 171,000 or nearly 10 per cent of all agricultural labourers. However, the terms of bondage suggested that engagement under such duress was not a lasting relationship and moving in and out of that dependency happened to be a regular event:

Bonded labour seems to be a transitory stage between periods of working as a free agricultural labourer. Whenever there is a bottleneck in the economic life of a free agricultural labourer he succumbs to the offer of the landlord to work as a *Hali* and gives himself up into such exploitation, but only for a certain period, say 1–3 years, and sets to free himself from the bondage in order to go back to the freedom as an agricultural labourer. (Marla 1981: 63)

I myself had expressed skepticism as to how strongly Indira Gandhi and her regime of emergency intended to protect landless labour and reduce the vulnerability of the rural proletariat at large. My surmise was that the new legislation on the abolition of agrarian bondage would remain as ineffective as the Minimum Wage Act that had become mandatory for agricultural labour. In my view the freedom declared could be seen as an attempt to promote the transition to capitalist relations of production by clearing away the remains of traditional forms of control over this workforce where they still prevailed.

Halipratha had become extinct in the villages of my research in south Gujarat. Nevertheless, dire economic need obliged farm servants to search throughout the year for as many days of employment as possible. Wages were paid at a rate far below the legally fixed minimum. Some emoluments were added for doing extra tasks or working more hours. Loans paid in advance to cover the shortfall of their basic requirements and to arrange for the cost of life-cycle events were subject to negotiation, either granted or not and in the latter case a ground for ending the relationship. At the same time servants avoided in their behaviour any expression of personal subordination and the stigma of inferiority attached to it. A labourer's wife often continued to work as *harekwali* to add badly needed income. She would do all kinds of domestic chores such as sweeping, cleaning and washing in the employer's household and still used to be paid in food and once in a while a trifling amount in cash. Her employer was not necessarily any longer the same one for whom her husband worked. Their offspring went to school now, boys more than girls, at least for a few standards, with many dropping out after short periods of time. Out of economic necessity the children still joined the labour process in and outside agriculture at a young age, although not automatically working for the same employers as their parents. Many changes had occurred in the labouring existence. Road-building and motorized traffic had opened up the countryside, leading to a more diversified pattern of employment. Members of land-poor and landless households started to work in growing numbers outside agriculture and the village in construction, transport, small industries, trade and services. Hired on a casual basis and without skills, they drifted around various work-sites without altogether giving up their mooring in agriculture, the prime sector of the economy. It meant a mixture of occupational identities that reflected a modified profile, extended and watered down from agricultural to rural labour at large.

2 An End to Servitude?

Rural-to-Rural Labour Circulation

At the time of my first round of research in the early 1960s a sizeable contingent of the tribal castes in my research locales already took off for faraway destinations after the monsoon to work for the next five to six months in salt-pans or brick-kilns. The growing labour mobility seemed at variance with the system of bondage that I found still lingering on, but later in this chapter I shall elaborate on their interdependence. First, however, comes the question why the pace of labour migration went on increasing from the 1970s onwards. In the villages of my fieldwork, the departure of these land-poor and landless households was matched by an influx of migrants during the peak seasons in agriculture from the tribal belt on both sides along the eastern border of Gujarat, Maharashtra and Madhya Pradesh. I decided to call this kind of labour mobility circulation rather than migration. Migration is conventionally understood as leaving one's place of origin and settling down in a new destination, but the movement I documented was short-term, lasting no longer than the duration of the dry season – at the end of which the wokers who had gone off came back instead of staying on in the usually rural locations to which they had travelled. They did not establish a foothold wherever they went and in whatever they did.

In my accounts of the fieldwork I conducted at both ends of their ventures away from home, I rejected the standard assumption that labour was made mobile because of an oversupply at the point of departure and a shortfall at the destination. The huge circulation I came across in the countryside stemmed from lack of sufficient paid work in the villages of origin and was driven by the imperative need to leave and search for wherewithal elsewhere in order to survive. However, un- or underemployment at home in my south Gujarat villages was not so much related to the absence of waged work but to replacement of local by outside labour. The rural economy was now fully structured on a capitalist footing and this explained why farmers as well as other employers had started to show a strong preference for migrants who were considered cheaper and much more pliable. I monitored the footloose army included in rural-to-rural wage labour circulation in my successive bouts of fieldwork; those engaged worked in brick-kilns and sugar-cane cutting in particular, but I also traced them in salt-pans, stone quarries, paddy harvesting, road construction and fruit-picking, either where they were at work or back in their native place. Often I tried to meet them at both ends of their trek. What made me reconsider my earlier conclusion that labour bondage no longer existed in the terrain of my research was that the floating workforce at the bottom of the rural economy was made mobile in a state of immobility. The Congress Party's prime minister, Rajiv Gandhi, announced in early 1987 that the 'Government would appoint a National Commission on Rural Labour (NCRL) to look into the working conditions of this vulnerable section of our society and the implementation of social legislation for their protection.'

The NCRL was established to investigate the predicament of these large masses of working people who had been objectives of planned change in India. A sober note was added to this fact-finding commission in the acknowledgement that policies and programmes devised for the realization of targets set for improving their condition had not achieved expected results, with the consequence that the benefits and gains of development had not been available to all. Why was this so and what could be done to solve the problems identified? To begin with, the tenor of the account submitted is at stark variance with the report of the first National Commission on Labour in 1969. This document had been crafted by civil servants and officials belonging to the state machinery committed to executing the planned economic transformation. When the promised improvement did not materialize, the ready excuse was that it would take more time for the proposed transformation, laid down in a proper frame of ordinances and acts, to be brought about. The NCRL was critical of what had happened, whether or not by design, because its members instead of being government servants had been appointed for their expertise as senior research scholars intimately familiar with the subject under study. In official reports, marked by an insider's bias, the government tended to be foregrounded as harbingers of progress, while the new report on rural labour not only spoke out against policymakers' top-down approach but also stated that the government was not infrequently more an obstructive than a catalyzing agent – as here, for instance, in a stern comment on moves to prevent agricultural labour organizing to fight for a better deal:

Generally, the attitude of the administration towards the cause of agricultural labour and its movement has been unfavourable, and even there are cases of use of repressive methods against agricultural labour. (Government of India, Ministry of Labour 1991, vol. I: viii)

The definition of rural labour was clearer than before. It was said to comprise the classes of people living and working in rural areas subsisting partly or wholly on waged income and engaged in agricultural or non-agricultural activity. The definition also included self-employed workers – identified as small and marginal farmers, tenants and sharecroppers, as well as artisans who had living conditions that were equally vulnerable. The estimated total of this workforce was around 150 million in 1987–8.

The report elaborated upon the new political economy that had emerged. It showed that rural poverty had persisted and perhaps even intensified. Economic exploitation and social oppression continued to discriminate against segments of the population. While the mixture of Scheduled Castes and Scheduled Tribes[1] were singled out as the most victimized communities, the account failed to register the pitiable conditions in which the equally disadvantaged Muslims were forced to live. Instead of upward social mobility and higher life standards the dominant trend in the lower caste-cum-class echelons of the rural economy and society was towards downward mobility and immiserization. In agriculture, still the mainstay of work and life in the countryside, the land-poor and landless classes had not been equipped with productive assets to raise their income. Common resources of land and water in the village were privatized, appropriated by the landowning oligarchy. Despite two rounds of land reforms, the surplus land acquired for redistribution to the rural poor amounted to a negligible fraction of the total cultivated area. In both agrarian and non-agrarian rural households self-employment had declined over the years, a sign of dispossession made manifest in the proletarianization of petty owners losing out on their means of production. Agricultural and rural labourers at large were increasingly affected by casualization and had to cope with a lower number of workdays due to the introduction of modern methods of production that displaced manpower by capital. The green revolution launched in the early 1960s accelerated the pace of capitalist farming and was quite successful in raising agricultural productivity, of food grains in particular. But the new agronomic technology mainly benefited the more substantial landowners while the substitution of capital for labour led to a

---

[1] So categorized by the government in acknowledgement of their underprivileged social position, which qualified them for various positive discrimination programmes.

loss of employment for land-poor and landless households. The outcome was a further widening of the rural class divide.

Contributing to the lack of much visible progress among the unprivileged categories was a sustained neglect of human resource development – reflected in the sparse or absent access to education, health care, housing, drinking water and sanitation. Because of abysmally low and fluctuating incomes the need for social security was greater for the rural poor but they did not benefit from the few and inadequate schemes that had been introduced. The expenditure on social security in India hardly accounted for 2.5 per cent of GDP and was mainly spent on the well-organized class of urban labour, which stagnated at about one-tenth of the total workforce. Still, and as the report duly pointed out, a sizeable increase had been generated in agricultural production. It was one more way of drawing attention to the increasing inequality in the countryside. In the transition to capitalism the vested interests seemed to have become more vested than before:

The political clout of large farmers has increased considerably. They have been able to influence Plan priorities and policies for the rural sector in a direction not quite favourable to the rural labour. The deficiencies in the implementation of poverty alleviation programmes are largely attributable to the dominance of vested interests in various rural institutions. (Government of India, Ministry of Labour 1991, vol. I: vi)

The NCRL urged the government to come out in forceful support of the rights of rural labour and defy the privileged position of the rural elite. Such a change of sides would indeed be a major feat because the voices of the dispossessed were muted or not heard at all in the village councils in most parts of India – and those of women least of all.

Although many voluntary organizations try to promote the interests of the proletariat, such well-meant intervention usually remains localized – and by and large has had little lasting impact. Protests such as strikes and demonstrations that challenge the structures of power spring up off and on. But collective action against non-representation or downright exclusion has rarely solidified into sustained and organized agency. The striking marginality of rural labour in economic, political and social terms is exacerbated by the unwillingness of the government to enforce legislation, e.g. the Minimum Wage Act (see also Breman 1985: 143–55). Has there been no improvement at all? There has been change for the better, but not enough by far. Among the down-and-out there is little or no awareness of the laws, ordinances and schemes supposed to mitigate their immense misery. Official agencies do not bother to disseminate information on how targeted recipients can avail themselves of such relief. The Indian bureaucracy has proved tardy in providing the benefits stocked up for its deprived citizenry. The masses at the margins of the economy and society have to find their own way – an effort that comes at a cost – to access the class-selective and discretionary goodwill of the state. One of the recommendations the NCRL made was to legislate waged work as a fundamental right. The idea was to operational-ize it in an employment guarantee act similar to the one that existed in Maharashtra. It would take many years to pass the National Rural Employment Guarantee Act: the attenuated format that then became operational could moderate the fall in employment in the best-performing states but was unable to redress the huge lack of paid work for the swelling reserve force of labour at the bottom of the rural econ-omy. The only way to escape destitution was to move out in the slack season and search in forays of varying length for whatever work could be found elsewhere.

Tying Down Labour Again

The NCRL report's explanation for mobility relied on the conventional wisdom that labour flocked to areas where it was in short supply and so found a better deal than it could get in the area from which it came:

High wages in the irrigated areas where Green Revolution has made an impact co-exists with low wages – often much below the statutorily fixed minimum wages – in the less-developed regions where the growth in agricultural productivity is slow and the demand for labour is sluggish. In the developed regions, on the other hand, farmers have generally taken to capital-intensive agriculture, partly in response to prevailing high wages and shortage of local labour. The prevailing big differential in wages between different regions has induced the migration of labour from the poorer regions to the areas of Green Revolution. Large-scale migration of Bihar to Punjab is a classic case in point. There are now more than 10 million rural migrant labourers in the country. Inter-regional migration of labour in the process of development is inevitable and is also desirable from the point of view of raising agricultural productivity as well as improving the incomes of labour. (Government of India, Ministry of Labour 1991, vol. I: vi-vii)

The impression created in this quotation from the NCRL's main report is misleading on several counts. In the first place the quantity of labourers driven to mobility, although higher than accounted for in the rounds of the National Sample Survey, is far above the estimated figure. While the study group of experts charged to discuss migration did conclude that circular movement in particular had been inadequately covered in the surveys conducted (and extensively referred to my fieldwork findings in

South Gujarat to scale up the understated figure), its own appraisal of 10 million was still much too low. Second, as previously stated, it is a misconception to argue that labour migration is a balancing act between plenitude and shortage. The misrepresentation is not at the departing end, which is marked by labour in abundance that remains unemployed; it is at the opposite end, where the demand for labour power cannot be met from a supposedly deficient supply. It so happens that migrants are often hired to replace readily available local labour. In the third place, the short-duration circular migration is not from lower to higher wages. The expert group confirmed that migrant workers tend to be preferred because they are cheaper and easier to exploit than the ones locally and abundantly at hand, a point of view emphatically stressed in my investigations on footloose labour. In other words, the mobility was due to acute distress, an imperative need to get out and compensate for the shortfall of sufficient earnings for bare survival:

All labourers are not able to withstand strenuous and torturous working hours, dehumanizing work conditions and repeated insult from the contractors or employers. The situation becomes unbearable when they did not get wages in time. Some labourers resist and revolt against the situation. But they are not allowed to form trade unions. Hence, their struggles are short-lived. Some try to run away to their native place. But it is not easy as the contractors create an iron curtain with the help of their musclemen who prevent the workers from leaving the work without repaying the advances given to them. These musclemen keep watch on workers and their activities and if necessary beat up the workers who defy the instruction of the contractors. This was the main complaint of the workers at the Sardar Sarovar construction site [my note: a dam built in Gujarat with labour fetched from Andhra Pradesh]. If all these fail and workers manage to escape, they are implicated in trumped-up criminal cases, arrested and then forced to return to work. (Government of India, Ministry of Labour 1991, vol. II: K 39–40)

It comes as no surprise to read that terms and conditions wherever the labourers go are horrendous, much worse than at home. This panel of experts concluded that migrant workers – in agriculture or non-agricultural sectors – are forced to accept abominable conditions. They are not only underpaid and obliged to work for longer hours but also have to make do without drinking water, accommodation, health care etc. They are treated by employers as subhuman, only worth the low-priced labour power they provide. All this is in line with my conclusion that bondage is the organizing feature of rural-to-rural wage labour circulation. Practices of bondage were explicitly discussed by another group of experts who had been asked to advise on how to identify, release and rehabilitate the workers thus entrapped. Several of them were high-ranking civil servants who, when they were still within the bureaucracy, tried to find more leverage in their designated field on this issue. I came to know them not in their official capacity but as unwelcome messengers of what they had advocated in the corridors of power. Both B. N. Yugandhar and S. R. Sankaran were instrumental in formulating the Bonded Labour (Abolition) Act 1976. Another was Laxmidhar Mishra, joint secretary in the Ministry of Human Resource Development. He toured the area of my fieldwork to check the accounts I had published and in his report backed up my writings on the exploitation and oppression of the floating army of sugar-cane cutters coming each year for the duration of the campaign. The experience of these bureaucrats made them public whistleblowers, anxious to open up the Pandora's box of bondage. However, none of the recommendations in the NCRL report induced policymakers and politicians to take the action proposed. In addition, the advice to set up a National Authority for Bonded Labour, to overcome the tenacious obstruction of law enforcement, remained unheeded.

The swarms of contemporary labour-nomads wandering across the country are pushed out of their rural abodes, driven to indebted dependency to work off the loan advanced to them at the moment of recruitment. In this one respect it is a form of 'voluntary' attachment that shows a striking similarity to how the tribal communities were denied access to land in south Gujarat and fell into agrestic servitude in a remote past. But the *halis* were contracted and dealt with in a quite different modality of employment to the one the much larger army of migrant workers faces

Figure 2.1 Pushed out of the rural economy in search of urban work

today. These proletarians are made footloose but entangled in immobility, which I have labelled as neo-bondage. What are the contrasting features between the unfree work regime now and long ago? First, the contract expresses a thoroughly commodified relationship, which means that nothing other than labour power is extracted from the body of the hired worker. The non-economic dimensions – which aimed at gaining more power and prestige for the master and insisted on deference and subordination on the part of his servants – are absent in this highly exploitative arrangement. It may still occur that other members of the worker's household – his wife and children – come along but then their ability and availability to work is explicitly specified in a higher advance paid out when the deal is struck. While the jobber pressurizes men to accept his deal, women and children brought along for the work on offer are forced by the males to accompany them. Recruitment is done in the slack season when, due to unemployment in the village, the land-poor and landless households are desperate for income. In acute vulnerability they are willing to sell their labour power, binding the able-bodied dependent ones among them for future work at a lower price than the going market rate. The jobber stands out as a major figure in the landscape of labour but his presence and role remains undocumented in the annals of the state.

Neo-bondage of migrants is often engagement for a limited duration because the activity for which the workers are taken on is seasonal in nature. Their presence is no longer required when the operations in which they are involved come to a halt. Another difference is that the workers are hired by a jobber who is authorized by the ultimate employer. His liaison stems from the need to bridge distance since the sites of demand and supply tend to be far apart. The labour broker is a figure with roughly the same identity as the recruited workers. The employer needs his agency to recruit the work teams or gangs in the desired quantity and quality and to distribute the money to bind them in advance. Having a similar background as his catch and often coming from their ranks himself, the jobber knows whom to select or reject. Those recruited should have adequate work capacity but also be willing to comply with the terms and conditions at the worksite, where the jobber continues to operate as a gang boss, supervising the output and keeping book of what they owe or are still due. He capitalizes on his familiarity with the situation on both sides as a crucial in-between and his acts as an honest broker, one who deftly links labour to capital, claiming to enjoy trust at both ends (Picherit 2009). The far greater risk nowadays of breach of contract makes employers wary of granting large amounts in cash as an advance on wages – all the more so because the implicit agreement to work when and as instructed is easier to terminate or even evade. Employers are often unable to recover the debt incurred, which is not legally binding. Wages are not settled while the work is going on. The jobber meticulously writes down what he has shelled out to the members of his gang and their day-to day production. Every week or two weeks he distributes an allowance made available by the employer in cash or kind (a grain ration) to his gang to take care of maintenance needs. Where workers are unable to reach the daily target set for them – because of illness, injuries or exhaustion – the allowance is cut. Slowly the debt is worked off, but even when that turning point is reached the same practice continues.

Neo-bondage is actually a mixture of advance and postponed wage settlement. It is only when the harvesting of sugar-cane is over – when the brick-kilns, salt-pans, stone quarries, mines and other open-air industries close down and construction work ends – that the net earnings made are paid out. They are paid only if any balance remains, because not all outstanding debts have been worked off to the full amount. Some may have taken higher advances from the jobber to allow for the cost of life-cycle events, marriage in particular, to spend on health care or to pay for housebuilding or repairs, etc. The size of these higher 'loans' is such that they cannot be worked off in a single season and leads to continuation of the same relationship for at least one more stint. It is important to note that the indebted workforce has no control whatsoever over the wage rate of the contract into which they have entered. The final settlement is fixed on the quantity produced daily and is piece-rated. Workers are only informed of what it amounts to – per 1,000 moulded bricks, ton of sugar-cane cut, *brass* of stones crushed, weight of cotton picked, square yards of roadwork laid, *bighas* of paddy harvested, etc. – at the last possible moment, when dismissed from further engagement. This procedure could not demonstrate in a more telling way the labourers' absolute lack of bargaining power. I have discussed the ramifications and repercussions of neo-bondage in a series of writings (Breman 1994, 1996, 2010a, 2010b, and 2013a; Breman et al. 2009). The upshot of these successive publications is that bondage and capitalism are not mutually exclusive and have to be understood in the context of the regime of informality that has come to determine the shape as well as the fabric of economy and society. This issue will be further spelled out in subsequent chapters.

Urbanization but in an Informalized Setting

So far I have discussed the acceleration in intra-rural labour migration, an understated theme in the literature. However, from the 1970s onwards I noticed that members of land-poor and landless households had started to move also to urban locations. It was in reaction to the compelling need for alternative or additional employment which, due to better and easier connectivity than before, could also be accessed in towns and cities. What I found was in tune with the discovery of 'the informal sector' in mainly anthropological case studies on the changing habitus of labour in what used to be called the Third World. The picture painted was of a workforce freshly arrived from the hinterland and drifting around in the lower echelons of the urban economy. They lacked skills and were commonly engaged in petty trades or services carried out under the open sky or in cubicles and stalls, the large majority of them in some sort of self-employment. The scene was analyzed as a waiting room in which migrants, still unskilled and unfamiliar with their urban setting, passed the time until they could move up to the formal sector. This implied that they had become upwardly mobile to a steady and well-regulated job with much higher pay. The switch from informal to formal employment would also enable them to set up a household and bring to the city wife and children who had stayed back in the village as unwelcome dependents. The imagined scenario still presumed that the planned transformation would happen – but in a more circumspect way. The age of industrialism and its massive employment had not yet arrived but the hope that a turn for the better was around the corner had still not vanished.

By the 1990s it could no longer be denied that the transition to a welfare state – duplicating the pathway of the advanced economies in the Northern hemisphere – had diverted from the laid-out track. The altered perspective led to a change in policy, handed down from the commanding heights of the globalized economy, which proposed that keeping employment flexible was not the problem but a solution in that it would speed up economic growth. The change not only frustrated dreams of upward mobility but also ushered in informalization, which deprived the organized segment of the workforce from the rights of well-regulated and protected conditions of employment they had gained in the preceding decades of collective action as members of trade unions (Breman 2004). Regular work is still the most common employment status in the urban economy but more than half of this expanding workforce is engaged on informal conditions without any employment or social security provided

Figure 2.2 Migrants remain footloose and without proper shelter wherever they go

by the employer. In the rural economy casual work dominates by far. Of this huge multitude only half is wage-dependent, hired whenever the occasion arises and then laid off again. The other half is self-employed. This latter category, also classified as own-account workers, is to a large extent a disguised form of waged labour and mainly consists of small and marginal farmers who have failed to get a proper job. The dismal switch in course to thoroughly casualized work in an endless rotation of hire and fire did not stop the trek to urban locations of labourers increasingly made footloose by their overcrowding in the nearby or faraway hinterland. The exodus from the countryside was reflected in the growing size of the population counted us urban, an upswing from nearly 29 per cent in 2001 to close to 38 per cent in 2011. For the first time since Independence the demographic increase was lower in rural areas. However, this census arithmetic cannot be taken at face value.

Not all of those arriving in the city are permitted to settle down in the urban habitat. In my final round of fieldwork, conducted in 2013–15 at the margins of the largest metropolis in Gujarat, I focused on rural migrants who sold their labour power in one of the morning markets to contractors or their touts for employment in the booming construction industry. Beyond the purview of the municipality they make their bivouac on the outskirts but many among this workforce, wandering around, pass the night as pavement dwellers in the city. In addition, many migrants who manage to establish a foothold in one of the slums are forced at the end of their working life, which tends to be around the age of forty to forty-five, to go back in 'retirement' to their native place. The cost of daily upkeep in the city makes it impossible for those without adequate earning power to stay on indefinitely. I followed up in my reporting on an earlier conclusion that labour circulation and informalization of employment are intertwined and reinforce each other in an escalating spiral. It boils down to footloose migrants being sent back to where they come from:

… urban citizenship is next to impossible for slum dwellers, blamed from day one as squatters with no right to the waste land, either in public or private hands, on which they have built their makeshift shelter. The space they encroach is required for building roads, bridges, canals, and power stations as part of an expanding urban infrastructure, or is taken up by housing colonies for people with higher and regular incomes. The squatters are forced to leave again before the construction works begin. Drifting around the outskirts of the city, they have to keep a low profile because they cannot afford to buy the plot on which they erect a bivouac of sorts since land prices are far beyond their budget. Without assets and contacts with the municipal authorities, these settlers do not, of course, qualify for property rights and tenure security. They are what I have called 'nowhere people' drifting around in a nowhere landscape. (Breman 2010b: 17)

Floating back and forth from season to season, however, is an ordeal different from the one faced by migrants who have managed to find somewhat more regular work, which allows them to hang on to life in the city at least until they are worn out. Many of them, for example the huge workforce in the textile industry engaged in power-loom sheds or in dyeing-and-printing mills, still do not earn enough to bring their dependents along. The production is frequently outsourced, which means that workers are not hired by the factory owner himself but by a (sub-) contractor. It is called job work, which means that the contractor continues the relationship if satisfied with the terms and conditions or he shops around to close a better deal with the owner of another plant. On his part the factory owner behaves in a similar way. The workers stick to their gang boss, but can also be tempted to accept the offer of another contractor who needs more manpower for the time being and is willing to pay a little bit more per square yard produced. The up-and-down swings in the textile market add to the complexity of this highly flexible type of industrial management, which is marked by constant rotation. In this fluid landscape, which I have classified as mercantile capitalism, the interdependency between the contractor and his band of workers is of crucial importance – with the gang boss resorting to neo-bondage to back up his hold over the core members of his gang. When workers get more skilled and increase their stock of social capital, they are less amenable to fall into neo-bondage as an utter and final stage of dependency. With the leverage gained they show themselves capable of moving around at their own behest in the work arena with which they are familiar.

My findings during my investigations in the city of Surat (Breman 1996) were corroborated in other studies on the same subject, with the added comment that money paid in advance for waged work does not always result in the immobilization of industrial labour. The rotation of the footloose proletariat among a variety of work sites undermines the strategy that employers apply to control their workforce. In reaction to the assumed turnaround in bargaining strength, these petty industrialists are prone to exclaim that they themselves rather than their subordinates are ensnared in debt-bondage (Carswell & de Neve 2013; de Neve 2019). In other branches of the industrial economy attachment in wage dependency is more rigorous, as in the case of children employed in carpet-weaving or of young women recruited on a postponed-wage contract to work in garment production (Kompier 2015, Mezzadri 2017). To conclude, neo-bondage is a form of labour attachment that is thoroughly capitalist in nature, widely prevalent in both the rural and urban economy, found in agriculture, industry and construction, as well as in other sectors, and in practice immobilizes migrant or local workers. The attachment varies in intensity, length, selectivity and shape but indebtedness is crucial to it. Conceptual confusion arose because the Bonded Labour (Abolition) Act 1976 focused on agrarian bondage as it still lingered on in backward regions, and overlooked practices of neo-bondage that became widely prevalent in the transition to capitalism both within and beyond agriculture and in the rural as well as the urban economy (Srivastava 2009). The workers thus victimized are doubly unfree in the classical sense, i.e. they own no productive assets themselves and are unable to sell their labour power in the open market. They have no or hardly any means of production and are forced to sell their labour power in advance to make a living for themselves and their dependents. Given labourers' availability in high numbers, the fact that the supply or workers is much higher than can be absorbed, why do owners and managers of capital find it necessary to tie contingents of them in shorter or longer spells of attachment? Reasons include: to reduce the fluidity that characterizes the labour market; to further weaken an already vulnerable workforce; to enhance the workers' pliability; to bring down the price of labour to an even lower level than it is at; and to withhold advantages that would otherwise accrue from the workers' contribution to gainful activity. It is in line with the dictum of predatory capitalism to increase profit by maximally cutting the cost of production and explains why in the informal economy in particular the percentage spent on wages has been driven down relentlessly.

Progressive Inequality

A second National Commission on Labour set up in 1998 was asked to suggest rationalization of existing labour laws in the organized sector and to propose an umbrella legislation for ensuring a minimum level of protection to workers in the unorganized sector. The request to do so came in the wake, earlier in the decade, of a decisive turn to globalization of the country's economic policy. The new government, dominated by the rightist Bharatiya Janata Party (BJP), appointed Ravinder Varma, a former minister of labour, as chairman of the commission. The change in the political constellation did not have major repercussions for the task ahead since the new brand of powermongers remained as much in favour of neoliberalism as the ones they replaced. The commission's terms of reference, loaded heavily pro-corporate business, were rejected by the majority of trade unions as being against the interests of the working classes. They boycotted the commission and strongly criticized its rec-ommendations. Collection of data and deliberations on it took much longer than expected and when the report was submitted four years later it included a note of dissent in which one of its members, also a trade unionist, scathingly repudiated the economic reforms ushered in and the negative consequences for labour. Saji Narayanan wrote that economic policy had headed in the wrong direction during the previous ten years. In the name of protection of capital and globalization, workers' rights had dissipated.[2]

Of the workforce, which rose to 406 million around the turn of the century, fewer than one in ten was engaged in the formal economy. More than half of the overwhelming majority in what was still addressed as the unorganized sector were self-employed or home-based workers and like the remaining plenitude without the minimum security all of them badly needed. The commission discussed in great detail the labour reforms pushed through in the residual formal economy, made manifest in a loss of bargaining power gained in struggles in the preceding decades. How-ever, the dismal plight of workers in the informal economy did not go unnoticed. The report gives due attention to the government's neglect

---

[2] Ten years later, having become president of the Bharatiya Mazdoor Sangh, the rebel who distanced himself from the second National Labour Commission Report had mellowed a great deal. His BJP-affiliated trade union had become the biggest in the country, catering to the interests of the much-shrunken regular workforce in the organized economy. 'We are known for reconciliation. We believe in talks and dialogue rather than having strikes.'(*Business Standard*, February 25, 2011). The former firebrand adopted the partnership role that he had decried as commission member and now strongly opposed the confrontational tactics he had then flagged.

since Independence of agriculture, which used to be referred to as the backbone of India's society and economy. Workers in agriculture get employment for less than six months in a year and close to half of them have to migrate in search of work in construction or other occupations in the off-season. Even then their income is not enough and to satisfy their basic needs they have to borrow money, an indebtedness that makes them more vulnerable. Umbrella legislation is urgently required for workers in the informal economy because of the flagrant violation of statutory rights on payment of wages, safety regulations, accommodation and health care, accident compensation, etc. The many omissions and loopholes in laws and ordinances must be closed, implemented instead of suspended and forcefully endorsed rather than ignored. How can it be that a spate of legislation in support of the informalized workforce – as e.g. the Minimum Wage Act, the Contract Labour (Regulation and Abolition) Act, the Inter-State Migrant Workers (Regulation of Employment and Conditions of Service) Act, the Bonded Labour (Abilition) Act, the Equal Remuneration Act, the Child Labour (Prohibition and Regulation) Act - have remained null and void? The report argued that the right to work, already a directive principle mentioned in the Constitution, should be made a fundamental right. Commenting critically on the exceptionally low budget for social security, a mere 1.8 per cent of GDP, the commission recommended that social security measures for unorganized workers should include health insurance, maternity and early child care, family benefits, provident fund benefits, amenities for housing, drinking water and education, compensation for occupational injury, retirement allowances, disability provisions and unemployment benefits. This wide range of care facilities follow from the right that citizens have to adequate means of livelihood irrespective whether they are at work or not.

What was the chance of this shopping list being accepted and endorsed by the National Democratic Alliance (NDA) coalition that had come to power? No hope, as the report duly comments, because difficulties might deepen with the increasing marginalization of labour under the regime of liberalization imposed. After all, social safety nets are only viable if the number of people who fall into them constitutes a small minority of the workforce. But if this is so, why ponder an umbrella legislation for more than 90 per cent of the workforce if it is already clear from the outset that the envisaged design is not going to reach the stage of endorsement – let alone of enactment? The second NCL produced a hefty document in two volumes (2002), full of inconsistencies and contradictions. Its contents read like a cop out, a lament phrased in the following passage:

Fifty years after Independence and the promulgation of the Constitution, if the 90% of the labour force do not enjoy 'guaranteed' rights, there is every reason to say that we have not practised what we have preached. This provides a fertile ground for the birth and growth of movements that aim at overthrowing the system, like the Naxalite movement or similar violent movements that we see in many parts of the country. One, if not the most important, of the ways of reversing this trend is to fulfill the promises the Constitution makes to the poor and under-privileged in the unorganized sector, in the rural and urban areas. Land reforms have not been implemented, in spite of reminders from many commissions and the manifestos of political parties. Employment opportunities are not adequate. Those in employment often do not get the minimum wages that have been guaranteed in law. Working conditions are deplorable, sometimes, inhuman. It is, therefore, necessary to construct a new legal framework and system of social security that will provide protection and welfare to the workers in the unorganized sector. (Government of India, Ministry of Labour 2002, vol. II: 72)

While conceding that there are contingents of labour employed under duress throughout the economy, the report's bland verdict without further qualification is that the Ministry of Labour had appropriately implemented the 1976 Bonded Labour System (Abolition) Act. The appreciation expressed is contradicted on many pages with statements conceding that e.g. in the construction industry a system of bondage exists and gets extended from one generation to the next through child labour and that agricultural workers slide into bondage when they are forced to borrow money to live on. Duly noted, also, is the important ruling by the Supreme Court that the need arising out of economic compulsion to accept work below statutory minimum wages should be considered as forced labour. At the invitation of the National Human Rights Commission a group of experts in 2001 drafted a definition that takes care of the changed setting of bondage. The NHRC report proposed that bonded labour be said to exist:

... when non-payment of minimum wages is combined with any of the following: an advance or debt, restraint of physical liberty, restraint on changing employment or the forced prevention of labour realizing its full market value. This way of defining bonded labour will cover labour or service relations involving both the payment of an advance and the promise of payment of wage as a lump sum at the end of the agreed contract. (quoted in Sethia 2014: 214–15; see also Sankaran 2009)

The overall conclusion that it would be wise to enact an umbrella type of law for unorganized labour that would guarantee a minimum of protection and welfare had been the point of departure and was included in the terms of reference. On the one hand urging the workforce not to take an antagonistic stance towards employers while on the other spelling out how labour laws were flouted by government agencies as well as private employers, the report got caught in a web of inconsistency. Delivering a set of incoherent, controversial and disputable recommendations, the second National Commission on Labour failed to do what it had been charged with. My last comment on the report is that it perceives the state as only engaged in governance but also piloting the economy. This perception is out of tune with a major change in the relative weight of the main stakeholding actors. The firm shift to neoliberalism since the early 1990s implied a loss of commanding control on behalf of the state over what capital and corporate business want, do and prevent or oppose. The central and regulating role ascribed to government was simply not there. Income inequality has substantially risen from the 1980s onwards. The top 0.1% of earners captured more growth than all the people in the bottom half combined. The decision to not any longer publish tax statistics after 2000 kept the spiralling inequality covered up (World Inequality Report 2018: 123). It is in this context that I have to bring up the consistent failure of the judiciary, from top to bottom and irrespective of the political formation in power, to protect and secure the rights of labour. As a matter of fact, the judiciary has not resisted being used as an instrument of governance, pliable in prioritizing the interests of capital and colluding in the repression of those of the working classes. In a pretence of alleviating the dismal plight of the working classes many acts and ordinances were framed while at the same time it was ensured that the judicial agencies of legality would prevent these obligations from becoming operative.

The Rejected Appeal for a New Deal

The lower echelons of the electorate did not buy the 'Shining India' slogan of the BJP-led NDA, which had favoured the better-off classes. The coalition was outvoted in 2004 by the United Progressive Alliance (UPA), dominated once again by the Congress Party. Promising a change in policy to benefit the people who had remained in the shadow of politics and policies, the new government committed itself to ensure 'the welfare and well-being of all workers, particularly those in the unorganised sector, who constitute more than 93% of our workforce'. This was a tall order, more so because of the paucity of concrete and reliable data on what goes on in the informal economy, activity that is to a large extent beyond the purview of the state. A panel of experts was commissioned to review the status of the unorganized/informal sector in India, including the nature of enterprises, their size, spread and scope, and the level of employment. Mapping the informal economy was an important task in itself but fact-finding would have to be accompanied by advising the government on how to upgrade work and improve the livelihoods of the common people referred to as the *aam aadmi*. Between 2004 and 2009 the National Commission on Enterprises in the Unorganised Sector (NCEUS) – headed by Arjun Sengupta, who was seconded by two main members, K. P. Kannan and R. S. Srivastava – produced nine reports. The final document sums up what the commission considers to be the overarching problem, which is the lack of adequate employment at a decent standard and a fair wage for the large majority of the population in the lower echelons of the economy. In its last report, submitted in 2009, the panel concluded that a large chunk of India's informal workforce remained in deep poverty. This was not welcome news in political circles that took comfort in figures apparently showing sustained high rates of economic growth. The report pointed out that the neoliberal reforms of the early 1990s had not generated more regular jobs. The rise in employment that took place was nearly exclusively on a hire-fire basis within the informal economy. In addition, real wage rates had fallen rather than increased. Thus, these years of high economic growth had not resulted in higher average earnings. The outcome was even more disappointing since, as worrisome as the drop in the quantitative growth of employment was, no improvement had occurred in conditions at work and neither had skill development been given the priority it should have been. Moreover, the UPA coalition defaulted on its commitment under the Common Minimum Programme as declared at the beginning of its tenure to enact comprehensive protective legislation for all workers in agriculture. Lip service continued to be paid to the need to relieve the worsening plight of the land-poor and landless masses in the rural economy. In the end the Congress Party reluctantly gave in to pressure from civil rights activists to start a workfare scheme that gave 100 days of employment to village households willing to take on unskilled manual work. The 2005 National Rural Employment Guarantee Act (NREGA – or in daily parlance *narega*) did improve the bargaining power of agricultural labour where it worked well (Drèze & Khera 2009). The alleviation of unemployment and the modium of political leverage it created for these underprivileged vote banks is said to have played an important role in the return to power of this political alliance in the general elections held in 2009.

The NCEUS panel met several times with the prime minister to apprise him of progress in the mission with which he had entrusted them. It soon became clear that they were not on the same wavelength and the clash of opinions must have come as a rude shock for both sides. The stance the prime minister, Manmohan Singh, took was along the lines of economist Hernando de Soto's suggestion that the majority of the people in the informal economy do not suffer from a total lack of savings or property but are hampered from making the unregistered capital that they do have more productive (Soto 1989, 2000). The recipe of this staunch admirer of petty entrepreneurship for how to promote capitalism in the landscape of poverty was admired and fully endorsed by the World Bank. In de Soto's script the poor manage to lift themselves out of misery and become self-provident. India's prime minister had expected the NCEUS panel to follow this up-to-the-minute wisdom and recommend policies that would create opportunities for the self-employed to start small-scale workshops or micro-businesses and generate their own means of production from scratch. However, this was not what the NCEUS brought to the table: their findings confirmed that poverty and lack of resources are closely interrelated. The years of high growth have made the middle and upper classes – barely a quarter of India's population – much better off than they were before, and an equal proportion may have succeeded in marginally enhancing their condition, but the large majority of the informal workforce have made only negligible progress or none whatsoever. The note in the commission's final report that productivity increased at the same time that employment stagnated actually means that labour tends to be squeezed to an ever-greater degree. Of crucial importance in the intensification of the workload is that the wages fixed are not time- but piece-rated. What passes for self-employment is often a disguised form of waged labour that easily boils over in self-exploitation because these workers are willing to exert themselves until the point of exhaustion for the sake of raising their all-too-meagre income. Even then there are those who lack the wherewithal to make both ends meet. They have to tap into savings in order to take care of ill health or of unavoidable expenses for life-cycle events in the household such as the marriage cost of a son or daughter. When deprived of assets that can be mortgaged or transformed into cash, these people have no other option than to sell their labour power in advance. It means losing the freedom to choose your employer or change the site of your employment until the debt is paid off – or rather worked off; and also then wage payment is often deferred until the moment of dismissal.

In its final and main report – *The Challenge of Employment in India: An Informal Economy Perspective* (2009) –the NCEUS pointed out that labour bondage is much underplayed in official statistics. It used to be found mainly in agriculture but attachment in debt has become a major feature throughout the informal economy, particularly among migrant workers. Subjected to economic exploitation, their identity as members of Scheduled Caste and Scheduled Tribe communities adds a social dimension to the extreme vulnerability faced by this mass of footloose labour (Report of the National Commission for Enterprises in the Unorganised Sector, Government of India 2009: 147–8). In his introductory summary the NCEUS chairman urged a drastic U-turn in economic policy: instead of growth being the overriding objective, social development and maximizing the quantity and quality of employment should be foregrounded. The panel of experts spoke out strongly in favour of inclusive development to reverse the trend towards inequality and exclusion. Instead of waiting for the trickle-down of what is left over from the benefits of growth, they insisted on the need for a bottom-up approach involving participation and equitable sharing. Avoiding the term formalization of employment, which is what they had in mind, the report-writers pressed for a levelling-up approach and the need to establish a social floor. A priority of the first order would be to ensure acceptable conditions of work in accordance with a modicum of human dignity. A national minimum wage with statutory backing should be introduced and enforced to allow for an income that meets the basic needs of the country's workforce. Social security was also included in the commission's terms of reference: the panel declared it a universal right for all workers and drafted a bill to back up this proposal (NCEUS 2009). In its Report on Conditions of Work and Promotion of Livelihoods in the Unorganised Sector (2006), the NCEUS had worked out a comprehensive strategy to upgrade production and services in the informal economy while insisting on decent employment practices. Most labour laws do not apply to employment in the informal economy and those specifically enacted for the protection and security of workers in this sector – as e.g. the Contract Labour (Regulation and Abolition) Act 1970 and the Bonded Labour Abolition Act 1976 – have limited coverage, are not properly implemented and lack enforcement.

Fully aware that the proposed agenda was bound to encounter strong opposition from vested interests, the NCEUS suggested beginning by adapting a rights-based programme of action promoted by a well-organized working class and a vigilant civil society. The reports were stonewalled by the political and policy elite – perhaps unsurprisingly, given that they were consistent in their policy formulations on how to repair the absence of job security, income security and social security in the informal economy. The Government of India did not acknowledge receipt of the final report; nor was it printed or made available to the general public. Since government agencies such as the august Planning Commission refused to deliberate its findings and recommendations, the initiative to do so had to come from other quarters. The Institute for Human Development in Delhi in May 2010 invited a wide range of academic scholars, public intellectuals, media professionals and representatives from civil society to discuss with the NCEUS panellists the recipe prescribed by the commission's team of experts, part-time members and colleagues. The gist of the dialogue held during the meeting made clear that the reports were seen as a turning point and a mine of information that was necessary for further studies. An ILO official who attended the meeting gave as his comment that the mission the NCEUS had completed 'is the largest single national effort in the world to encompass the characteristics and needs of what is known as the informal sector' (Breman 2010c: 46). The NCEUS had delivered an important message to politicians and policymakers: the economy cannot be split up into a formal and an informal sector. The two are interconnected and should be dealt with accordingly; the upper side cannot be privileged without harming the underside. Neoliberalism sharply distorted the imbalance that already existed between capital and labour. Not heeding the formalization remedy that the NCEUS had proposed was the consequence of the political decision to stay on a policy course of progressive inequality (Kannan 2014). From 1993–4 to 2011–12, a period that saw the upswing of neoliberalism, labour market dualism was given a further boost. It meant more prosperity for a minority of the workforce against sustained or increased poverty for the majority. Unwilling as well as unable to comprehend the political fallout of this linkage between gains higher up versus losses down below and blamed for widespread corruption at all governmental levels, the Congress Party was routed in the 2014 elections.

Debt bondage, as described and analyzed above, has become widely prevalent in the informal economy. It is a form of servitude in which, by my estimate, about 15 per cent of the total workforce, all those toiling without proper jobs and living in destitution – or presently more than 50 million men, women and children – are contracted (Breman 2010/ 2012). Following a United Nations formulation dating back to 1956,[3] servitude for debt is defined as an unequal exchange between creditor and debtor, where the latter borrows from the former and is constrained to work for the creditor until the debt is serviced (Lal 1977). The practice is of long standing and speaks of a highly exploitative and oppressive work regime. The common stance taken in referring to it is to ask what can be done to prevent, phase out and prohibit workers' loss of control over where, when and how to sell their labour power at a fair price and for decent work. A recently published article, however, suggests that debt

---

[3] United Nations Supplementary Convention on the Abolition of Slavery, the Slave Trade and Institutions and Practices Similar to Slavery, 1956.

bondage should be condoned instead of condemned (Bhukuth et al. 2016). The authors argue that allowing the practice to continue is the least worst of alternative solutions. Why? Because according to their reasoning – which is open to dispute – other choices would imply an outcome even worse than being constrained in bondage. An overview of the literature on the issue leads them to conclude that:

> The eradication of debt bondage could bring with it household exposure to serious risks, particularly a greater financial risk and an increased risk of violence. India's 1985 prohibition act[4] condemns the use of debt bondage and businesses caught using bonded labour are liable for a fine of Rs. 20,000 per bonded labourer. In this situation, the dependence relationship ends as the labourer cannot get an advance from the *maistries* in the village and therefore cannot migrate because of this broken relationship. The labourer is then forced to take a loan from other sources associated with financial risk and probably the risk of violence. In this case, such a law does nothing to either solve poor households' problems or address the issue of debt bondage because it further aggravates the situation of these indebted households. (Bhukuth et al. 2016: Conclusion)

It is a logic derived from the neoclassical school of economic thought, which also tends to label this form of bondage an arrangement from which both employers and workers stand to gain. The plausibility of this assessment is flimsy and can be faulted on several grounds. To begin with, it starkly contradicts the gist of another publication (Bhukuth et al. 2007) in which two of its authors (Bhukuth and Ballet) in collaboration with Isabelle Guérin spelled out the intense exploitation and oppression to which bonded workers in South India are exposed. However, more weight would have to be given to the argument that unfree labour needs to be eliminated because it grossly violates human rights and is in conflict with the tenets of social justice. Justifying its widespread persistence is essentially allowing politics and policies to keep the labouring poor framed in a brutal race to the bottom.

Achhe din or How to Frame the Policy of Exclusion

With its designated prime minister Narendra Modi, the BJP swept the polls in 2014 and returned to power with an absolute majority in the lower house of parliament. At the helm of the nation the leader's pledge was that *achhe din* (good days) were bound to come for each and every one. But right from the beginning his political agenda has been discretionary, exclusionary and discriminatory. An architect and manager of Hindutva politics and for many years a full-time executive in its

---

[4] This was an amendment to the Bonded Labour (Abolition) Act 1976.

hard-core front organization Rashtriya Swayamsevak Sangh, he was nominated chief minister in Gujarat in 2001 and in the years of his administration in this state built up a pro-capital and anti-labour reputation. His proclivity for small government made him the champion of neoliberalism in India. Modi successfully promoted economic growth and allowed crony capitalists to set up special economic zones funded with state subsidy, set free from public taxation and not imperilled by labour laws and trade unionism. In stark contrast to the praise he receives from a powerful lobby for his pro-business politics is his failure to improve the quality of life for the working classes. Between 1951 and 2011 the number of agricultural labourers in the country increased from 27.3 million to 144.3 million, a rise from 19.5 to 30 per cent of the total workforce. Employment growth has been consistently low and declined to less than 0.5 per cent annually between 2004–05 and 2011–12 (Papola & Kannan 2017: 148). The dire lack of regular, let alone secure, jobs and abysmally low wages are not addressed. Social care benefits are few and far between. Poverty is widely prevalent and continues to be ignored by the eoncomic policy followed. This finds corroboration in abominable standards of public health, education, housing and, of course, welfare above all. The man who has engineered the 'Gujarat model of development' gatecrashed to national power with the ambition to replicate it for the country at large. The reforms his government made are meant to ease the activities of big business and not to redress vulnerability. What in this jargon tends to be called the urgent need to remove labour-market rigidities means getting rid of the protection and security the organized workforce has fought for over many decades. Regular job-holders were flexibilized on a large scale as casual workers, hired and fired or rotated around by the contractors to whom employment has been outsourced.

An amendment to the Child Labour Prohibition Act in 2016 undid the earlier effort made to restrict the massive number of children engaged in waged work – in industries such as carpet-weaving, gem-polishing, bidi-rolling, lock-making and matchbox manufacture, but also as under-age domestic servants or 'helpers' in small-scale establishments – which often takes the form of bondage. Replacing 'Inspection Raj' with self-certification and making it tough for workers to engage in collective action, Modi cleared the desk for his 'Make in India' fantasy, which it is imagined will turn the country into a veritable manufacturing hub. The 100 million jobs he promised to generate when campaigning – 20 million in each successive year under his watch – have four years later not even begun to materialize. On the contrary, the demonetization drive pushed in late 2016 under the pretense of weeding out corruption has had a devastating impact on employment in the informal economy. Although it

Figure 2.3 Although prohibited, child labour remains widely practised

is still too early to substantiate its full impact, the introduction of the Goods and Services Tax (GST), which became operational in early 2017, will likewise have a counterproductive effect, in particular on the interests of the low-skilled workforce exposed to intense exploitation. The underlying strategy in both policy interventions to formalize the economy is meant to benefit the households well above the poverty line. The unprivileged masses lack the social capital required for access to formal employment and remain thoroughly excluded, not only as workers in the economy but also as citizens of the nation. Capitalizing on the instant availability of a huge labour reserve, underemployed as well as underpaid, the BJP supremo is willing to drive his destitute countrymen in a race to the bottom to create higher profits for corporate business. Rohini Hensman has correctly pointed out that workers have not given up fighting for their rights, including in the informal economy (Hensman 2014), but the battle in which they are engaged is an extremely grim one. On Labour Day 2017, Narendra Modi had the audacity to salute the determination and hard work of the country's workforce – and the big role they play in India's progress. Knowing quite well that in the informal economy the labouring poor are either made to toil ceaselessly or have to suffer bouts of unemployment with nothing to fall back on, the prime minister tweeted that 'the day marks the victory of workers' movement for eight hours of work. It also aims to pay tribute to workers' sacrifices in achieving economic and social rights.' Most trade unions have turned hostile to him and refused to show up for the address made by the minister of labour and employment delivered on 1 May to mark the occasion. His audience remained limited to leaders and a cadre of the party-affiliated Bharatiya Mazdoor Sangh and a broad sample of dignitaries from other organizations associated with the induction of an undemocratic *Hindu Rashtra*.[5]

Behind a populist posture of benign command from above and in a newspeak language, an authoritarian state is being built up that – in synergy with its dominating ideology – cultivates a hierarchically framed society. In this setting the twice-born rule the roost, an enemy-in-our-midst is identified to cement the people in 'nationalist unity' and the lower working classes-cum-communities are firmly kept in their place as subordinates. So far the political parties opposing the threat of major-itarianism have not been able to join hands on a common platform to halt the drift away from social justice, human rights, democracy and progress towards equality as objectives of the national order. For the time being they seem inclined to leave the field of resistance to public intellectuals and social activists. It is a small band that speaks up on behalf of civil society. To make visible what those in power want to keep hidden is more difficult when mainstream media become reluctant to give space to such voices. Harsh Mander stands out among these dissenters engaged in public action for having insistently raised the issue of labour bondage. With a team of associates he edited *The India Exclusion Report 2013–14* as the first of an annually published series. It has an excellent overview of the origin of the master-servant relationship in agrarian society, the change in shape to neo-bondage in the transition to a capitalist mode of production, the social identity of the huge workforce that falls prey to indebtedness, the failed attempts to weed out bondage, the political denial that bondage continues to exist and the callous indifference shown by the machinery of the state charged with its eradication. My conclusion

---

[5] But toeing the Hindutva line no longer goes all the way for the president of the BMS. Six years after he went on record as a protagonist of conciliation instead of confrontation, Saji Narayanan lamented in a new interview how the policies victimize labour while reforms benefit only big business and turn India jobless. With the agricultural economy in crisis, 'Half of India's population is still either below the poverty line or just near the poverty line. India is notoriously behind the majority of nations in the Human Development Index, Social Development Index etc.' (*Outlook Magazine* 14 October 2017). His frankly stated views must have made him a black sheep in the political company he keeps.

is that this pretended ignorance can only be sustained because of the political backing it enjoys.

Welfare and Workfare for Coping with Indigence

Over time several schemes have been established to enable households stuck in deep poverty if not to overcome then at least alleviate their adversity. The most important, the Public Distribution Scheme (PDS), dates back to the Bengal famine in the 1940s but rationing was reintroduced and much expanded when food shortage arose in the early 1960s. Although the network of fair price shops spread across the country does not deliver a sufficient quantity of subsidized grains (and some other basic items) to the targeted beneficiaries to meet their consumption needs, the PDS has made a major dent in food insecurity. Below-Poverty-Line (BPL) cardholders in the villages of my fieldwork in Gujarat nowadays spend a little above half of their cash income on their daily food intake, 20 to 30 per cent less than they were forced to do when I first came around more than half a century ago. It does not necessarily mean that they are much better fed than the former generation was. However, a larger part of their earnings, still highly deficient of course, has to be set aside for much-needed expenditure on health, housing, transport and education. Whether people are included or not in the public distribution scheme for food depends on a capricious and arbitrary administrative system. While BPL ration cards have been granted to a fairly large number of families who are not in dire straits at all, the problem I found far more disconcerting is that many heads of truly impoverished households were not entered or were withdrawn from the register sanctioning the provision. As I commented in my account of the way the list was cleaned up in Gujarat a decade ago, then chief minister Narendra Modi had removed poverty from his field of vision. His decision was not inspired by a reduced intensity of deprivation at the bottom of the rural economy but was the result of a political move to produce good news – to simply deny the widespread misery that existed (Breman 2007a: 421). The Antyodaya Anna Yojana programme launched in 2000 promised relief from pauperism for the most vulnerable segment among the poor, initially estimated to consist of 10 million families or 5 per cent of the population. The figure was later doubled to 20 million families or 10 per cent of the citizenry–without any elucidation. But according to media reports a few years later about half of the states had still not been able to complete the process of identification of 'the poorest of the poor' – mostly made up of the old-aged, widows and deserted women, disabled minors and adults – and were negligent in issuing ration cards to them.

Consequently, a high percentage of the targeted categories were still unable to access subsidized food rations (Breman 2016: 201).

In its terms of reference the NCEUS had been asked to review the social security provisions available for workers in the informal economy and to make recommendations for expanding their coverage. On the basis of an inventory of central-government and state-level initiatives and having appraised the action taken by non-governmental organizations to promote and protect the well-being of this workforce, the committee tabled the draft of an Unorganised Workers' Social Security Bill (NCEUS 2006). With strong opposition from the neoliberal lobby in and outside parliament, the final wording in 2008 was a much watered-down version of the carefully crafted proposal that had been submitted. Even in this 'lite' formulation the act lacked proper enforcement, as I found out during a new round in my south Gujarat villages of fieldwork (Kannan & Breman 2013). A large majority of potential recipients who had reached old age, had become widowed or were disabled failed to receive their legal dues. The provisions, however meagre and erratic they might be, give a modicum of relief without which the recipients' lives would be even more miserable and intolerable. The very high percentage of non-inclusion cannot be attributed mainly to the incapacity of the non-labouring poor to access the social welfare schemes. The state is to be blamed much more for not reaching out to lighten the burden of its poorest citizens. This is not due merely to a failure to understand why the most vulnerable people are unable to access social protection allowances; it also results because the machinery of governance has neither the efficiency nor the effectiveness required for operating these schemes. The downtrodden who dare to intrude into the corridors of power find that officials are indifferent to their problems. Being illiterate, they need help from higher up to see to it that their applications reach the appropriate office and desk. Without in-betweens and paying the price this mediation implies, they cannot get the forms, cannot fill them out and cannot get them authorized and passed through the layered channels of officialdom. Living in isolation and at the margins of society, this grossly neglected clientele tends to perceive receipt or not of their statutory benefits as good or bad luck, not something they can claim as their right but a favour, over which they lack control and which can be withheld as arbitrarily as it has been granted.

The neoliberal doctrine of self-reliance dictates that social security has to be provided by the poor themselves. It means making transfers from the working members of the households to the dependent ones. This long-standing policy was backed up by the World Bank in its World Development Report 1995 that:

Financial help from relatives remains the principal form of income support and redistribution in developing countries. The extended family system is an important way of providing extra income and security to individual workers and their immediate household. Private transfers play an important insurance function in addition to reducing income inequality: they provide old age support and ameliorate the effects of disability, illness and unemployment. In most developing countries, especially in rural areas, older generations rely on the young to supplement their income. (World Development Report 1995: 87)

The Government of India has bought the hands-off remedy with gusto. The way in which the National Social Security Initiatives operate illustrates the reluctance or even outright unwillingness with which policy-makers took the first steps towards solving the social question. They were motivated not by an urge to empower the underprivileged but by the realization that further delay in enactment would cost them at the next election. After restricting the sparse benefits to BPL households and drastically cutting back the size of this underclass, they introduced conditionalities that excluded many destitute people. It meant that the survival of the non-labouring poor was entrusted to the working and earning members of households, the assumption being that a fund of subsistence solidarity existed in the countryside that motivates the coping poor to help the improvident segment in their midst to keep going.

The Mahatma Gandhi National Rural Employment Guarantee Act (NREGA) of 2005 aimed to provide at least 100 days of wage employment a year to every rural household willing to do unskilled manual work. It was hailed as the largest public works scheme in the world and was introduced under mounting pressure from civil-society activists to acknowledge the right to gainful work. Did its nationwide execution enhance livelihood security? No doubt the scheme is considered a nuisance by landowners and industrialists who resent the fact that land-poor and landless classes stand to benefit from the additional employment that workfare provides. Regional variations make it difficult to determine whether this large-scale intervention has been successful in generating worthwhile employment with a lasting impact. In south Gujarat the public works programme has little or no meaning. During an early spell of fieldwork I found that in three of the four localities of my recurrent research localities no job cards had yet been issued. Neither the members of the local village council nor the people I met in the neighbourhoods inhabited by the land-poor and landless had any idea what *narega* was all about. Officials in the sub-district town told me that since ample work was available in the region there was no need to generate more employment. They insisted that the influx of a huge army of seasonal migrants at the high tide of the agrarian cycle indicated that local labour was in short supply and forced employers to bring outsiders from far away to harvest the crops. However, when I came back for another round in 2009–10 *narega* had become fully operational. With the district development officer of Navsari I visited several sites he had sanctioned to get a first-hand idea of what was going on. These are all local initiatives for which prior approval of the Village Council is required. In the next stage, the projects proposed are assessed by officials on their technical merits, logistical format and financial feasibility. In the budget made, the quantity and cost of manpower is calculated for executing the project, and with authorization from officials at the district headquarters the Village Head is given the green signal to proceed. He assembles one or more work gangs which are supervised by a Mate. This is an educated young man who handles the administration – stamp job cards brought by the workers, keep a muster roll for daily attendance, measure the work done by each gang member and write down the payment to be made for it. A petty Engineer from the sub-district office checks on the progress made and collects the work-lists maintained by the Mate. The project administration report is sent to the district headquarters for sanctioning and should result in payment of the wages earned within a fortnight. The amount is deposited in a bank account which is opened for each card-holder. The procedure sketched follows the official manual in minute detail. The impression created is that of a waterproof and fail-safe scenario, one with the greatest possible public transparency – with every project detail being accessible online, from beginning to end – with the strictest adherence to a bottom-up procedure, founded on the close and cordial collaboration of government, local authorities and the labouring beneficiaries. (Breman 2013b: 326)

I went back unaccompanied to the same and other sites and found out in one sub-district about the construction of a veritable Potemkin façade. Most projects (64 out of 81) reported to have been successfully completed turned out to exist only on paper. However, the budget for all of them was spent, sometimes overspent. Social auditors whom I met confirmed the fake I had come across but were threatened or bribed to keep the fraud covered up. The existence of a racket that I slowly came to know about in my grassroots investigations was vindicated in writings published from the end of November to early December 2010 in *Diviya Bhaskar*, a leading daily in Gujarat. Petty and senior bureaucrats, bank officials, postmasters, village headmen, district politicians and members of the legislative assembly had all teamed up to profit from a scam going on in the name of creating waged work for the rural poor. It is certainly not true that corruption has spoilt *narega's* record everywhere. Much better results have been achieved in the southern states of India, in particular, where brands of populist politics have conceded more space for agency and assertion from below boosting agricultural wages (Drèze & Khera 2009; Kannan & Jain 2013). But even when workfare has been implemented according to the rules and regulations, the number of days of employment has remained much lower than mandated and the need to migrate to search for work outside agriculture and beyond the village has not abated. Even where the programme has been successfully implemented, it has only made a dent in rural poverty. The lesson learnt by officials is not the need to broaden the range and scope of public workfare as has been recommended (Papola & Kannan 2017: 155) but to phase it out. In line with its pro-capital and anti-labour policy the BJP government announced in late 2014 that *narega* would be downsized. The funding for the following year was cut by nearly half of the earlier budget.

Gujarat is admired as a great neoliberal success story that resulted in a much higher rate of economic growth than elsewhere in the country. Moreover, some claim that the rapid increase in state domestic product was accompanied by a sharp fall in poverty and major improvement in social sectors such as health and education. It is a development performance more laudable because good governance saw to it that the outcome was inclusive and fair. However, this wonderful story has been uncovered as a fable. A volume of essays on the 'Gujarat Miracle', edited by well-known social scientists (Hirway et al. 2014), argues that the state became one of the fastest growing in the country by ignoring or even sacrificing major development goals. The policy frame has been one of exclusion rather than social inclusion. Excessively low wages for men and women in both the rural and urban economy as well as new forms of child labour clarify why the state ranks at the bottom of the national wage heap (Papola & Kannan 2017: 150). Gujarat is not an exceptional case, and the difference is one of degree. Nevertheless, what makes this state remarkable is the paradox of a weak or even absent commitment to the well-being of the masses existing alongside a strong promotion of growth benefiting a small minority. Narendra Modi as its high-profile driver went out of his way to placate big business with favours. The chief minister of Gujarat ushered in a climate of crony capitalism, and the overt plus covert support he got from these quarters is meant to enable him now to proceed in the same direction countrywide. The huge tax breaks and subsidies granted to corporate India has been at the cost of public funding for the social sector, which explains why on this expenditure Gujarat lags behind in the nationwide score. The percentage of the public budget to gross state domestic product spent on primary education, health, family welfare and social protection went down between

2000–01 and 2009–10 and this decline was the steepest in Gujarat (Breman 2014b: 27–9). This growth model built on progressive inequality has become the agenda for the country at large.

Covering up the Dismal Plight of the Labouring and Non-Labouring Poor

The first part of this book has chronicled how labour came to be written up in the annals of the state. In my publications based on my empirical research regarding the labouring and non-labouring poor, I have time and again criticized the official data base for the documentation of work, employment and labour relations in India's economy. The statistical data collected on a regular basis by the National Sample Survey Office (NSSO) has over the years been a major source of knowledge and is also referred to in the chapters of this monograph. Expressing my reservation on the exclusive use of aggregate data to report on the changing landscape of employment and labour, I have argued against mere reliance on quantified data and on techniques of measurement resulting in undue fixation on drawing a poverty line (Breman 2016: 27–30). The perception brought to the fore in my own investigations is that a thorough study of poverty involves investigating not just the conditions of deficiency but also the relationships between the poor and the non-poor. Although the facts and figures collected and analyzed in the NSSO rounds are an important source of information and cannot be ignored when investigating the economic fabric, more is needed to find out what transpires in the realm of work and income. Other research methods are required. But do we really want to know what remains hidden? The response to this question was certainly positive on behalf of the politicians and policymakers who took the initiative to monitor the economic lay of the land in the early post-Independence era. An agency was set up, in a system designed by Prime Minister Jawaharlal Nehru, to provide the input of data meant as yardsticks and checkpoints to inform and guide the country's planned economic development. The founder of the Indian Statistical Institute in Kolkata, the eminent scholar P. C. Mahalanobis, became the architect of the statistical agency that was established. The NSSO came into being in 1950 charged with collecting systematically and consecutively sets of big data through nationwide surveys on a variety of socio-economic aspects, mainly for poverty and labour force estimations. After a managerial reshuffle in 1970 the agency was entrusted with all tasks – from the scheduling of sample rounds, preparation of enquiries, framing of instructions, training of field staff, and processing/analyzing of data to writing and disseminating the reports.

Branched off as a separate government organization, the NSSO has operated from 1999 onwards under the umbrella of the Ministry of Planning and Program Implementation.

For a number of reasons there seem to be grounds for casting doubt on the validity and veracity of statistical data presented in NSSO publications. This can be illustrated for instance in the recurrent count of jobs. The NSSO has discontinued its quinquennial Employment and Unemployment Survey (EUS) with the intention of replacing it with an annual Labour Force Survey, which used to be carried out by the Labour Bureau. This department acknowledged in its report for 2014 that 'labour statistics in its present form is dated and of poor quality, thus limiting its reliability and use' (Singh & Mitra 2018: 30). The issue as stated in this citation is of a technical nature but much more seems to be amiss than just logistical problems in the collection of data. A note from the former chief statistician of India reads like a minute of dissent. Pronab Sen wrote that notwithstanding the country's long history of labour regulation none of the sources he referred to has been found useful in monitoring employment trends in the country:

This is partly because of the fact that India has a very large proportion of its non-agriculture labour force in the unorganized sector, specially in own account enterprises, which do not come under labour legislation. Nevertheless, even for the organized sectors of the economy, these data sources have not been found to be particularly accurate (Sen n. d.: 4)

The NSSO has already backed out of its announced plan for a job count each and every year. What has been going on in the corridors of these government agencies? In addition, the decline in quality could no longer remain unnoticed among insiders. When the NCEUS panel of experts, all economists, had in its series of reports[6] pointed out that much of what transpired in the country's informal economy was understated and misrepresented in official statstics, tackling the problem of data reliability and improved measurement could be put off no longer. The National Statistical Commission constituted in 2010 a Committee on Unorganized Sector Statistics 'to identify major data gaps relating to unorganized enterprises and unorganized workers and to suggest ways of developing a statistical database on the unorganized sector with standardized concepts, definitions, coverage and comparability over time and space' (Government of India, National Statistical Commission 2012). The chairman and several members of the committee are well-known

---

[6] See in particular NCEUS Working Paper No.3 entitled *Definitional and Statistical Issues Relating to Workers in Informal* Employment, New Delhi 2009.

scholars thoroughly versed in the intricacies of the informal economy. But it seems that, other than in the case of the NCEUS panel, the members who wrote the report were nominated ex-officio and relied on their administrative staff. It may explain why the political economy of informality does not seem to have been part of the deliberations, even though this would have been relevant in deciding how to establish a statistical database that stands the test of reliability as well as inclusive coverage.

In its attempt to accomplish the task set, the committee's report quite understandably leans heavily on the views adopted by the Fifteenth International Conference of Labour Statisticians held in 1993 under the auspices of the ILO in Geneva, on the United Nations-endorsed System of National Accounts (which in cryptic terminology comments on activity that escapes formal statistical measurement as 'the-so-called-not-observed-economy') and last but not least on the substantive methodological contribution made by the NCEUS. The committee suggests that the problem of statistical measurement is partly due to the growth of the informal economy and employment. It is a disputable notion since most economic relationships and transactions – rural and urban, agrarian and non-agrarian – were informal from the very beginning and never lost that stamp. Rather than a change in the economy's shape and composition, the way in which it was statistically recorded in the past needs to be critically reappraised. No doubt, it is a difficult exercise but I wonder if the way out of the quagmire of debatable measurement should be to exempt from statistical data collection the intricate forms of employment in agriculture or what is often incorrectly classified as income from self-employment. Hardly less problematic are inventories of occupational multiplicity and side-earnings to the main household income. However, to desist from quantification of such issues, and there are many more than the ones mentioned, is to lose out on coverage and accuracy. Behind a stiff-upper-lip façade much remains unregistered as exemplified by the following citation:

Though the surveys of NSSO/CSO are supposed to have covered informal financial services no data have been reported separately for this sector. The enterprise surveys do not collect loan-wise details such as interest rate and duration of the loan. As such, it is not feasible to measure the extent of financial accommodation and interest paid on these loans to the informal credit agencies. (Government of India, National Statistical Commission 2012: 38)

It is a striking instance of subterfuge, a veiled suggestion that helps keep the wide-ranging practices of debt bondage firmly beyond official purview. I shall further comment on this omission in the third and concluding part of this book.

The report ends with a clarion call to stakeholders, informants and the general public to answer survey questions truly, noting that a good database depends upon the cooperation of respondents. Such an appeal to the goodwill of all and sundry reflects a naive disregard for the fact that lack of transparency is the essence, the alpha and omega of the informal economy. Not to open up what is going on in the economic circuit but to hide it – a practice in Gujarat labelled as *number be* or *kalum* – is the very reason why the drive to informalization was launched by the taskmasters of global capitalism and became readily accepted by all those accountable for India's governance. It is therefore only natural that the tabulation of statistical data should also bear the imprint of manipulated fabrication. In this endeavour and irrespective which the ruling party is, political leaders and policymakers have from the beginning of the 1990s consistently subscribed to the tenets of neoliberalism, bringing the interests of capital to the fore and victimizing those of labour. Elaboration of this agenda would have inadvertently brought up the nature of the political economy in a more encompassing analysis than the Committee cared to deliver, possibly because it was too far detached from its mandate.

The report's concluding part consists of a set of recommendations meant to improve the quality and credibility of statistical presentation. The constraints identified are mainly of a technical nature, respectively listed as: reduction in the number of sanctioned posts of NSSO field investigators and their supervisers; failure to initiate surveys; reductions in sample size, along with deficient sample frame; and unacceptably large revisions that damage public credibility but also diminish their usefulness for making policy decisions. It is clear that these deficiencies are caused by a major squeeze of the budget allocated to the NSSO. An implied operational change – outsourcing data collection to hired consultants – may reduce costs but the price paid is a lack of qualified enumerators and consequently a growing unreliability of statistical data. Much more crucial than highlighting the problem of professional staffing, which after all is the result of the fetishism of neoliberal privatization, would have been to foreground that a major issue for the future of the NSSO is its character as a government undertaking. Since it is part of the state apparatus it has less autonomy to freely and fairly report on work and employment in the informal economy. But even drawing attention to the critical constraint that labour issues are not only hugely understated but also consistently misrepresented in the annals of the state still does not touch on the heart of the matter. The problem overriding all others is that those in power do not want to be briefed on the dismal plight of the men, women and children in the lower ranks of the labour hierarchy. Having turned their backs on the dispossessed among the labouring and non-labouring poor, the ruling powers are no longer willing to be informed on the miserable plight of this very sizeable chunk of India's huge workforce. Data, statistical or not, are unwelcome and considered redundant to demand in official quarters.

Part II

Destitute in Bondage

The song of a *hali*
I go in darkness
I return in darkness
My whole life is full of darkness
There is no ray of light
                    Cited in Chakravarti 1985

3   The Commodification of Agricultural Labour

Bondage Re-examined

In the first part I demonstrated that there are various grades of bondage, along a continuum from mild to harsh. Lack of control over one's labour power can also differ in duration, stretching from being held in life-long captivity to more temporary forms of engagement in servitude. My contention in this section is that this fluidity holds equally for the distinction between free and unfree labour. While the extremes at both ends are clearly articulated, the range in between is more ambiguous and difficult to classify – not least because it can change according to time and place. The two forms of labour bondage that I focused on in my local-level research in south Gujarat are both based on indebtedness. At least, that is how they have been documented in the literature, although the setting in which they came about was highly dissimilar. The variant I put on record in my field-based research when it was already on the verge of being extinguished derives from the pre-capitalist past, when bondage was a hereditary relationship attaching a landless servant in beck-and-call availability to a landowning master. The *hali* was born in bondage and became domesticated at young age in the master's household. Children started to work when they were six or seven years old; sons to graze the cattle and tend the beasts in the stable, daughters to join their mother (*harekwali*) performing domestic chores in the master's house and courtyard. Getting married, sons would continue to serve their father's *dhaniamo*, while girls joined as maids the household of their husband's master. To fix the beginning of bondage at the time of marriage is therefore quite arbitrary. Once the relationship was established the *hali*'s allegiance to his master's household was supposed to pass on to the next generation.

In my endeavour to trace the origin of the domination-subordination opposition in an indeterminate past hidden from the historical record, I proposed that in a process of colonization of 'wild lands', Hindu civilization expanded through the invasion by peasant castes of regions inhabited by tribes. In his seminal work D. D. Kosambi has shown how in the precolonial economy tribal communities were dispossessed and tied down in bonded dependence:

Many tribal people had fallen into servitude in times of famine, and one step away were the tribal castes or poorest cultivators who had at the same time incurred a debt which could not be repaid by generation after generation. This accounts for the retained castes such as the Cheruman in Malabar, the Koltas of Jhaunsar-Bawar in the Himalayan foothills near Almora, the Halis of Gujarat, and the like. (Kosambi 1956: 353; see also Lorenzo 1943: 122)

Retracing the evolution of the caste-tribe frontier in south Gujarat, I took my cue from finding out how land was settled and cultivated in the colonial era (Breman 2007b, Chapter 1). The newcomers brought with them a more advanced agricultural technology in which the plough and early well-irrigation played a pivotal role; the introduction of sedentary agriculture enabled the settlers to rise to the position of landlords. The bands of intruders may have been peasant owner-cultivators where they came from but now began to exempt themselves from tilling the soil. It was a ritualized avoidance of labour considered degrading that marked their slow but steady elevation to dominant ranking. Their upward movement in the caste order was made possible by the simultaneous subjugation of the dispossessed local tribals to predial servitude. Not all tribals relegated to landlessness were attached in bondage, although finding sustenance without a benefactor must have been arduous. The unattached segment remained embedded in or fell back on a tribal mode of existence, a mixture of food gathering and slash-and-burn cultivation of the still abundantly available wasteland. Were they not engaged because the supply of subordinate labourers exceeded demand or did they lack the qualities required of a *hali*: a display of diligence, obedience, loyalty and deference? Were the *halis* indeed better off than the unattached landless, as reported in early colonial accounts, or was this a biased opinion put on record by relying on information solicited from landlords?

For lack of factual evidence these questions can only be answered speculatively by comparing South Gujarat's *halipratha* to identical practices of institutionalized bondage found elsewhere in the south Asian subcontinent. In a study of the *malik-kamia* system of bondage that was prevalent in Bihar, Gyan Prakash argued that the relationship that held tribals captive to Hindu landlords resulted from the introduction of capitalism in a colonial setting (Prakash 1990). The earlier servitude that existed should be understood, he argues, as the outcome of an unequal power configuration. In his view it was only during colonial rule that *kamias*, until then dependent servants of dominant landlords, were reconstituted as unfree labourers attached to big landowners. I am in agreement with Prakash as far as the overriding importance of instilling social and political hegemony in a feudalistic setting is concerned. These features were the organizing principle of what I classified as patronage in my elaboration on past bondage. Nevertheless, the articulation of inequality, of pairing domination to subjugation, was – quite apart from being a goal in itself – part of the process of laying claim to labour power (for instance, of Dublas in south Gujarat and Bhuniyas in south Bihar) for land clearance and cultivation. This was, after all, the economic base on which the ascendancy of the caste Hindus who ventured into these still unsettled regions was founded. To highlight the political and social ramifications in the pre-capitalist type of bondage but to disconnect these features from the economic moorings of the practice is in my opinion uncalled for. I still stick to Hermanus Nieboer's original premise that scarcity of labour produced by a high land-to-man ratio was a powerful force behind an intruding social formation, which claimed exclusive ownership rights, forcing others to work for them (Nieboer 1910). However, to squeeze out ever more labour power at the lowest possible cost was not the driving force in this mode of employment. Exploitation needed to be balanced by a measure of security and protection, as Max Weber explained in his treatise on *patrimoniale Herrschaft* (patrimonial rule):

> The master 'owes' the subject something as well, not juridically but morally. Above all – if only in his own interest – he must protect him against the outside world, and help him in need. He must also treat him 'humanely', and especially he must restrict the exploitation of his performance to what is 'customary'. On the ground of a domination whose aim is not material enrichment but the fulfillment of the master's own needs, he can do so without prejudicing his own interest because, as his needs cannot expand qualitatively and, on principle, unlimitedly, his demands only differ quantitatively from those of his subjects. And such restriction is positively useful to the master, as not only the security of his domination, but also its results depend on the disposition and mood of the subordinates. The subordinate morally owes the master assistance by all means available to him. (Weber 1922: 682)

Exploitation and Patronage

The security that servitude promised must have been a good enough reason for tribals who were deprived of their customary means of livelihood to surrender their freedom because hunting and gathering with rudimentary agricultureis is a vulnerable and risky way of life. They were given a daily food ration not only on days at work but also when out of work in the slack season. On such days of forced inactivity *halis* used to come and hang around the landlord's residence doing odd chores in the courtyard and feeding the animals, although they mainly turned up to collect the grain ration that would see them through the next couple of days. *Khavathi* (from the word for 'to eat') was the name of their daily sustenance. They were supposed to get their regular allowance even when they were ill or too old to work. Payment of wages not earned, in the sense of not worked for, was how the livelihood guarantee used to play out during the long spells of unemployment that characterized the uneven and not highly work-intensive agrarian cycle. The quantity given 'freely', that is without labour power in return, increased the cumulative debt of gratitude the servant owed his master. This is why I defined *halipratha* as marked by both exploitation and patronage. I should qualify this contradictory duality by pointing out that the landowner was willing to make up the livelihood deficit of the landless on the condition that subordinates would acquiesce in their state of servitude. Exploitation was conditioned by patronage, and vice versa. The income *halis* were able to get out of the deal fell short of their minimal requirements to stay alive and bear at least the cost of reproduction. Everything the patron was willing to provide to his landless clients over and above their daily food allowance, though much-needed, was a discretionary supplement, extras that made the shortfall somewhat more manageable. In addition to having labourers at their disposal when they needed them, patrons bene-fitted from a show of humility and deference from servile clients who did their utmost to extract more than was their apportioned due in terms of food, shelter and care. On opposite sides in this interlocking spectrum of servitude the two parties must have manoeuvred to maximize their dues and minimize their obligations. However, neither master nor servant intended to terminate the relationship they had agreed upon. The better-off landowners engaged *halis* not only to cultivate their fields and look after the cattle. They were driven by their desire to lead leisurely lives, to excuse themselves from working on the land and so to gain in prestige and power. Displays of servile behaviour added lustre to the master's household. The number of servants a patron had under his protection indicated his standing. His main consideration in deciding whether to take on another *hali* was not how many he needed to work for him but how many he could afford. Patrons went bankrupt when they had surrounded themselves with more clients than they could maintain on the terms stipulated. Their carrying capacity also dried up rapidly in times of adversity. Servants taken on in boom periods were released again in years of famine, as happened towards the end of the nineteenth century: '*Halis* are no longer maintained as the Anaolas find it hard enough to feed themselves, let alone their *Halis* (Machonochie 1897; see also Census of India 1901, vol. XVIII, part 1.1: 72–3).

Did compliance also imply that the servitude had become internalized? This was certainly the image of *halipratha* that landowners wanted to project: the faithful servant as a grateful recipient of the generosity bestowed on him. The perception that bonded labourers were to be envied rather than pitied resonated in the name given to the master: *dhaniamo*, i.e. 'he who confers well-being'. The presentation of *halipratha* as a reciprocal bond beneficial to both parties fits with the language of patronage. It suggests that *halis* subjected themselves not only willingly but also unconditionally to the goodwill of their master. It is a biased appraisal that ignores the negligence, abuse of power and denigration they endured. The claim to security and protection could in daily practice be denied and boiled down to favours the patron might capriciously grant or withhold. As a token of his displeasure the patron could refuse to provide a 'loan' when he was asked to do so and instead of graciously handing out the grain ration at the end of the workday, scold his servants for the poor quality of what he had ordered them to do:

Fear of eviction from the house site, fear of recall of loans, fear of loss of the additional income from a piece of land gifted to him and lastly, the security taken from a farm servant in the form of deferred wages to be paid only at the harvest, are more powerful and terrible sanctions than what the ordinary law may provide. (Sivaswamy 1948: 30)

There was, of course, an in-built tension in a relationship that was structured on the pretension of partnership but rooted in deep inequality. How did the landless clients react to the loss of their promised or imagined entitlements? In the first instance, no doubt, with efforts to placate the boss, to go out of their way in proper clientelist fashion and beseech him to leniency. Such were, after all, the rules of the game in the domination-subordination equation. But the discord might easily escalate and feed feelings of animosity lingering from long before. Rather than risk an open confrontation that he was bound to lose, the servant might resort to obstruction, sabotage, feigned ignorance, evasion and other weapons of the weak. It was 'misbehaviour' well captured by the ethnographer of the tribal community from which most *halis* originated:

... obstinacy of temperament is a common feature of Dubla life whether it represents a man, a woman, or a child. If a Dubla has made up his mind not to work on a particular day, it is generally difficult to make him change his mind; also when he makes up his mind to do any work, it is equally difficult to divert his mind to other pursuits. If he is well fed and treated well, he can stand hours of work in the field and can turn out good crops; he is, however, sensitive to bad treatment and if jolted, the output of work is at once brought down. (Shah 1958: 25)

When grievances were neither admitted nor solved and dissatisfaction on both sides mounted, falling out with each other was the next stage of the rising conflict. It usually took the form of the servant deserting the master. In the archival sources I did not come across cases of patrons becoming fed up with the subversive, impudent behaviour of a subordinate and sending him off in disgrace. In the course of my fieldwork I found out how such rascals were brought to heel with killing brutality (Breman 2003: Chapter 2). If *halis* did run away where did they go? Often to the wife's village, but this was not a safe haven since members of the dominant caste of landowners were supposed to inform the master where to find his absconding *hali*. Under their prescribed code of conduct they were not to employ him and if they nevertheless did they were fined when found out. However, the patrons sparred with each other to increase their power and prestige by attracting a larger clientele and to undercut their rivals by persuading his *halis* to change allegiance. The servants were aware of the competition that split the ranks of their superiors and ran off or were lured away to join the household of another patron. Their desertion, instigated or not, aimed at finding a master who would give them a better deal and was not inspired by the prospect of 'freedom'. It was an act of desperation, when discontentment heightened to resentment, but the break could still be a temporary one. Having expressed their deep anguish by making themselves scarce, it so happened that many *halis* did go back to their old master (Kishore 1924). Toeing the line of bondage was unavoidable so long as no other employment opportunities came around. A short reprieve opened up with the construction of railway lines, which traversed the plain of south Gujarat in the second half of the nineteenth century. Tribals in the region were recruited as coolies for infrastructural work and in addition many *halis*, attracted by the much higher wages, left their masters. But the opening of the labour market turned out to be a short-term windfall and the laid-off coolies were reported to have gone back again to their 'safe and secure' *hali* existence (Enthoven 1920–2 , vol. I,: 347).

The resistance reported was highly individualized. In the early colonial accounts no mention is made of any collective action against bondage – presumably because there was hardly any space left to act in unison and certainly not when protest took the shape of challenging the power of the dominant landowners. The servants were sheltered in huts on sites close to the master's abode, instantly available if their presence was required and kept under close surveillance. Foregrounding the patron-client axis

meant that work and life ran along ties of verticality and left subordinates
little time and opportunity to retreat into a horizontal sphere of communal solidarity. The regime of subservience saw to it that the tribals had no
regular or intensive contact with members of their own community. The
ethnographer of tribal lore, P. G. Shah, described them as leading loose
and diffident lives, with the implied suggestion that the *hali* and his wife
interacted more with their master than with each other (Shah 1958: 42).
This phrasing may have been a veiled reference to the sexual abuse to
which the *hali*'s wife and daughters in particular, were subject at the
hands of males in the master's household. The accounts on which
I depend for reconstructing the past system of bondage avoid discussing
this 'custom' as one of the prerogatives of patriarchal domination. But
the violation of female bodies (and not rarely those of young boys as well)
among the downtrodden and oppressed remained customary, as I found
out in the course of my fieldwork. Forced sexual intercourse is still a
taboo subject but its incidental or regular prevalence cannot any longer
be denied and covered up as it used to be in the past. With the passing of
time the rise of assertiveness from below seems to have opened more
space to prevent, oppose or even prosecute perpetrators. However, at the
high tide of servile bondage the agony such intimate abuse caused must
also have found an outlet in efforts to find healing among the like-
minded. Through ties of kinship *hali* households were wont to articulate
their own tribal identity and share in the life-cycle events of the community of which they were part and parcel. They also set up a *panch* to codify
a list of do's and don'ts and if called upon gathered in meetings to sort
out trespassers. Communal togetherness existed, although it was understated in accounts that portrayed *halipratha* as a bond of patronage above
all. This portrayal suggested that mutual affection existed between
master and servant and characterized the servant as having been admitted to the intimacy of the master's household. But this was a thin veneer,
at odds with the way subordinates tainted by an impure way of life were
treated. Prone to eating meat, drinking alcohol, singing and dancing on
festive occasions in which men and women freely participated and given
to other forms of 'licentious' behaviour, these uncouth and inferior
people needed to be kept at arm's length. The relationship of domination
also extended to the cultural domain, expressed in a disdain for their
backward status as non-Hindus. Still, having lived from generation to
generation in the shadow of landowners who had raised their own religious status as twice-born Hindus by dispossessing and subjugating tribal
communities, the latter were classified in colonial records as semi-
Hindus who had incorporated some traits of Hinduism in their social
life. Tribal castes would be a better alternative label – and this was how

Kosambi classified them. According to conventional wisdom, tribals were too poor to adopt a proper Hinduized life style. I would like to emphasize that apart from being unable to spend on rituals and festivals, members of these communities also refused to bow down under the pressure of social reformers to accept their submission at the tail-end of the caste hierarchy. They tenaciously stuck to their separate identity in demonstrative resistance, aptly expressed by Tanika Sarkar:

Within the outer arch of assimilation and hegemonization by the ideology of dominant groups, an inner, almost completely closed world, of primitive survival existed for slaves and bondsmen. This was their 'living space', an area of autonomy set apart from their master's domination and control. It was also a comprehension of their dark, helpless, primeval and precarious existence which they elliptically identified as their entire universe. (Sarkar 1985: 122; see also Chakravarti 1985)

Colonial Interference

How did colonial authorities react to the agrarian bondage they encountered in south Gujarat? In reply to an enquiry ordered by the metropolitan headquarters in the first half of the nineteenth century to report on the existence of slavery in the possessions of the East India Company the system of *halipratha* was indeed described as slavery. From Surat, regularly administered by the British from 1800 onwards, district collector and magistrate W. J. Lumsden wrote:

The Dessaees Buttela Brahmins in Parchole Soopa, and some other purgunnahs, possess as large a portion of slaves as may be found perhaps in any part of India. Those, who are frequently attached to the soil, as well as bond-servants who voluntarily engage to labour in payment of loans made to them for their marriages, or the like occasions, at times run away from their masters, and such cases are brought before the Magistrate. Sometimes the master is to blame, and sometimes the servant, and no particular inferences arise on the cases of this I am acquainted with as to the treatment of slaves. The slaves are all of the Coolee Doobla, and other poor classes of the Hindoos, who are in this zillah, much addicted to drinking toddy, and a very debauched, improvident and inferior race. I believe the slaves to be more comfortable than the free portion of their respective castes. (8 August 1825 in Slavery. Accounts and Papers. 1837–8. Vol. 16. 15 November 1837–16 August 1838: 433)

★ ★ ★

The queries to which this official responded were part of a large-scale survey conducted in preparation for a forthcoming debate on slavery in the British parliament. The views expressed differed in assessments of its seriousness, magnitude and shape and advice from the wide range of colonial officials consulted on how to deal with it was also varied. As the collector of Surat District, Lumsden concurred with the majority of his colleagues who recommended that the usages of the land should not be interfered with and that the servitude that had come into existence under native rule should be allowed to continue undisturbed. In the passage just quoted the Company's official in charge of south Gujarat indicated why this was also his considered opinion. Firstly, because the practice did not have its origin in coerced imposition but was entered into voluntarily by labourers eager to become attached. Secondly, because the bonded landless were much better off than the free ones in their midst. Thirdly, the 'hereditary bondsmen', in local parlance known as *gulams* or slaves, belonged to inferior tribes willing to stick to their masters because they did not mind their lack of freedom. When all was said and done, slavery was not thought to be so abominable as to call for its instant abolition. Maybe that step would have to follow in future but action should be taken in moderation rather than in haste. The notion that should take precedence was that without masters taking care of them such people, unable to stand on their own feet, were bound to perish. In this assessment the immense poverty of *halis* is not seen as being caused by bondage but a consequence of the improvident lives they led. But a hands-off policy did not go far enough according to another school of colonial administrators who claimed that remaining impartial and not taking sides in disputes was ill-advised. They argued that the interests of the masters should be given priority and their control over labour bonded in debt to them be enforced as a legal right. In 1837, the political commissioner for Gujarat, J. C. C. Sutherland, warned that any other strategy would contravene the sense of justice of the main landowning class:

Claims for the restoration of fugitive slaves are by no means infrequent; and in such a rude state of society as exists in this province, non-compliance would not only be regarded as a great injustice, but be apt to lead to acts of violence and retaliation. I would, therefore, suggest that, except when decided ill-treatment appears to have taken place, I should be authorized to interfere to cause the restoration of run-away slaves, or compensation and satisfaction for their owners. (Banaji 1933: 318)

What actually happened was that in the judicial-bureaucratic language of colonial rule the *hali* was henceforth no longer portrayed as a slave or agrestic serf. He was dealt with and also codified as a workman who had been free but chose to contract himself in bondage. He had, on payment of a loan, forfeited the freedom to dispose of his labour power as and when he saw fit. Prevented by lack of possessions from returning what had been advanced to him, he was considered to be duty-bound to serve the landowner until his debt was redeemed. To employ him was after all the only way the creditor could get a return on his investment. The authorities therefore felt obliged to return runaway servants and authorized, by a letter from government of 19 April 1822, the magistrate of Surat district 'to apprehend and return to his master any Halee who may abscond' (J. Vibart, principal collector of Surat district, quoted in Report from the India Law Commissioners and Papers Relating to Slavery in the East Indies 1841: 164). Although this was now supposed to be standard procedure, not all the Company's officials went out of their way to track down deserters. They sometimes roundly refused to attend to complaints of 'owners' who wanted to file a case against a defaulting servant. 'Wretched' was the term used in colonial accounts in the middle of the nineteenth century to describe both the condition in which the *halis* lived and the treatment meted out to them by their masters. Such colonial officials probably acted out of compassion, unwilling to add to the miserable plight of the landless workforce, but did not desist from the prevalent view that the tribals themselves were to blame for their destitution. The manner in which bondage was now framed brought to bear the contractarian thinking that had gained much ground in the dispensation of colonial legality. The abolition of slavery in 1843 made it necessary to indicate in revised officialese, firmly eschewing the jargon of servitude, what debt bondage stood for and why it should be backed up by law. It was redefined as an employer-employee relationship and could be submitted for judicial arbitration in case of breach of contract:

Halees are rather bondsmen than slaves; these persons or their offspring who have sold their labour for an advance of money, are bound to serve the lender and its heirs, until they are able to repay the sum. Their children remain bound until the debt is discharged. Halees may acquire property but cannot be transferred or sold ... They almost entirely consist of Dooblas and other low castes of Hindoos ... The master is bound to feed and clothe them, give them a piece of land and to defray their marriage expenses, the sum laid out on the latter however being added to the original amount, for which their services became his. (Letter of 22 February 1836 by G. Grant, Acting Judge, Surat District, quoted in Report from the India Law Commissioners and Papers Relating to Slavery in the East Indies 1841: 157, 164, 171)

Prabhu Mohapatra (Mohapatra 2009) has argued that the juridical construction of free labour relations under colonial rule had the paradoxical effect of reproducing and legitimizing unfree labour relations. The new policy had its origin in local ordinances promulgated in Calcutta, which in slowly growing jurisprudence from 1814 onwards held native workmen accountable to colonial masters to provide goods or render services that they had obliged themselves to deliver. The deal, which applied to craftsmen as well as domestic servants, was sealed on receipt of advance payment – as customarily practised. Initially restricted to the Company's headquarters, the contractarian codification extended in the first half of the nineteenth century to rural areas and other parts of the colony. It allowed for the criminalization of 'free' labour that could be prosecuted and punished – specifically, not redeeming the debt incurred; and, more generally, not adhering to what had been mutually agreed upon. Prior payment of a small cash amount as earnest money and then not abiding by the employer or his agent's orders as to when to report for work or disobeying instructions on how to do it were now considered an offence. This ordinance was enforceable from 1819, with penal sanctions, on the pretext that civil procedures were ineffective at preventing workers from deserting. Working under duress, as the *halis* did in south Gujarat, was validated by colonial law and accepted as being in accordance with standing practice also in south India, as also Meenu Tiwari has pointed out:

The language of 'debt' and 'contract' was, however, employed without qualification by missionaries and state officials alike, making for an ill-fitting description of Pariahs' relations with their landed caste overlords and unwittingly contributing to the impression, shared by some state officials as well as some modern historians, that these so-called loans were the very source of bondage. The persistence of bondage did not depend on contracts any more than it depended on courts. More common and highly effective tools were in place, such as landowners' monopoly on the means of production, Pariahs' lack of alternative employment, and violent disciplining. (Tiwari 2014: 29)

The legal course taken implied that the colonial authorities backed up arrangements privately made and culminated in the Workmen's Breach of Contract Act in 1859. Although this act at first only addressed agreements secured with a down payment in cash, the notion of criminalized breach was soon broadened to deprive workmen of control over the free use of their labour and, once they were engaged, prevented them from bargaining for better terms of employment. In the wake of the abolition of slavery the colonial government had given in to pressure to facilitate large-scale recruitment of coolie labour for deployment to enclaves of capitalist production within the country and in other dominions under British rule in the global South. Mines and plantations required a workforce that could be exploited and oppressed in ways similar to the erstwhile slave armies. Indenture was coined as the legalized formula that amply met this requirement, while the worker was denied all protection against abusive treatment for the duration of his or her contract. In a case study of the plantation economy of Southeast Asia I have elaborated on how the taming of coolies in capitalist bondage took place as part of a collusion between the colonial state and corporate agribusiness (Breman

1989). The colonial government resorted to introducing a contract to tie down Indian labour to European employers. The Workmen's Breach of Contract Act in 1859 was not intended to regulate relationships within the colonized peasant economy. The agrarian servitude that had its origin in dispossession of customary rights when tribal communities were subjected to the emerging caste order was allowed to continue uninterrupted.

Commodified in Debt Bondage

The attachment of labour such as had taken shape in the *halipratha* system was not declared out of bounds within the rules and regulations of the colonial state. The contractarian ideology that came to shape colonial governance gave landowners a new handle to keep their bonded servants in check. Throughout the Indian subcontinent the former serf was now reconstituted as a labourer legally compelled to work off his debt. Formal sanctions could be solicited to back up the informal power of the landowning elite in the exploitation and subordination of their landless workforce:

Landlords and labourers ordered their relations as contracts founded on advances of loan. They executed written deeds representing their relations as debtor-creditor ties and approached the courts as parties bound by contracts. Contributing to this liberation of the kamias from slavery and their reconstitution as bonded laborers was the objectification of agrarian relations. While this objectification, gathering increasing force by the late nineteenth century, founded on social relations in contractual exchange of things – advance of money, grain, and land for labor – it was the juridical process that helped define these exchanges as creditor-debtor transactions. In effect, therefore, the two processes acted in harmony, making the kamias manifest as innately free persons bonded by debts. (Prakash 1990: 222)

The changing character of the master-servant relationship was much affected by the growing commercialization and monetization of the rural economy. The social history of south Gujarat does not confirm the assumption of a closed and subsistence-oriented village community that in the pre-capitalist era remained disconnected from the outside world. Market linkages were already of long standing and local products found their way to faraway destinations by wheeled transport over land and by ship from small ports. From the tribal hinterland, still covered with forests, timber was carried by bullock cart along country tracks to coastal towns at the river mouths and shipped from there to Bombay, Surat and Kathiawar. Salt-pans along the coast also produced a commodity required for common use and not merely for local demand. Food crops were consumed by the producers, bartered within a narrow range for other goods and services or brought to weekly fairs held in the vicinity. Among a large variety of grains, rice in particular was traded outside the region by country boat. In the lands around Surat cotton was a major non-food crop sold to village- or urban-based traders, while in the southern *talukas* sugar-cane manufactured by the cultivators to brown sugar played a major role in the gradual commercialization of the peasant economy. The pace of this commercialization began to accelerate from the middle of the nineteenth century onwards. The total area under settled cultivation expanded and the conversion of dry to wet land in the central plain resulted in higher crop yields. But the agrarian technology did not change much since the wells dug for irrigation, still shallow and without masonry, failed to last beyond a year. More important was improvement in overland connectivity, which boosted marketization of food and non-food commodities now purchased using standardized measures and weights. The completion of the railway line from Bombay to Surat in 1864 was followed by the subsequent construction of west-east sidelines that cut across the central plain and facilitated traffic into and out of the interior of the district. Bridges and fair-weather roads, although not yet paved, gave better access to the *taluka* headquarters in which agricultural and handicraft products from the villages around were collected and traded for transport elsewhere.

Cash money, and no longer of the locally minted sort, had over time become accepted as means of exchange and was also used for payment of the land tax that the government collected from landowners. However, between the various agrarian classes and with other castes at the village-level transactions were, as before, settled in kind. At the end of the workday *halis* were given their wage in the form of a grain ration or *bhata*, handed out to them in a hollow wooden receptacle. They received the same quantity by way of advance if they remained idle in the slack season. A few coins that the master would add as a bonus on festive occasions or when servants were charged with chores different from or additional to their normal workload were typically spent on liquor bought from the local distiller and which his tribal subordinates were reported to relish beyond moderation (Gazetteer of the Bombay Presidency 1877, vol. II: 199–201). This economic transformation not only found expression in changed modes of production and distribution but also led to new patterns of consumption among the better-off cultivators. They could afford to buy items unheard of until then, demonstrating a lifestyle that set them apart from the large majority of the peasantry, as the collector of Surat commented at the end of the nineteenth century:

... the present men as they live less labourious lives ... have more expensive tastes than their forbears, and to gratify them will refer to the savkar [note: =moneylender], if there is no money in the house. Formerly the ordinary cultivators to a man wore country cloth; now they must have it of finer texture from Manchester. Cheap local rice, *dal* and *gul* were enough for the daily food; now vegetables, imported rice and refined sugar are in demand. A most luxurious generation seeks after *pan-supari*, *chiroots*, hired servants, sweetmeats, and American watches, and will borrow money to get them. (Settlement Report on Bardoli Taluk, Surat District 1895: para 6.)

Gone were the days when the *dhaniamo* joined his *halis* for the midday meal and shared with them the food brought from his house – as was said to have been the custom in the past (Gazetteer of the Bombay Presidency 1877, vol. II: 199). It marked the beginning of a distancing that would profoundly separate master and servant.

Cotton cultivation in south Gujarat expanded considerably when a ready market was found for the commodity in Britain during the American Civil War. The price producers received for the exported crop rose to a higher level than ever before. In the years of boom that followed a class of peasants who had always been self-cultivating landowners started to attach landless tribals. Was it because the cash crop turned out to be more labour-intensive and required additional hands that the household could not provide? It is arguable whether growing cotton generated much more employment. The eagerness with which the middle class of peasant-owners took to this crop was undoubtedly driven by the prospect of gaining a higher income. But the realization of this objective, worthy in itself, also allowed the cultivator to set himself and his wife free from backbreaking agricultural work:

It is even asserted by careful observers that the keenness of cultivators to grow cotton is due not only to the fact that they can make good profits from it, but also to the fact that it is an easy crop to grow and leaves them plenty of leisure. (Keatinge 1921: 145–6)

In emulation of the rural elite enjoying conspicuous leisure and consumption, a lesser class of landowners followed suit and began to attach landless labourers to their household. Economic progress enabled them to upgrade their social standing and allowed them to lay claim to a higher ranking in the caste order. To have one or more servants was a major feature in the lifestyle adopted and what had been the prerogative of a dominant minority was practised more widely in the final decades of the nineteenth century. Refraining from manual work as much as possible did not occur overnight but was a gradual process in which upwardly mobile middle-class peasant households began to exempt some of their members from demeaning work – for which a domestic help was hired. J. B. Shukla reported in his study of Olpad *taluka*, conducted between 1929 and 1932, that the rising price of cotton in the preceding years had prompted men and women in Kanbi Patidar households to abstain from working in the fields, tending the cattle and doing domestic chores such as cleaning vessels, fetching water, etc. Supervision of the work that others were doing for them and purifying their behaviour from unclean duties was how they aimed at and succeeded in raising their caste status (Shukla 1937: 124; see also J. M. Mehta 1930: 132–3). However, the labourers employed were held captive in a state of bondage that differed from the way *halis* used to be attached.

While the onset of servile labour in remote history remains a matter of speculation, there is no doubt that the feudal-style unfreedom that had been customary changed shape as well as pace. This was due to the intrusion of capitalism in the rural-agrarian economy towards the end of the nineteenth century, as Sudipto Mundle (Mundle 1979) and Gyan Prakash (Prakash 1990) have argued. In south Gujarat an up-and-coming class of farmers imbued with the spirit of the new mode of production wanted to attain power and prestige. But not in the way landlords under the *ancien régime* had sought and attained domination as patrons surrounded by subordinated servants who owed their master allegiance in exchange for protection and livelihood security. The patronage features disappeared and what had been a comprehensive relationship of clientelism eroded to a new type of bondage with no other dimension than the maximization of labour utility to increase monetary profits by reducing labour cost as much as possible. It did not lead to a much lower wage rate because the daily provision of a grain allowance was already at or below the survival level. The discretionary favours – added as advances on future wages, out-of-work work allowances, bonus or gratuities and other 'loans' – which went a long way to diminish the budgetary deficit – were now more sparingly granted. In other words, the new type of bondage was more exploitative than even the former *dhaniamo-hali* tie had been. In his monograph Shukla summed up the disappearance of the flavour that had marked the earlier relationship in no uncertain terms:

'If the master's work does not suffer in the event of the Hali's sickness, he may be allowed to rot in his cottage.' (Shukla 1937: 123)

The contractarian ideology that had infused colonial legislation neatly corresponded with the rationale of capitalist enterprise. Accumulation of capital in a monetary and market-driven economy was now identified as the measure of wealth rather than status-related investment in a needy clientele that constituted a drain on the further amassment of property and income. It did not mean that *halipratha* faded away since the supervisory class of farmers that had come to rule the roost continued to employ labour in debt bondage, though treating them even more callously than had been done before.

Why did the landowners still insist on labour-tying arrangements to get their work done? According to Mundle, bondage was necessary to prevent the landless from going off in search of other and better employment. He suggests that in south Bihar the exodus of labour from agriculture had reached such proportions that landowners could only be sure of keeping the landless under their control, especially given the very low wages they were willing to pay, by denying them the freedom to leave. In my view this appraisal overstates the widening spread of the rural labour market at the end of the nineteenth century. Such an enlargement in scale was certainly not noticeable in south Gujarat. As before, some better prospects elsewhere might unexpectedly open up but these were windfalls of short duration and did not result in a permanent departure. Several landless tribals from my fieldwork region managed to join the Indian Labour and Porter Corps that was set up at the start of the First World War. This coolie workforce of half a million men was sent for porterage duties, building army camps and other grueling toil in Mesopotamia, East Africa or France. On the termination of their contract those who survived the brutal detainment they had endured went back home again.

While opportunities to escape agricultural labour remained few and far between, more *halis* than before chose not to stick for the duration of their life to the same master who had engaged them at young age. If they seemed to have gained more room to manoeuvre, it was because in the transition to the new mode of production the cohesion and collaboration that existed among landowners was also eroded. They no longer closed ranks and did not feel bound to send back a *hali* who had broken his bond. Although the new master was still obliged to settle the *hali's* debt, he would bargain for a lower amount than the old master claimed:

The system had now broken down, not so much because the masters cannot afford to keep the 'halis', as because they will not stay. Imbued with the new sense of independence they run away to get higher wages, omitting to repay money that has been spent by the old master in marrying them or in other ways. The frequency of such instances has made the Anavla Brahmin chary of keeping them at all, at any rate on the old family footing. (Report of the Revision Survey Settlement of the Jalalpur Taluka, 1900: 99)

As we shall see, the opinion expressed by the collector of the Surat District was premature. The number of cases of desertion, although higher than before, should not be exaggerated. But more important is to take note of the last words in this quotation: ... *at any rate, on the old family footing.* This comment highlights the changed conditions of employment, pointing to the loss of features of patronage that, however grudgingly provided in the past, still gave some space for bargaining on the part of the servant. His docile and deferential behaviour did not persuade the new generation of masters to generosity. Left with terms of service that boiled down to relentless exploitation, the landless tribals reacted by giving release to their pent-up feelings of despair and animosity. It was not a sense of independence that encouraged them to run away but hope of finding better treatment at the hands of another master.

The downward slide to an even more repressive work regime did not remain totally unnoticed. Although the colonial high command absolved itself from taking steps to halt the progressive dispossession and immiserization of the tribal population, the authorities of the princely state of Baroda were more alert to the tension building up at the bottom of the rural economy in the sizeable territory of south Gujarat under their jurisdiction. Accounts of a breakdown in the relationship between landowners and landless labourers expressed concern for the brutal victimization of the underclass and indicated the need to do away with debt bondage:

The labourers run away not because they get better terms elsewhere but because the treatment given to them is not at all sympathetic. Most of the labourers are Dublas and Dhankas, members of the aboriginal classes, illiterate and ignorant. The employers sometimes maltreat them and to avoid further trouble they run away to some other places. To force these people to stick to the cultivators and sometimes work under degrading conditions would be cruel. (Report of the Baroda Economic Development Committee 1918–19, 1920: 131–2)

For their part, the landowners saw the disloyalty of their subordinates as proof of bad faith, a refusal to perform the duties they had committed themselves to on becoming bonded in exchange for the credit the *dhaniamos* had invested in them in the form of 'loans'. In the master's view desertion was tantamount to breach of contract and with the risk of this eventuality in mind, they became even less generous and forthcoming. In order to retrieve absconding servants, landowners in Bihar commonly filed court cases and submitted written deeds of the loans they had advanced to them (Prakash 1990: 222). In contrast masters of *halis* who had eloped in south Gujarat were reluctant to back up their claim with such documents. Magistrates had shown themselves hesitant to accept these receipts as legitimate evidence, as the deputy collector of Surat District, N. M. Parakhji, testified (Census of India 1921, vol. VIII, part 1: 221). Possibly they feared that such bills had been thumb-printed under coercion. In 1923 the State of Baroda declared the system of forced indenture illegal and authorized the tribal serfs to reclaim their freedom if they chose to do so. But the order carried little weight and remained ineffective due to sabotage in the lower ranks of the bureaucracy (Census of India 1931, vol. XIX, part 1: 255). The clerical staff of the district-level machinery hailed from the rural gentry and maintained close ties with the village elite. It meant that *halis* lacked the connections and clout in the corridors of power required to end their bondage.

An altogether new argument put forward in colonial accounts was that *halipratha* was unsound in economic terms, as G. C. Mukhtyar observed in the village-based study he conducted in 1927:

It is obvious that the average of wages paid to the Hali is higher than paid to the free labourer, while the actual output of work per day by the former is only equal to, if not less than, that of the latter, as the former, unlike the latter, is an irresponsible fellow. Thus evidently the Hali system is uneconomical and inefficient. (Mukhtyar 1930: 170; see also Shukla 1937: 130)

In line with the logic of capitalism officials went out of their way to convince landowners that keeping debt-bonded labourers employed throughout the year was not cost-effective. Clearly, to engage free labourers on a casual basis would be much cheaper. They might have to be paid a little bit more on a daily basis, but the employers would be spared the nuisance of providing loans on and off that enabled the landless to meet their non-daily needs. Furthermore, they would not have to spend on wages in the slack season when there was no work. But it soon became apparent that the farmers did not buy these arguments. They explained that their preference for permanent rather than casual employees was based on purely economic considerations. In a condensation of the replies to his queries on this subject, the district collector put forward this opposite point of view:

At first sight this arrangement scarcely appears an economical one to the masters but they have assured me that, everything considered, it is financially better than keeping no farm servants, and engaging labourers when they are wanted. For, when any of the principal operations, such as ploughing, reaping, &c., are in full swing, the demand for labourers is often far greater than the supply; and not to have sufficient hands at such seasons must mean a heavy loss. In the dull season these servants, or halis (cultivators) as they are called, are employed in various ways, such as repairing and building rice embankments, converting jirayat [note: dry fields] into rice land, carting manure, & c. (Settlement Report on Bardoli Taluk, Surat District 1895: 7)

The information provided essentially confirmed what I would be told more than half a century later when I questioned landowners in the villages of my fieldwork why, despite their dissatisfaction, they continued to employ farm servants. In addition to what is stated in the above quotation, they pointed out that fixing some labourers permanently also gave them access to the much larger pool of casualized labour in the midst of whom their servants lived.

The contractarian way of thinking had entered into the jargon that the landowners used to justify their control over the landless workforce. The rural elite seemed no longer to care for the caste-based code endorsed at the local level that enabled them to keep *halis* immobile in previous generations. But they had found new weapons to promote and protect their interests. They claimed that labourers who deserted them had defaulted on the employment contract they had entered voluntarily and which the employer had backed up by shelling out a loan. As stated before, it made little sense to prosecute deserters in court since they had no possessions with which to pay off their accumulated debts. What the creditors insisted on was to be in control of the supply of labour and to achieve this objective they needed the help of the government. This demand was repeated some years later in a memorandum presented to the Royal Commission on Agriculture that toured the country to examine the condition of the agrarian-rural economy and make recommendations on how to improve people's welfare. The deputy director of agriculture who represented the interests of landowners in Gujarat called for the introduction of an identity card with details of the labourer's work record, which he could show to a new master as proof that he had fulfilled his debt to the previous one (Memorandum by Rao Sahib B. M. Desai in Royal Commission on Agriculture 1928: 577 and 601).

Agrarian Servitude Reaffirmed in the Struggle for National Independence

Although some colonial reports at the beginning of the twentieth century announced that *halipratha* was on the verge of breaking up or had already disappeared due to dissatisfaction on both sides of the relationship, this was not borne out by local-level investigations. In his prolonged study (1929–32) of the pattern of agricultural employment in a sub-district of Surat, Shukla unambiguously concluded: 'We (too) have failed to observe any signs of disappearance of the system, at least in the near future' (Shukla 1937: 132). In another village study conducted around the same time, Mukhtyar reported similar findings:

In this village, and, in point of fact, in the whole of Southern Gujarat, there still obtains a system of labour called the Hali system in which a labourer mortgages his labour to the farmer for a loan he takes for celebrating his marriage. A capitalistic cultivator keeps one or two Halis for performing field operations. He is bound to maintain them whether he exacts work from them or not. He, therefore, deems it wise and profitable to occupy them in sugarcane-cultivation (Mukhtyar 1930: 75)

The landowners were now more open to the argument of economic rationality than they had been before. In order to bring down the cost to maintain *halis* their masters allowed them to leave the village in the slack season and work in brick-kilns and salt-pans near Bombay 'to effect a saving of so much wages, which he must pay without exacting any work' (Mukhtyar 1930: 169). Three decades later I would again find and report on the same practice in a nearby village, the location of my fieldwork in the early 1960s (Breman 1974a: 132–3). *Halipratha* did not fade away but the relationship between master and servant was put on a new footing in the late-colonial era. In the course of time and in tune with capitalism making further inroads in the agrarian economy, servitude had acquired the imprint of a labour contract. To gain their freedom *halis* were forced to work off the 'loans' they had run up. The conversion of these 'advances' into monetary terms meant that they had landed in dire straits; stifled, as before, in a labour-tying arrangement, subjugated to merciless exploitation and no longer compensated by features of patronage. The wages paid to them remained stuck at a level far too low to satisfy their basic needs let alone to seek redemption from what had become known as debt bondage.

Failure to heed the interests of the land-poor and landless peasantry was a major flaw of the government's handling of the agrarian question in the post-Independence era, as has been widely noted. But the needs of these groups have been ignored for much longer still. Long before social ranking was 'discovered' in the mid-twentieth century, the differential configuration of political power in the peasant economy-cum-society was disregarded, while the disjunction between the main landowning castes and dispossessed communities was glossed over. In Gujarat this divide played out in the distinction made between the *ujliparaj* and the *kaliparaj*. Their separation and the mutual antagonism it aroused did not end when what were called tribals were converted into castes since the change in stratification now came to coincide with the contrast between 'those higher up' and 'those down below'. Throughout the centuries an ideology and practice of ingrained inequality was maintained. However, the leadership of the Indian National Congress began to appeal to the rural masses by flagging the cherished image of an undifferentiated amalgam of self-cultivating peasants. Without much further ado the interests of the dominant class-caste of landowners were prioritized in its canvassing strategy. Gujarat was selected as a testing ground for mobilizing the support of the peasantry in the struggle for Independence. In protest against the steady increase in the colonial land tax two campaigns were launched in Bardoli in 1922 and 1928. My main concern here is at what point the leadership of the freedom movement became aware of the *halipratha* system and how the high command, while raising the freedom slogan, dealt with the existence of unfree labour within the ranks of the peasantry.[1]

Gandhi himself came to south Gujarat in the early 1920s to start the non-cooperation campaign and went around the region to familiarize himself with the conditions of the peasantry. He was shocked to hear that participation in the scheduled civil disobedience would remain restricted to the *ujliparaj*. His hosts from the dominant landowning castes told him that the *kaliparaj* were traditionally discounted as part of the population. In their shacks at the edge of the villages the Dublas outnumbered by more than two to one the main landowning castes that they served in bondage as landless labourers. Gandhi discontinued the civil disobedience he had launched, much to the annoyance of the committee of notable landowners surrounding and accompanying him on his tour through the region. The violence that had broken out in a town in North India – the Chauri-Chaura incident – was given as the formal reason for the abrupt decision to call off the scheduled no-tax campaign. But the Mahatma's anguish at the non-inclusion of three-quarters of the population in the planned agitation must have been of no lesser importance. In a later column Gandhi expressed his grievance that the dominant landowners had not delivered on what they had promised him:

They took a pledge to eradicate untouchability, to uplift the Kaliparaj community, to put an end to the suffering of the Dublas, and to spread *khadi* throughout Bardoli ... I know that Bardoli is not quite prepared for this. The question of course is, will it ever be prepared? When will it be? What have they to say? (Gandhi 1927b: 15 June 1924)

His disciples stayed back in the area and from the Swaraj ashram established in Bardoli the Gandhian movement began what passed for 'constructive work' meant to uplift the tribal communities from the state of backwardness ascribed to them. They were taught to abandon their wayward life by abstinence from drinking alcohol and eating meat on festive occasions and were instructed in the use of the spinning wheel to

---

[1] For a more elaborate discussion of the Bardoli *satyagrahas*, see Breman 2007b: Chapter 3.

meet their basic needs. The enthusiasm with which the gatherings of the *kaliparaj* welcomed these missionaries waned when Kasturbai Gandhi and Vallabhbhai Patel tempered the militancy expressed in demands for the return of dispossessed land and higher wages. Both Sardar Patel and Gandhi's wife Kasturba lectured the *halis* on remaining obedient to their masters and warned them not to go on strike. Docile obedience to the better-offs was and remained the message that the Gandhian shepherds preached to their flock. Resistance against the invading Hindu culture and social order was condemned rather than condoned. Indeed, putting an end to *halipratha* was for the time being removed from the Gandhian agenda. To put the struggle of the freedom movement in south Gujarat on public record, the Surat district authorities commissioned a special publication on the social history of the tribal communities in the late colonial period. It reported, in line with the bias of received wisdom, that the Dublas' improvidence was a fatal flaw. They were held to be lethargic, without the zest to qualify for a better and more respectable way of life. Twenty years after the start of the reform movement, this depressed community remained – to use one of Gandhi's expressions – untouched like a lotus in the water (Desai 1971: 157).

As the Gandhian activists learnt, the landowning masters did not permit outside interference in their control over the labour they had attached. When the activists opened a night school in one of the villages to teach children of the landless labourers how to read and write, the infuriated Kanbi Patidars landowners immediately put a stop to it. Encouraging these children to read and write would discourage them from tending the master's cattle and working in his fields. Thus ended an early attempt to give voice to labour shut up in bondage. Jugatram Dave, the frontman of the Gandhian movement in south Gujarat, frankly explained that after this incident in 1924 no further action was taken that would have betrayed the trust of the main landowning class in the Independence movement:

We could recognize that to serve the Halpatis [note: the new name with which the Dublas were blessed in 1939] was not so simple a task as it appeared to be. It involved an age-long economic tradition. We should first patiently secure the confidence of the farmers' community. Only by a long service of many years, we shall be in a position to awaken in them the feeling of human sympathy and justice for Halpatis. So from 1924 to 1938 we, the voluntary workers, never raised this issue. (Dave 1946: 35)

The leadership in the struggle for national independence had become aware of the lack of freedom in rural society but from political opportunism chose to remain silent. The top-down approach was justified by the absurd argument that bondage was as degrading to the masters as it was to their servants. A change for the better in the mindset higher up – which failed to materialize - was given precedence over action to lift the landless out of the yoke that harnessed them. In the Gandhian cadre there were differences of opinion and dissenting voices strongly protested against a policy of tolerance or even compliance in collusion with the ruling caste-class. They pointed out how the landowners had become much better off while reducing the Dublas to the state of animals:

They are slaves, they live as *halis* or landless agriculturists on the farm of well-to-do farmers. When they marry, they incur debts of Rs. 50 to 200 and provide drinks to their relatives. They begin to work for people they borrow money from and sign letters to repay the debt. The debt, of course, is never over. Both the landowner and the Dubla are aware of this. The landowner maintains accounts in such a way that interest multiplies and there is more credit than debit in the accounts. This whole issue has become quite knotty now because the landowners (*dhaniyama*) claim that they do not benefit from hiring a Dubla instead of a casual labourer. I don't believe this. If hiring Dublas was not economically advantageous, thousands of men would not be engaging Dublas. They are certainly not being hired for altruistic reasons. (Mehta n.d.: 234)

In 1925 the colonial government announced its intention to increase the land tax by 30 per cent in Bardoli *vibagh*, which had experienced rapid economic growth as was illustrated by the larger and better houses built in recent years, the higher land prices and tenancy rates and the boost in the price of cotton – the main cash crop (Settlement Report on Bardoli Taluk, Surat District 1895). The Bardoli Congress Committee urged its members not to accept the higher land tax and to prepare for public agitation. In anticipation of the *satygraha* to be launched and in protest against the proposed hike in the tax rate, an enquiry was carried out to back up the argument that due to a steep rise in production costs most farmers, far from making a profit, suffered heavy losses. Narhari Parikh started his report with a profile of the agrarian workforce in which he identified the landless Dublas as the real tillers of the land:

But their condition is almost like that of slaves. Whether the crop yields are good or poor, whether prices realized are more or less, the remunerations they receive are the same, as they have been over the ages. Therefore they have no personal interest of any kind in the cultivation. Work done under compulsion can never be good and hence the condition of agriculture is deteriorating by the day. Still the farmers believe genuinely that that their interest lies in the preservation of *halipratha*. This system has lowered the Dubla community from human existence to the state of animals. Morally the practice is harmful even to the farmers who are considered as masters of the Dublas. But these masters believe that the *hali* system is economically beneficial to them. It is not. (Parikh 1926: 26 September 1926)

Parikh pointed out in his report that the cost of a *hali* amounted to six *annas* a day (Parikh 1932). This was the value of his food in the morning and at noon, to which was added the grain ration at the end of the day, given irrespective whether he had worked or not. Over and above this basic allowance came small amounts of money (spent on buying alcohol) and perquisites in kind (some clothes for the *hali* and his wife on festive occasions in the master's household, a cover in the winter, etc). The initial debt at the start of the relationship also gradually went up when the *hali* bargained for new loans. The wage bill added up to nine *annas* a day or at least Rs. 150 a year. Over and above this lump sum Parikh included in his calculation several tens of rupees for what he called interest on the farmer's investment in labour as well as an amount for depreciation. It was a stark example of commodity fetishism justified with the argument that the master could not reclaim the money he had laid out on the *hali*, a loss that was compounded by the risk that the latter might die or run away (Parikh 1926: 3 October 1926).[2]

'You Are Men, You Are Not Dublas'

Vallabhbhai Patel agreed to take charge of the agitation that the Bardoli landowners had in mind. They did not consult Gandhi, whom they suspected to be set against to their class interest and biased in favour of redeeming the tribal communities from their dire poverty and lack of freedom. Their mistrust in Gandhi and faith in Patel, of Patidar stock himself, was well founded. The difference in opinion between the two men on how to address the agrarian question was not made public. Gandhi had nominated Patel as leader of the Congress movement in Gujarat, gave him in 1924 the name of *Sardar* (Lion) and consented to his leadership of the new civil disobedience campaign launched in early 1928, which coincided with the date the government had set for collecting the first tax instalment. The Bardoli *satyagraha* lasted for six months and was run like a military operation with a daily bulletin published to inform the rank-and-file and outside world on progress. A committee of front-ranking landowners, all from *ujliparaj* castes, urged the farmers to refuse payment. Two-thirds of the agrarian population, the communities of *kaliparaj* vintage, were not represented on the panel that decided the

---

[2] The colonial government did not buy the argument of labour value lost. In their reaction to this calculation in the *Report of the Bardoli Enquiry Committee* (1926), Broomfield and Maxwell thoroughly discredited it. 'It is a difficult matter to reduce that rather uncertain quantity, the Dubla, to rupees and *annas*. But anyhow we cannot regard this method of accounting for him as satisfactory' (Broomfield & Maxwell 1929: 63).

course of the agitation. The rallying cry to join the movement included all who depended for their living on agriculture. Next to large and small landowners, tenants, sharecroppers and agricultural labourers, the largest class of all, were identified as *khedut* (peasant) even though the land tax did not apply to them. Many farmers, afraid that their possessions would be confiscated, were hesitant to join the movement and others were requisitioned to assist government officers in carrying off the forfeited property. They were put under pressure not to do so and, acting as commander-in-chief, Sardar Patel spurred them on in strong language:

You are men, you are not *dublas.* Spurn that appellation of degradation. *Dubla* means weak and cowardly. Weak and cowardly are they who would exact labour from you. (Chopra 1991: 132)

Confronted with a solid and well-organized block of opposition, the government was willing to compromise and lowered the increase in the tax rate from the initial 30 to an acceptable 6 per cent. This proposal ended the agitation and was rightly declared a major success for the Congress movement, which had demonstrated its capability to mobilize the peasantry or at least the better-off landowning classes among them.

The image invoked in the early nationalist literature of a village community with a simple hierarchy in which self-employed cultivators exchanged part of their grain harvest with non-agrarian castes in a relationship of reciprocity could no longer be upheld. It was at variance with the dynamics of the rural economy, already commercialized and monetized, in the late-colonial era. Gandhian social activists had from the early 1920s been in direct and regular contact with tribal peasants and landless labourers. Implementing their agenda of constructive work, they had observed the contractual servitude of their depressed clientele to the dominant landowners at first hand. The *halipratha* system was now a recurrent subject of discussion among the proponents of the freedom movement. And yet, in the run-up to the agrarian agitation, the Congress leadership did not for a moment hesitate in siding with the castes and classes higher up while disregarding the excessive poverty and subalternity in which the landless half of the population in Bardoli remained sunk. Those in command of the struggle for Independence not only became cognizant of the deep inequality that existed but also used it for political ends. According to Sardar Patel, the peasant alliance that he forged expressed the harmonious solidarity that existed between high and low castes. He paid no attention to reports clearly stating that a common stand had been achieved by the exercise of pressure and intimidation. The denigrated and dispossessed classes of south Gujarat were reputed to have accepted or even internalized their subservience. According to Mahadev Desai, the official chronicler of the Bardoli campaign, *halis* had rushed to defend their master's property and were wont to benefit from their unwavering loyalty:

... the refusal on the other hand of the ordinary Dubla to help in the *japti* [confiscation] was bound to have a wholesome effect on the relations between the landholders and the Dublas who worked for them. Those who had been up to now no better than menials and slaves came now to be looked upon as friends and brothers who had their share in the fight no less important than that of the landholders themselves. (Desai 1929: 64)

Behind the campaign banner of 'each and every one', it was the front-ranking landowners who had been at the forefront of the agitation. Some Gandhian social workers were critical of the leader of the movement who himself had urged the lower castes to dutifully obey their superiors. The caste awareness to which the campaign strategists appealed related not only to the code of good conduct that all were bound to follow but also reaffirmed the subjugation of the lower ones to those who ruled the roost:

Patel told untouchables, Dublas and artisans that it was their dharma to be loyal to their masters. The government wants to divide you and the *shahukar* [moneylender], but for you, your shahukar is everything. You should laugh at and consider him a fool if somebody says that you should change your shahukar. It is just like saying to a *pativrata* [chaste and dutiful wife] that she should change her husband. How can you leave your shahukar who has helped you in your difficulties? (Shah 1974: 10)

Congress had indeed succeeded in mobilizing the peasantry but the nationalist movement achieved this worthy goal by allying themselves with the rural elite. The well-to-do peasants of Bardoli celebrated the outcome of the agitation that had vindicated their claim to power and status. The strategy was driven by political opportunism: It enabled the leaders of the freedom movement to avoid taking issue with the unequal distribution of ownership and the existence of unfree labour in the ranks of the peasantry. The inevitable consequence was that the large majority of land-poor cultivators and landless labourers remained invisible and without voice. In accounts of the no-tax campaign in Bardoli the class conflict within the agrarian economy has been consistently understated. Not Gandhi but Sardar Patel became lionized by the dominant land-owners who were the main beneficiaries of the anti-colonial protest. The statue erected at the entrance of the town is not of the Father of the Nation but of the peasant leader, a member of the caste of Kanbi Patels, now dignified as Patidars throughout Gujarat. Likewise, the national museum that has been built in the grounds of the Swaraj ashram does not carry the name of its founding father, Mahatma Gandhi, but that of his disciple Vallabhbhai Patel, venerated to this day as the one and only hero of 'the people of Bardoli'.

Some of the social activists who joined the agrarian agitation were shocked to find out that the cause they were asked to serve did not align with the way they themselves perceived the agrarian question. The fight against colonialism as it now took place in the countryside was going to benefit an upper segment of the peasantry only. But these dominating owners were the same ones who, often with the support of colonial officials, had appropriated most of the property on which the tribal communities used to make their living. The people who were the original owners of the land had become dispossessed and become tenants, sharecroppers and landless serfs. It was the rediscovery of this history of dispossession that induced Indulal Yagnik, Dinkar Mehta and several other activists who came to participate in the Bardoli *satyagraha* to break away from the Gandhian movement and Congress politics in the aftermath of the campaign. They did so out of disillusionment at the contradiction between what was preached and what was practised. As Yagnik phrased it in his autobiography:

While a lot of activity has been promoted in recent years to carry on temperance and spinning activities among these unfortunate people, nothing has been done to snap or even relax the chain of slavery in which thousands of these Dublas, men and women, live under the oppressive yoke of the so-called higher classes. (Yagnik vol. V, 1971)

The Patidars had gained the upper hand at the expense of the landless labourers, who remained locked in subordination. In fact, the dependence of the lower castes on the dominant ones had been reinforced by Gandhian policy, which through wishful thinking aimed at bringing all castes and classes together in the downfall of colonialism. What explanation was given for tolerating the ongoing exploitation and oppression of bonded labour? Two motives are prominent in the accounts of the agitation. Firstly, that no solution could be found to ending the *halipratha* system while the landowning masters continued their abusive ways. Would a more confrontational line not persuade them to change their unjust and inhuman code of conduct? As a proper disciple of Gandhi, Narhari Parikh rejected the radical approach to accelerate the process of emancipation that a number of hotheads, as he branded them, had proposed. In his preface to Jugatram Dave's book on *halipratha*, he showed his unwavering faith in the Gandhian doctrine:

Some old social workers of the Bardoli taluka sense an attempt to create class conflict in the activities of workers to bring about an awakening among the

Halpatis. But Jugatrambhai has made one thing very clear in this booklet, which is that efforts to secure human treatment and justice to the Halpatis should be made on the basis of truth and non-violence and never in a manner which would breed class conflict. (Dave 1946: 10)

By invoking the impelling need for social harmony, the class conflict that existed and in fact raged in full force was covered up and denied. The second reason that Gandhian activists, while engaged in what was labelled constructive work, did not free the landless from their bondage was because these do-gooders from upper-caste stock had bought the idea that the victims owed their misery to a defective way of life. The mission of charity prioritized reforms to lift them out of their tribal customs, which permitted eating meat and drinking alcohol, and trans- form them into proper Hindus. The guidance provided in this civilizing trajectory would in due course lead to the desired outcome, but its accomplishment would take a great deal of time and zealous effort. The indolent behaviour of this community explained why they landed them- selves in ever deeper debt and were incapable of planning for today, let alone for tomorrow. The weapons of the weak to which they resorted were not acknowledged in those terms. Even observers who commiser- ated with the landless – as, amongst others, Sumant Mehta did – held the Dublas accountable for their pauperized lifestyle:

A Dubla lived in the *wadi* (field) behind my house. His chief occupation was to smoke *bidi* and drink *toddy*. His wife was tall and emaciated. She would leave for earning her daily wages (*majoori*) every morning. She bore a child every twelve months, hence there was an army of starving children in her hut. One of her children was three months old. When the mother left for work, all the children would cry their lungs out and fall into silence out of exhaustion. The mother would extract milk from her breasts and leave it for the young child in a dirty saucer. The young child would be fed this milk by his six-year-old sister. The family ate only *jowar* (millet) gruel for food and nothing else ... I tried hard to drive some sense into that Dubla's head. I offered to employ him for sundry tasks so that the children would at least have something to eat. He was simply not ready to give up smoking and fooling around with women of his age. Never mind if he also starved, but he would simply not work. He finally took up the responsibility of working at a *toddy* shop so that he could have some *toddy* on the sly. (Mehta n. d.: 233–4)

What it boiled down to was that they were *halis* because they lacked the resolve to live and work properly. It is the timeworn argument that slaves become slaves because they lack the zest and aptitude to live and work in freedom. Being lazy and improvident by nature made them fit for servi- tude. Work or no work, they were assured that their master was willing to satisfy all their basic needs. Virtues such as diligence, moderation and sobriety were alien to them and only by growing used to such civilized behaviour would they be able to break their chains. This meant that outsiders, no matter how well intentioned, could in good faith claim that they were at a loss to bring about what the Dublas themselves evidently did not want: to be free labourers. Addressing large crowds during the Bardoli *satyagraha*, Sardar Patel clearly showed his prejudices against the landless underclass. But he came closer to peasant life and lore than Mahatma Gandhi ever was in his insistent style of simplicity. In a speech during the campaign Patel spoke of the need to clean up the village and get rid of filth and stench all around. In plain language he blamed his audience for being untidy and unclean, showing a lack of respect for women and negligence of sanitary degradation. Radical changes were needed, and the imminent Independence would bring the ideal village, as he saw it, closer to reality. In that cherished setting there would be no place for the impure behaviour embodied in the Dubla as in no one else. In his speeches he scolded the farmers for not properly disciplining their uncivilized servants:

What type of Dubla have you appointed? Who don't have the manners to go to the latrine, who are drunkards and who themselves are so dirty! I feel so wretched while drinking water from a farmer's house when I go to a village. But where should I go? All these dirty people are my brethren, therefore I have to drink water somehow or the other. What is bad in doing the work with your own hands instead of keeping a Dubla so dirty and getting work from him? I shall prefer to draw water for myself instead of asking such a dirty man to draw water for me. Reform him if you want to get work from him. Make him give up drinking and set him right. Your fears are baseless; a reformed labourer can give you 12 hours work done in just four hours. And if he continues to be illiterate, he will whimper about the whole of the day and his work shall lack cleverness. Such a foolish person does not listen to what you say, does not carry out your orders properly and runs away as and when it comes to his mind. If he is a bit sensible, you can make him understand what you want him to do. But you yourself give him money for drinking and turn him into an animal. (Quoted in Chopra 1991: 302)

Patel refused to listen to members of his staff who wanted him to place the predicament of bondage on the agenda of the campaign. Dinkar Mehta, one of the students from the Gujarat Vidyapith in Ahmedabad that Gandhi had established in 1920, came to Bardoli as a volunteer eager to participate in the Bardoli agitation in the entourage of its leader. In an interview about this important episode that made him change his political leanings, Mehta describes how upset he felt at how landowners mistreated their agricultural labourers. When he mentioned this, Patel curtly replied that the time was not yet ripe to solve this problem. The hero of Bardoli sharply reacted when Mehta insisted, telling him plainly not to bring up the issue again. The young activist noted that the reluctance of his chief was more than just a matter of convenience:

We also got the impression that he and some others were not very sympathetic to them. We came to know that when Narharibhai [note: Parikh] and myself went to the areas called Dublawadas (the area where the Dublas stayed). None else tried to go there ... I used to write to Kaka Kalelkar [note: a close associate and confident of Gandhi] that the condition of Halis and Dublas was horrible, but that issue was not taken up by anybody. But we did not complain about that. That was our discipline. (Mehta 1975: 33)

In contrast to Sardar Patel, Mahatma Gandhi was mild-mannered and patient, more considerate and unwilling to denigrate values that he did not share. He told his disciples that they should practise humility in their work of tribal emancipation. Persuading these people to adopt a purer lifestyle should not, in his opinion, be inspired by contempt and arrogance. It was precisely with such sentiments that Jugatram Dave, the founder and head of the Vedchi ashram in the hinterland of Bardoli, rejected the accusation that he showed no respect for tribal culture. 'You want us to preserve what we want them to forget', was his indignant reaction to this reproach. Gandhi neglected to temper the self-righteous zeal of his disciples and gave them a free hand in what he saw as the fulfilment of a civilizing mission, to convert the tribals to a Hindu identity (Hardiman 2003: 146). At the same time, he did not shy away from condemning the brutality with which the dominant landowners treated their workforce. In no uncertain terms, he chastised the cruel way in which the masters used to browbeat their servants as 'Dyerism'.[3] But even Gandhi did not stand in Sardar Patel's way and he allowed him to lead the campaign as he wished. The outcome of the no-tax agitation was to consolidate the exploitation and oppression of the tribal peasantry. Gandhi did not waver from the stance he took – either then or later on. Antagonism and confrontation would not be tolerated in efforts to solve the agrarian question. If that meant avoiding confrontation with landowners when they imposed their diktat, so be it. Parikh gave the example of a master who was forced by his fellow caste member under threat of boycott to take back land he had given to his servant on a sharecropping basis. The Kanbi Patel himself was too busy as a trader to supervise its cultivation and had decided to contract it out to his *hali*. He had to cancel the agreement under pressure because Dublas were agricultural

---

[3] R. E. H. Dyer was the British general who in 1919 ordered his troops to open fire on an unruly crowd in Amritsar. Several hundred people were massacred.

labourers and raising one of them to the status of sharecropper was seen by the other landowners as unacceptable (Parikh 1926: 3 October 1926).

The account of the no-tax struggle – Mahadev Desai's *The Story of Bardoli*, published a year after its successful outcome – carried the stamp of hagiography with undiluted praise for all who took part in the campaign. The political strategy that had led to victory came in for more critical discussion after Independence. These more detached writings suggest that the landless were held in a relationship of subordination that left them no other choice than grudgingly to comply with their master's domination, as Shankardass (Shankardass 1988: 85) and Mehta (Mehta 1984: 187) have argued. In similar vein Dhanagare concludes that 'probably the poor trusted their masters as being their only hope of improving their conditions' (Dhanagare 1983: 104–7). The impression created in these accounts is that, when all was said and done, the Dublas accepted their fate and remained faithful to those who had attached them. But were they indeed as passive and docile as these subsequent judgements seem to suggest?

4   The Class Struggle Launched and Suppressed

Turning a Page in the Class Struggle

The tribal communities in south Gujarat who had been shifting cultivators until well into the nineteenth century were receptive to certain features of the Gandhia mission of 'uplifting'. Although eager to join mainstream society, they refused to become stuck at the tail-end of the Hindu hierarchy. To prevent that happening it was crucial for them not to acquiesce in the loss of their land rights to moneylenders and drink-dealers. This chapter will document how they sought confrontation with these vested interests and strongly opposed their degradation to the status of indebted tenants and sharecroppers of the fields that were once their property. Their militancy would lead to their reinstatement as owner-cultivators in the aftermath of Independence. The *kaliparaj* peasantry – upgraded by Gandhian missionaries to *raniparaj* (people of the forests) – gave in to the strong pressure to participate in the Bardoli *satyagraha* of 1928, but they did so with their own agenda and not in subservience to the *ujliparaj*. These tribes – split up between Dhodhia, Chodhari, Gamit and Naika – had retained their own habitat in the much-less-populated hinterland of south Gujarat and were somehow able to distance themselves from the invading Hindu culture. The Dublas by contrast, who were the largest community amongst them, had already been made thoroughly landless in the central plain of fertile soil many centuries ago. In their dispossessed predicament they were attached to well-to-do households and lacked physical as well as social space of their own. Forced to work and live in the shadow of their masters, they were ordered around on beck-and-call duty. The chain of servitude prevented them from developing a collective identity and sense of solidarity. For this agrarian underclass the obstacles to asserting themselves and gaining in confidence and self-respect were much greater than in the case of the tribes who, while also subjected to dispossession, were inhabitants of less settled tracts of land and still not totally detached from their ancestral property to which they managed to hang on as tenants or sharecroppers. With the exception of a small minority, these land-poor peasants had not become the bonded servants of the dominating landowners.[1]

However, the impression that the Dublas remained docile and obedient in the 1928 no-tax agitation is wrong. Reading between the lines of the chronicles and reports on the campaign, one is struck by their mood of resentment and recalcitrance against the hegemony of the main landowners and the alliance of the Congress leadership with these vested interests. What the Kanbi Patidars were wont to consider as the lethargy of the Dublas was the latter's sustained unwillingness to conduct themselves as devoted farmhands toiling for a wage lower than their basic needs. The landowners insisted that the *halis* received what they needed for sustenance, but they cheated their servants by giving them less than they were customarily entitled to. The latter had no other choice than to make up their livelihood deficit by asking for further 'loans'. The *halis* showed their impudence by not turning up for work, pretending to be ill or just too tired, complaining that were not able to finish what they had been asked to do, saying they had misunderstood the master's orders and other acts of overt or covert sabotage. While the Gandhian workers were prone to reaffirm the image of 'the good master' and 'the faithful servant' bound to each other in a tie of reciprocity, sometimes the tension in their relationship could not remain hidden and erupted in a clash of temper on both sides. Disunity rather than harmony prevailed and could burst out quite unexpectedly, as in the incident which Mahadev Desai narrated in *The Story of Bardoli*:

During our tour with the Broomfield Committee,[2] we went to a village to collect preliminary information. We were asking about the condition of the Dublas, and whether the Kanbis gave them the proper measure of rice. The men said, 'Yes'. One of the women who were carefully listening to us from inside, rushed out and exclaimed: 'No lies before these friends. Let us confess that we do not give the proper measure. The Dublas trouble us a lot, and we also do not deal with them fairly. That is why we are in such a wretched plight'. (Desai 1929: 138)

---

[1] Those who had slid down to that predicament of unfreedom were not only members from the other tribal communities mentioned before but also included a segment of the Kolis, a community that had already left their tribal identity behind and were classified in colonial documents as a low Hindu caste. Those among them dispossessed from all agrarian means of production and who for that reason had fallen prey to debt bondage were set apart as *gulam* (slave) Kolis.

[2] The colonial government had appointed two officials, R.S. Broomfield and R.M. Maxwell, to conduct an enquiry into the feasibility of the proposed land tax rate. During their tour around villages they were kept company by members of the Bardoli Enquiry Committee who had collected the evidence for the report that signaled the start of the agitation.

In their low-profile resistance the farm servants resorted to 'the weapons of the weak'. From generation to generation, *halis* and *dhaniamas* must have developed a routine means of interacting with each other in order to keep the fragile complementarity of 'benevolence' versus 'deference' intact. But the trend towards commercialization and monetization that articulated the transition to a capitalist mode of agricultural production brought new cleavages. These further tilted the imbalance in a relationship that from the very beginning was characterized by excessive inequality. The Dublas were dependent on the good will of their masters and that made them vulnerable to the occasional or indefinite denial of perquisites, such as their right to *chas*, the buttermilk that the *hali* came to collect early in the morning and which was an indispensable ingredient in his diet. He may have taken to his hut fallen and damaged fruit from the master's orchard, cut grass in his field as fodder for the cow or few goats that he kept at home or gathered firewood on the master's land without asking permission to do so. These were favours the master could grant or withhold at his whim. If the *hali* continued to satisfy his customary needs unauthorized, he stood accused of theft. But the farmhand would no longer be cowed by the master's anger, beg for forgiveness and promise to mend his ways. Instead, he and his wife might go on undeclared strike, stay away from the employer's abode or, worse, go elsewhere for casual work. This refusal to behave with propriety and respect led increasingly to conflicts. Times were changing and the master would go to his labourer's hut – formerly unheard of – to try and persuade him to tend to the cattle or go to the field. He would find his *hali* still asleep inside. On being aroused by his master's shouts the servant, still lying on the ground, would put his toe in a pot of *bhadku* (gruel made of *chas* and grain) to see if he had enough food for the day. If there was, he just refused to get up and went back to sleep. Such stories were proverbial among the high-caste farmers – and during my fieldwork several decades later they were still common (Breman 1985). Behind annoyance about the indolence of the Dublas, the inability of their bosses to enforce obedience even under threat of severe sanctions was a major source of frustration.

Had this defiance increased in frequency and intensity over time? This assumption would seem to be confirmed by landowners' complaints put on public record in official reports and other archives. As for the opinion of the labourers, there is a dire lack of oral or written information on their social consciousness. In addition, the accounts of Gandhian activists rarely included such details. In so far as they came into contact with the Dublas, and that contact was sporadic and fleeting, they would report from the perspective of their own mission of upliftment rather than from that of their informants they had haphazardly met. But the 'vertical solidarity' so praised in the Congress chronicles of the no-tax campaign is more a matter of propaganda than an account backed up by factual evidence. The few testimonies I could find that are not founded on bias and prejudice do not corroborate that the farm servants had indeed surrendered in unconditional subordination to their masters. From what Dinkar Mehta suggests, an attitude opposite to the cherished image of harmony seems to have been prevalent – an antagonism expressed in an almost steadfast refusal to side with the landowners in the Bardoli *satyagraha*:

The Dublas and Halis neither joined the movement nor attended our meetings. They complained, 'This movement is of the Dhaniamas, our masters. What have we got to do with it? We won't get more than four annas even if their revenue is reduced, we don't get more than five annas'. That was the way they used to complain. So they did not participate, they did not sympathize with the movement, because they realized that their condition was not going to change. (Mehta 1975: 32)

During the first round of the Bardoli agitation in 1921–2 Mahatma Gandhi had told the *ujliparaj* landowners in plain words that they could only consider themselves fighters for freedom if they put a stop to the exclusion and repression in their own midst. The message fell on deaf ears but must have percolated to the landless underclass to some extent – enough to strengthen their resistance and to make their grievances felt by joining hands. There are no references to any such feelings of solidarity among the Dublas in the annals of the no-tax campaign, but the colonial authorities became aware of this changing perception. Broomfield and Maxwell reported on it in the following passage:

... the Dublas are undoubtedly becoming more independent, and more capable of combining in defence of their rights and interests. If they think they are stinted of their food ration and not paid a fair wage they will desert their village in a body, as happened this year in Afva,[3] Vankaner, Timberva and other places. (Broomfield & Maxwell 1929: 15)

While individual acts of defiance went on as before, the Dublas had now also started to resist bondage more collectively.

---

[3] About half a century later, this village became one of the locations of my fieldwork in the region. See Breman 1985.

From Weapons of the Weak to Concerted Action?

Two senior disciples had detached themselves from Gandhi's entourage because they saw the agrarian question to be first and foremost a matter of improving the plight of the land-poor and landless peasants. Both Indulal Yagnik and Dinkar Mehta broke away from their *guru*, as well as from the Congress movement, when they were refused permission in the mid-1930s to establish a political niche that would cater to the interests of the poor peasantry. Sardar Patel strongly opposed their attempt to do so and, having lost first Gandhi's and subsequently also Nehru's support, these dissenters gave up their hope of setting up a more radical peasant organization within the Congress fold. In close collaboration with Sahajanand Saraswati, who founded (in 1936) and chaired the All-India Kisan Sabha (AIKS), Indulal Yagnik was a member on the board of this organization and took charge of its provincial wing in Gujarat. The trade union concentrated its activity on the lower ranks of the peasantry and mobilized them with an agenda of agrarian reforms that had at its top the demand that ownership rights over land should be in the hands of the actual tiller. Despite the suspicion of militant radicalism that the AIKS immediately aroused, it was a typical multi-class association in which the sharp segmentation within the agrarian order remained understated. Attention was focused mainly on self-cultivating peasants converted into tenants or sharecroppers and eager to reclaim their lost property in the recent past. In south Gujarat it was customary for indebted tribal peasants to hand over half of the harvest to the moneylenders, who were put on record as the legal owners of their land. The new wave of agrarian agitation was meant to put an end to this system of *adhbhag* and reduce the share they were forced to yield to one-third. The mass of landless labour hardly came into the picture and calls for their improvement remained restricted to the suggestion that land still not under cultivation should be set aside for them. Just like Yagnik, Dinkar Mehta had become aware of agrarian bondage in south Gujarat during the Bardoli *satyagraha* of 1928. As a prominent member of the Gujarat Congress Socialist Party, he drafted a resolution to abolish the *halipratha* system. Throughout the Surat district he organized meetings and demonstrations from 1935–7 to achieve this goal, now as a member of the Communist Party of India, which he had meanwhile joined (Mehta 1975: 135). In an article in *National Front* Mehta explained that the masters of the *halis* were capitalist landowners and that even the smallest among them held Dublas in bondage on the basis of loans ranging from Rs. 75 to Rs. 100. To further the same cause, Yagnik arranged for the reprint of a colonial report, included in the Census of India 1921, which compared the *halis* – an agrarian workforce estimated at 57,010 in the Surat district – with the slaves on American plantations before the American Civil War and held the government accountable for setting them free (Census of India 1921, vol. VIII, part 1: 219–23).

An excellent opportunity to draw wider political and media attention to this problem came when in early 1938 the All India Congress Committee held its annual session in Haripura, a village close to Bardoli. In preparation for the occasion Swami Sahajanand toured around the tribal habitat and in his speeches strongly criticized the agrarian policy of Congress in the provinces where it came to be vested with power to rule. Holding such a high-profile meeting in a rural location required all kinds of facilities to be provided for the large number of people that would attend. The committee charged with making these arrangements called on thousands of Dublas from the vicinity to build a tent camp for the delegates to the convention and the infrastructure of the venue, such as access roads, latrines and canteens:

... the big advantage was that in this way a sense of togetherness developed among them. A mentality to work in a group was born and they got an idea of the advantages that could be gained. What is Congress and why such a large congregation takes place, were the things they slowly came to learn about. Thousands of men and women and children of this community attended the meetings held by Congress to spread information on what was going to happen. As a result, awakening to a considerable extent took place in this class and the roots of uplift were planted and the spirit of this community woke up, which was before totally ignorant of their state, life or the world at large and which had remained content for so long in their backward and down-trodden condition. (Desai 1971: 161–2)

The landowners did not approve being deprived of their workforce while the construction was going on. Many came to fetch their farm servants back who, tempted by the much higher wages, had not asked their masters permission to be absent. Social workers of the Gandhian ashrams in charge of the whole operation were instructed not to have any contact with Kisan Sabha activists and to warn the workers they supervised against troublemakers. But clashes between these very different brands of political activity did occur and were communicated to the Congress caucus. Sardar Patel, who hosted and chaired the convention convention, reacted furiously. The next incident was of a more serious nature, the long-awaited march that the Kisan Sabha organized to interrupt the AICC deliberations. The event, which Congress had in vain tried to prevent taking place, was a great success:

Bands of Kisans started from different centres. They walked ten, twenty and thirty miles carrying with them the Red Flag and the national tricolor and Kisan and anti-imperialist slogans. They held meetings all over the route. Their number swelled to thousands. All the processions merged at a distance of two miles from Haripura. From there a mighty procession started for the Congress Nagar. It was a wonderful sight. Five thousand peasants, shabbily dressed, covered with dust, worn out from the long march, yet full of enthusiasm formed themselves into a procession. The procession marched through Vithalnagar with hundreds of banners and slogans and terminated in a rally attended by over ten thousand peasants. (Bukhari 1938: 8–11; for another report on this meeting, see Yagnik vol. V, 1971: 117–18)

The bulk of the participants in the rally seem to have been peasants from tribal communities who were sharecroppers. In addition to having to pay for all costs of cultivation themselves – buying seed, keeping draught cattle to till the land, tools and their own labour cost – they were also vulnerable because the moneylending landowner could terminate the contract if its outcome did not suit him. The tribal unrest in south Gujarat now also spread to the talukas of Bulsar[4] and Pardi. Moneylenders and merchants had seized the land of Dhodhia peasants. The grass now growing in the field they used to cultivate was sold to Bombay, where cattle breeders had opened up large stables in the suburbs to provide milk for the city's inhabitants. News of these protests spread and the landless Dublas also took courage and went on strike:

The months of April and May witnessed a series of these labour strikes against their bosses. There were sporadic scuffles and struggles. Some serfs were beaten up by the Pathans and other servants hired by their masters. And the Kisan leaders in [the village of] Lavet promptly repaired to the scenes of these little rebellions, backed the cause of the serfs and tried to secure freedom of service and adequate wages for them. This was the united front of the small tenants and agrarian workers realized in the course of the struggle. (Yagnik 1938a: 12)

In Mota, a village near Bardoli and a center of Kanbi Patel power, 500 *halis* refused to report for work in the monsoon of 1939. They resisted their employers who wanted them to bring their midday meal to the field and not go home for it. They also stopped their wives from doing domestic work for the *dhaniamas,* as noted by the Intelligence Branch of the colonial government, which kept a close watch on the agrarian turmoil (e.g. Government of Bombay 1938–40: Home Department, file S. D. 2867, first half of August 1939). A delegation of the dominant landowners appeared to give in and agreed that the Dublas would no

---

[4] Bulsar was the name for the southernmost district and its headquarters in Gujarat during the colonial era. Both the district and the town are nowadays called Valsad.

longer be employed as *halis* but as casual wage workers and would henceforth be paid in cash. However, the success turned out to be short-lived as the farmers exerted considerable pressure to force their servants back to the old regime, including the use of physical violence. *Halis* who refused to toe the line were blacklisted and found no employment in their village.

Among the board-members of the All India Kisan Sabha there were different opinions on the strategy to follow inside or outside of the Congress movement. Swami Sahajanand gradually came to the conclusion that the union had grossly understated the interests of landless labour, which was the largest peasant class. In a lengthy essay entitled 'Who Cares for the Poor?', he examined the origins of landlessness and the social identity of the people who belonged to this residual class. In the introduction, written while he was in prison in 1941 for his political radicalism, the Swami commented that the Kisan Sabha had many members who fought for their own interests while exploiting labourers who toiled in their fields. The critique showed that he was acutely aware of the rift in the ranks of the peasantry. During his repeated visits to Gujarat the Swami became acquainted with the *halipratha* system, strikingly similar to the *kamiauti* bondage with which he was thoroughly familiar in Bihar. While this practice of subjugating the landless to the power and whims of landlords was in his view no longer at its height in the country, the regime of serfdom seemed to have been preserved in south Gujarat:

Beating and assaulting the *halis* is common. And the remarkable thing is that whereas in other provinces the *kamiauti* system and similar forms of bonded labour are dying out of their own accord, the *hali* system is gaining momentum. Now, however, through the agitations of the Gujarat Provincial Kisan Sabha even this system is being rooted out. Once a *dubla* youth in the area of Haripura in Gujarat, narrated to me his story. He explained that he worked like a slave in the home of a Parsi. He had to go there at four in the morning, boil the water and bathe him. The slave had to soap and rub his *malik's* body and wash him. In this process, if the Parsi felt the least irritation from the rough hands of the *dubla*, he would slap him. But the slave had heard the speeches of the Kisan Sabha and this gave him courage and one day when his Parsi owner gave him a slap, he returned the slap and since that time he has been free. (Quoted in Hauser 1994: 78–9)

Yagnik was initially full of hope, claiming that once people have broken their chains they are determined to stay free. By the end of 1938 the euphoric mood of a half-year before may still have lingered on but the political tide had turned. The Kisan Sabha could not consolidate the terrain it had gained, although the association did not fade away immediately. The Gujarat wing was able to maintain its hold on tribal tenants –

and sharecroppers in particular. They formed the bulk of the membership, which stood at 9,000 in 1939. The mood of resistance among this
class of small and marginal peasants had not abated, the colonial authorities concluded in the early 1940s on the basis of intelligence reports that
expressed dismay about 'the growth of a spirit of lawlessness' (Notes
Regarding Kisan Movement 1940–1: 175). The opening session of the
sixth conference organized by the Gujarat Kisan Sabha in 1953 was
attended by more than 20,000 tribal peasants. In order to pre-empt the
land reforms that were due, many absent owners had evicted their
tenants overnight from the agrarian property of which they had been
the original owners. In what was called concealed tenancy, this land had
often been given for cultivation to agricultural labourers who received
half a share or less of the crop yield they produced. The speeches
highlighted these new abuses, and while intra-class differences now came
to the fore, the *halipratha* problem as such did not figure any more on the
agenda. Under the tenancy legislation of 1956, reluctantly enacted, a
sizeable number of tribal peasants in south Gujarat were partially or
wholly restored to their former property and, for the time being,
reinstated as owner-cultivators. Having realized the main objective of
their struggle, these small and marginal landowners then left the Kisan
Sabha, which for two decades had fought for their rights (Vishwanath
1985). The coalition that the Gujarat Kisan Sabha had forged between
land-poor peasants and agricultural labourers broke down. The split
between them was partly driven by conflicting class interests and partly
by their separate tribal identities. With the downfall of the association,
also, the voice of bonded labour and those speaking on its behalf seemed
to have faded away again.

The Congress Remedy, a Faked Solution

Had the status quo ante indeed been brought back, as if nothing had
changed? That would be a misreading of what happened in the aftermath. In their programme of constructive work among the agrarian
underclass, the cadre of the Gandhian movement steered clear from
mobilizing the Dublas to attain freedom from bondage. The dominating
landowners did not tolerate any interference in what they considered
their domain and showed no sign at all of being uncomfortable with the
system of unfree labour. The Gandhian do-gooders had explained their
inactivity on this issue by suggesting that the landless themselves were no
less attached to *halipratha* than their capitalist employers. Subordination
to a master gave what they required for their daily sustenance and did
away with the need to take fate in their own hands. Such an easy-going

mentality frustrated well-intended efforts to raise the Dublas – roughly half of the population in the area around Bardoli – to a higher economic and social plane.

What happened by the end of the 1930s to change the view that the *halis* felt no urge to be free? No reference at all was made to the campaign launched by the Kisan Sabha. Records of the Gandhian movement that I have scrutinized make no mention at all of the important role Yagnik and other radicalized activists played in their more critical perception of the agrarian question. The colonial authorities, alerted by the growing tensions in the countryside of south Gujarat, had started to monitor in fortnightly reports the threat that peasant agitation posed to political and social stability. On the other hand, Congress ignored in its publicity the support that the land-poor and landless now openly expressed for the radical cause. The impression created was that the fight against colonialism had the backing of the peasantry irrespective of their differential ranking in the agrarian hierarchy and that Mahatma Gandhi's teachings would guide the solution of land and labour issues once *Hind Swaraj* (Indian Home Rule) were realized. For the AICC session of 1938 in Haripura preparations were made in this spirit of an all-inclusive commonweal. The excitement in the run-up to the convention was intensified by word of mouth and created an expectant atmosphere. The Dublas in the surrounding villages came to understand the aim of the meeting – national freedom – as the announcement of their own freedom. The Gandhian front man in the region would later comment on this episode as follows:

How can the people who were ignorant, distressed and caught in slavery, grasp the understanding of *Hind Swaraj* all of a sudden? In fact they could follow the simple and straight meaning of *Swaraj* as freedom from the bondage of *halipratha*. Hundreds of Halpaties began to dance with eagerness inspired by two thoughts – hope of freedom and journey to Haripura Congress. Had the Propaganda Committee not made efforts, these people would have hardly realized up to the last moment that there was something like Congress and that a *Maha-Yajna* [great sacrifice] of *Swaraj* was going to be performed. All this for securing human rights for people like them. (Dave 1946: 36)

There was a clear divide between the approach of the Kisan Sabha agitators and that of the Gandhian social workers. While the left-wing political activists spoke in a style that invoked solidarity in their efforts to mobilize the land-poor and landless peasantry, and considered the struggle they had embarked upon as a precondition on the road to emancipation, the quotation from Jugatram Dave's brochure on the Halpatis showed that the Gandhian reformers remained at a distance from their target group. The landless labourers were seen as ignorant, unable to come to terms with what went on around them. They were prone to react with childish stupefaction to rumours that promised liberation. Their freedom would be managed by benefactors who remained invisible and about whom they knew very little. The impression of a magical metamorphosis was strengthened because it was so unexpected, a sudden reversal of their fortunes rather than the result of gradual changes in the agrarian regime spread out over a number of years – and, moreover, a change they themselves had brought about.

To counteract the Kisan Sabha campaign of mobilization, in mid-December 1937 Sardat Patel addressed a crowd of Dublas gathered from twenty villages round about. He told his audience that the forthcoming liberation of the country from colonial rule made it intolerable that the slavery that persisted here, as nowhere else in India, should be permitted to go on as before. Over the heads of the assembled agricultural labourers, he addressed their masters:

The custom of Dublas (bonded labourers) is a shame on us, because it deprives us of human rights and reduces us to the state of animals. I told you when I came here last time [note: in 1928], that it is better to be animals in the houses of farm owners than to be bonded labourers ... because special place is provided for the animals in the farm owner's house. When the animal is hungry at night the farm owner or somebody from his house gives food and water to the animals and caresses them. Then when the farm owner provides [a] place to animals, it is a sin to keep human beings in bondage. But though we are men, we have lost our rights as human beings, not only that but alas! We have lost rights as animals also. See your dwelling houses, even animals can't be kept there. Your huts are made of grass, that is not painful, but the huts are in very bad condition. The tenderness with which the animals are given grass and other cattle food, who gives you bread with such tenderness? They give you bread but it is thrown in your face, because it is not given out of love but out of disgust. That is the reason why I tell you that your condition is worst than that of animals. (Quoted in Chopra & Chopra 1996 vol. VIII:65)

There is nothing amiss with this outburst of indignation about the inhuman treatment of the workforce. The Congress leader's style of speech bears witness to his intimate knowledge of the lives these landless peasants led. Yagnik or Swami Sahajanand could not have expressed it better. The difference was that both these men were not only more familiar with the lives of the underdogs but also knew how to approach them as equals. This was clearly not the case with Sardar Patel. After having expressed his compassion at the inhuman treatment to which the Dublas were subjected, he carried on to lecture them sternly on their uncouth way of life. If a man marries he must be able to support his wife and children without landing himself into debt; if he cannot do that, he should not get married in the first place. And then he scolded the *halis* for having habitually accommodated themselves in bondage. He ended his diatribe by calling them fools for their failure to comprehend the gist of what he blamed them for:

But you will not be able to understand all this. The bird which is habituated to live in a cage, if it is made free by the person who maintains it, then it gets scared, and returns again to the cage. Similarly if the farmer owners free the labourers, they will return to the masters because they have no hatred towards slavery. (Chopra & Chopra 1996 vol. VIII: 65)

Next came the turnaround: how should they mend their defective ways? Sardar Patel urged the labourers to be diligent, work loyally and adopt a decent and civil lifestyle. His tone was that of a stern father who corrects his foolish children. He not only listed the failings that stood in the way of emancipation but also appeared to see these manifold shortcomings as unavoidable confirmation of their stigmatized backwardness:

As we have knowledge about our rights , similarly we must have knowledge about our duties also. What type of behaviour one who wants to enjoy should have? He should not use abusive language nor he should use indecent words, but he should utter words which are decent. He should not insult anybody, he should not scold anyone, nor should he use foul words. He should learn how to use decent language. You should change your names if the names are not decent. It does not behove to give the names of dogs and cats to human beings. As soon as you enter schools, get your names changed by the teachers and call everybody with respect. Similarly, you keep your body clean. As soon as you return from work take a bath. You keep your looks clean. Similarly, you also keep your mouth clean. The mouth from which you offer sweet words and pray *Ram* should not be used to gulp down wine or toddy. It is a sin to do so. It has done most of the damage. If you think it relieves you from fatigue, however that is not a fact. It deprives you of money as well as energy. (Chopra & Chopra 1996 vol. VIII: 66)

Patel continued his diatribe in subsequent lectures. He undoubtedly felt this was necessary in response to the more assertive and more successful agitation stirred up before and after the Congress congregation in Haripura. The Congress leader continued stubbornly to avoid mentioning the Kisan Sabha's presence in his public appearances. He did, however, warn the Dublas that they must be patient because when small children who learn to walk run too fast, they risk breaking a leg when they fall. In reply to pleas from *halis* to be set free from bondage, he coolly answered that they must stop borrowing from landlords to get married. The amount they spent on this and other life-cycle events needed to be reduced and besides they had to earn it themselves. They should manage by saving up the extra income they made during the harvest peak. After all, Sardar Patel added, they could make do with little money for their daily sustenance. 'If you get enough food to eat, open space to live in, and clothes to cover your body, all needs are fulfilled.' (Speech of Sardar Patel at the Halpati conference held at Varod village in Bardoli taluka on 15 December 1937 in Chopra & Chopra 1996 vol. VII: 43). Cutting down their basic needs to enough food, simple shelter and one pair of cloth was his favourite theme in telling his audience how to live within their means. In another lecture he remarked: 'You require only one *dhoti* and one shirt, nothing more. You can get your cloth, even from the cotton which is blown away from the field. It is not at all difficult.' (Speech held at the Halpati conference in Bardoli on 26 April 1938 in Chopra & Chopra 1996 vol. VIII: 108). At the same meeting Sardar Patel commented that the only thing bonding his listeners to their employers was their own weakness. He advised them to maintain cordial relations with the landowners. Just as a pair of bullocks is required to pull the plough, farming requires cooperation between landowner and labourer. If they quarrel, both will suffer. So Halpatis should stay calm and not cause trouble, he said, in a veiled reference to the confrontational attitude the Kisan Sabha activists were taking. 'If any farmer gets angry and slaps you, do not return the slap. If you do you will be suppressed' (Speech held at the Halpati conference Swaraj ashram in Bardoli, quoted in Chopra & Chopra 1996 vol. VII: 108–10).

For Gandhi, non-violence was a moral principle to which no concessions could be made, even in situations of extreme oppression. But Sardar Patel was more pragmatic. Where Sahajanand saw the slap a Dubla boy gave his master as symbolic of an urge for freedom, Sardar saw this act of resistance as a failure of the obedience inferiors owed their superiors. His speeches, as quoted above, show that he held the Dublas accountable for their state of pauperism. He warned them not to challenge those who stood in the way of their advancement. Like other *kaliparaj* the Dublas would have to mend their rough and uncivil behaviour and needed to be taught how to discipline themselves. On the systemic and enduring violence the agrarian elite used to keep their workforce in check, Sardar maintained a steadfast silence. In his style of leadership he mixed his praise for non-violence with the acceptance of violence according to the need of the moment:

The backward classes were in fact encouraged to preserve the status quo. Curiously, the 'weapon' of nonviolence, supposedly intended to strengthen the weaker sections of society, actually disarmed them and exposed them to greater exploitation by those who could manipulate them for their own ends. Patel had no commitment to nonviolence; he adhered to it and discarded it at his convenience. In the (19)20s and (19)30s when Congress was in the process of ascending, Patel considered nonviolence useful in keeping control over widespread movements. In the (19)40s when Congress was strong and entrenched, he was willing to use violence against rivals and opponents. In Patel's hands nonviolence and other Gandhian methods were tools to be used for wider political goals. (Shankardass 1988: 87)

Underlying the lack of approval of violence was a rejection of militant action – on the grounds that it did not solve the conflict of interests but only threw them into sharper relief. The Congress ministry that in 1937 had come to power in the province of Bombay took the side of the landlords in south Gujarat. The party's stalwarts maintained that the widespread violence that had erupted gave them no choice but to force-fully counteract the class hatred preached by the agitators and their followers. It was in fact the same argument that colonial authorities had always used at times of agrarian revolts to justify sending in armed police to restore peace and order.

Declaring the Halpatis Free

Having kept the *halipratha* system in abeyance throughout the 1920s, the political climate changed a decade later – meaning it was no longer possible for the Congress movement to wash its hands of the widespread existence of unfree labour in the agrarian economy. The inroads Kisan Sabha had made in south Gujarat forced a change of strategy that would, without alienating the main landowners, have a pacifying impact on the by now frantically contested agrarian question. As a reward for their hard work constructing the premises in which the AICC convention was held, Sardar Patel had promised the Dublas release from bondage if they gave up drinking alcohol. In the Swaraj ashram, located in Bardoli town, he called on the dominant landowners of the sub-district – each village was represented by a few of them – to set their *halis* free. In separate talks held with spokesmen of the Dublas – all of impeccable Gandhian vintage, but none from the landless community – he notified them of this intention. At the end of his deliberations with representatives from both sides, a compromise was reached in which the main clauses were:

1. Abolition of *halipratha*, including cancellation of the debt. *Halis* who had worked for the same master for twelve years or more would no longer be expected to pay off their accumulated debt. Those who had been employed for a shorter time had to pay back a twelfth part for each year less than twelve years.
2. The daily wage was set at 4 *annas* and 8 *paisa*, and at Rs. 80 a year for annual contracts. If a farm servant had a debt to pay – which was always the case – 1 *anna* daily, which added up to Rs. 15 per year,

would be deducted from these amounts. The rates only applied to men. The daily wage for women was 3 *annas* and, in addition, women and boys received a small amount for domestic chores or tending the cattle.

3. The wages had to be paid in money. The custom of providing meals was discontinued and the other payments in kind, of which the daily grain ration was the most important, would also be stopped.

4. A *panch* of supervisers was to be appointed by employers and employees to ensure that these rules were duly implemented and complied with. Each village had such a council to settle disputes, and if that failed the cases would be submitted for arbitration at a higher level.

The formal declaration that the landless workforce would henceforth live in freedom and that the landowners would have to comply with the agreement reached was without doubt the crux of the compromise. Wages stayed at the same level as before, far too low to live on. That the daily remuneration was set at 4–5 *annas* (at best!) showed that Narikh Parikh had ten years earlier grossly exaggerated when he estimated the cost of a *hali* at 9 *annas* a day. Changing the payment from in kind to cash was meant to improve the Dubla's self-respect. By having to arrange for his own food and sharing the yield of his labour with wife and children in his own hut, the labourer could retire at the end of the day into a homely atmosphere and learn to take charge of the members of his household dependent on him. The settlement was also attractive for the farmer's wife who no longer had to provide meals for the labour attached to the household.

The covenant immediately turned out to be a bone of contention. Only a few villages cooperated in setting up a *panch*. To begin with, the landowners had always dictated the terms and conditions of employment and did not like the idea that they would now have to negotiate these with representatives of the landless peasants. It was even more difficult to persuade them to settle wages in cash. As the compromise had been reached in their absence, they did not feel bound by it. On their part, the labourers presented more of a solid front and refused to work if their employer did not abide by the new deal. However, this imbroglio did not last long since the landless did not have the resources to maintain their collective protest for more than a couple of days. The outcome was that the old practice of payment in kind went on uninterrupted. The compromise had also not spelled out how the demand for and supply of employment would take place on a day-to-day basis. Dublas who had always worked for the same farmer were supposed to give him priority before offering their labour to another one. But the landowners were worried that the labourers would disregard this unwritten rule just out of spite. How to solve this tricky issue? By way of experiment, one village agreed on a meeting place where the Dublas would assemble early in the morning to wait for landowners who needed one or more hands for the day. Alternatively, at the end of the day farmer and worker would make arrangements for the next day. When drawing up the rules for an eight-hour workday, Sardar Patel had allowed for it to be extended to ten hours in the peak season. But the landowners complained that the labourers were not punctual, arriving for work much later and leaving much earlier. For their part, labourers said that the bosses kept them back long after the agreed length of the workday. The solution to this problem was the installation of a siren that sounded the start and end of the workday.

In the presence of Gandhi, Nehru and five ministers from the Congress government of the Bombay Province, Sardar Patel announced the formal end of *halipratha* on 26 January 1939. He chose to do this on what was already celebrated in Bombay as Independence Day, in the hope that this date would also become known as 'Bonded Labourers' Liberation Day'. In a touch of irony, the ceremony was held not in Bardoli's Swaraj ashram, but on the premises of Patidar Gin. This was where the cooperative enterprise for cotton ginning in the region had its headquarters. The chosen venue for the occasion symbolized the hegemonic power of the dominant caste of Kanbi Patels. In his opening speech Patel admonished the Dublas to do what according to him they had so far obstinately refused to do: work diligently and live frugally. He pointed out that the supply of labour in agriculture was greater than the demand, and that the landless therefore would have to find side-activities to live properly. Spinning and weaving would earn them 2–4 annas a day additionally. Urging them to maintain harmonious relationships with the farmers, he called on the landless not to steal standing crops in the fields, even when they were hungry. On their side, the landowners must stop protecting their property with security guards who were notorious for the brutal way they treated the Dublas (Chopra & Chopra 1996 vol. VIII: 35–6).

The proclamation Patel had written was submitted to Gandhi for his approval. The Father of the Nation gave his consent, but not without commenting that the labourers' wages were unjust. In Gandhi's view the farmers had proved themselves stingy by fixing the wage level for men and women far too low. He said that both were entitled to a daily wage of at least 8 *annas* for an eight-hour workday. But he qualified his criticism by rhetorically asking why he should veto an agreement that landowners and labourers had entered into of their own accord. His comments were shocking because they implied that he was, or pretended to be, unaware that the landless proletariat had no bargaining power and did not have a say at all in the level at which the wage rate was settled. Like Patel before him, Gandhi also suggested that the eight-hour workday would leave the Dublas ample time to supplement their meagre income by spinning and weaving. With these words the Father of the Nation confirmed the liberation of the *halis* and on this auspicious day also officially gave them their new name. Their identity as Dublas implied weakness; they leave that blemish of a dark past behind. They should forthwith be known as Halpatis, lords of the plough, a blessing meant to dignify their agricultural work. The traditional name for the landlord, *dhaniamo* ('he who confers prosperity'), would also no longer be used, since it referred to a time that was forever gone. The festive celebration ended with a song and even the landlords present, who had been forthright to the very end in their resistance to the abolition of *halipratha*, joined the chorus at the top of their voices: *chhuta thaya re, chhuta thaya, Halpatis chhuta thaya re* – or, 'the Halpatis will be free'.

The joyful mood was short-lived, however, and discord soon regained the upper hand. Landowners in the villages of the Bardoli sub-district, beyond which the compromise did not apply, were unwilling to adhere to the terms of the settlement their spokesmen had reached with Sardar Patel. In response, the Halpatis refused to continue working under the old regime. But their bosses already knew in advance that they would not have the resilience to go on strike and stay away for more than a few days. As the wave of unrest escalated, the next step came from the weaker side. The wives of the *halis* refused to perform the domestic chores entrusted to them, such as fetching water, washing clothes, tending the cattle and cleaning the stable in the master's house. Alarmed at the rising conflict, the Gandhian activists rushed to the scene of these disputes and tried to persuade the landless workforce that it was their beholden duty to work as before. Determined not to give in, the landowners set about doing manual tasks themselves: tilling the land, picking the cotton, loading the harvest on carts and taking it to the cotton gins. In effect, they did what Gandhi used to tell them to do, to once again become self-working peasants who did not shy away from manual work. To alleviate the economic distress of the Halpatis, the social reformers came to their rescue by arranging public works. The dominant landowners turned against such 'troublemakers', some of whom had come to live in the neighbourhoods occupied by the landless, and chased them out of the village (Dave 1946: 42). As time passed the turmoil subsided because there was no adequate political, economic and social space left to keep up the resistance from below.

Sardar Patel thought, or pretended, that he could achieve the end of *halipratha* by relying completely on the free play of social forces. Why didn't he turn to public authority to issue an order banning unfree labour? There had been a Congress ministry in Bombay Province since 1937 and it would have taken little effort to obtain official endorsement of the legal abolition of bondage. In his speech on what would be proclaimed as Independence Day, he pointed out that bonded labour had no legal basis. Still, it was no reason for him to call on the authorities to proscribe the practice and enforce compliance with the ban. Using local councils with no formal authority – and which could do no more than persuade the opposing parties to accept a compromise – essentially meant that the whole exercise was a façade and doomed to failure from the beginning. It is easy to guess why this charade was chosen in the first place. The political leaders of the struggle for freedom had closely allied themselves with the dominant landowners, did not want to antagonize them by introducing radical reforms to the agrarian regime and were not overly concerned with the predicament of the landless masses. Intelligence reports solicited by the colonial authorities concluded that the agrarian elite sabotaged the agreement:

It is reported that the resolution deciding to abolish the 'hali' system, to which reference was made in my letter for the second half of January last, has not been implemented in many of the villages of Bardoli taluka (Surat District) and that some of the Dhaniamas who are opposed to the settlement are conducting vigorous propaganda against it. The opposition is said to be receiving support in other talukas in the District in which the system obtains. The Congress supporters of the settlement are carrying out counter-propaganda and there have been signs of tension at meetings held by the two sections. (Government of Bombay 1938–40, S. D. 718, first half of March 1938: 3–4)

A special note in 1940, prepared by the district superintendent of police in Surat and elaborating on the kisan agitation, confirmed that the leadership of the freedom movement had become unpopular with the landlords of south Gujarat because of their pledge to put an end to the *hali* system. His report shows that even before national independence had been attained the rural elite no longer supported Congress (Notes Regarding Kisan Movement 1940–1).

Waiting in Vain for Collective Action

Congress and Gandhian workers initially tried to continue their efforts to improve the plight of the landless underclass in the agrarian economy. To vacate this terrain would mean to leave it open to left-wing political agitation, an eventuality that had to be avoided. The idea was to set up a trade union that would bear the Congress stamp and the AICC session in 1938 deliberated on the proposal. Pamphlets were printed – meant for the outside world and therefore in English language only – to explain the aims and strategy of the new association. A conference would be held to announce the birth of the All-India Khet Mazdoor Sammelan, with Sardar Patel as its projected leader. The design was no doubt supposed to occupy the space filled so successfully by the Kisan Sabha, as Swami Sahajanand rightly commented many years later. With barely repressed glee, he added that:

... for whatever reason such a conference was neither held nor did Sardar Vallabhbhai become its president. But this makes it clear who was behind the agricultural labourers' movement and what their motives might be. There is no one who doesn't know that Sardar Vallabhbhai is perhaps the greatest enemy of the Kisan Sabha. (Quoted in Hauser 1994: 3–4)

The initiative to organize a trade union for the agrarian underclasses, presumably along the lines of the Majoor Mahajan Sangh that Gandhi had founded for the workforce of the textile mills in Ahmedabad, was revived in 1944 by the Congress movement in Gujarat. A committee was nominated to explore how best to launch an association that would cater to the interests of the land-poor and landless peasantry and met with Gandhi to discuss its scope. He spoke out against the top-down model the conveners had in mind and was more democratic and progressive than they had been, suggesting that the membership be restricted to the tillers but not the owners of land:

From my point of view genuine Mandal could consist of only one class. It is the class which actually works and which does not own any land. We work only for such class. This may be considered ideal advice. Everything less than that is inferior.[5]

The issue was raised and discussed but nothing happened afterwards. The collapse of Kisan Sabha in the late 1950s, torn apart by factions that had gone their different ideological ways, also ended the need for Congress to outflank a competitor.

The agrarian question was no less urgent than before, but at the apex of the political establishment the desire for mobilizing the peasants had waned. What did the radical agitation under the late-colonial regime achieve? For the rural proletariat stuck at the bottom of the class hierarchy nothing at all. Although this massive workforce had slowly become more visible, its presence and interests were consistently played down in the nationalist discourse. Even unions committed to a militant agrarian

---

[5] The minutes of the meeting with Gandhi held in his Sevagram ashram are included, together with the report of the committee, in the collection of Congress Papers deposited in the Nehru Memorial Museum and Library in Delhi.

policy rarely reached out to the landless. When they did so it was on an ad hoc basis rather than systematically. The political turf occupied by the Kisan Sabha movement during the 1930s was further eroded in the years that followed, perhaps not everywhere but certainly in south Gujarat. When I started my fieldwork in the Surat District in the early 1960s, it was hardly conceivable that at the dawn of Independence this area had been the scene of a fierce struggle for the emancipation of the exploited peasantry. It does not mean that these masses remained dormant in the past. The records and literature dealing with the Hindu-tribal frontier are replete with tales of how *adivasis* resisted being dispossessed and incorporated at the tail-end of the intruding mainstream order. This entanglement of losers and winners in a drawn-out trajectory, taking place in temporal disjuncture throughout the subcontinent, has largely been glossed over in the annals of peasant protest. But it would be misconceived to label such revolts merely an expression of tribal revivalism, a harking back in despair to lost identities. From sources close to the stage of operation we know that political activists often did not have to urge tribal peasants to rise up in revolt. They themselves attempted to seek outside support from higher up in order to redress the injustices to which they were subjected – seeking to reduce rent or land tax, secure their property, be free of debt or get higher wages. There is factual evidence to conclude that this was the case in the struggle of *halis* and sharecroppers in south Gujarat.

The records show that the Kisan Sabha movement spread in most provinces, but there is little information as to what membership entailed, how it was registered and who was in charge of the agenda of activities. Instead of relying on formal procedures and written communication, contact was through small-range networks and made by word-of-mouth. Administration hardly existed, not even for raising funds. A small core of local-level activists disseminated what went on, operating on a shoestring and working with great zeal but without much comprehension about who was responsible for what. None of the top-ranking leaders belonged to the targeted milieu themselves. Yagnik and Mehta were born into high-caste families of the urban bourgeoisie in Gujarat. Both displayed a social engagement at young age and became disciples of Gandhi. Their subsequent radicalization was inspired by having become disillusioned with the consistent refusal of their venerated *guru* and of the nationalist movement to end agrarian exploitation and oppression. Swami Sahajanand was of rural stock but also came from a landowning family. Although all three of them had a great affinity with and compassion for poor peasants and landless workers, there was a wide gap between them and the masses whose interests they defended. It was a world of working and living with which these outsiders felt empathy, but which remained for them difficult to approach and understand. These leading activists had to be highy mobile in their day-to-day life. They were continually on the road, attending to mundane politics and factionalist infighting. Their very busy agenda prevented them from gaining the detailed knowledge required to effectively articulate local-level events and interests. The gap could have been filled by training cadres from among the workers who had their origin down below and giving them authority to canvass followers and initiate grassroots activities. Mobilization of the membership, however, remained strongly top-down, as was apprehended in the aftermath:

The rural poor could squeeze their nominees only into the *taluk* or the *thana* and the village committees (also known as the 'primary committees'). But even these were so overwhelmed by the directives of the educated, petty bourgeois District and Sub-Divisional leaders that they enjoyed hardly any opportunity for originating a move or taking a crucial decision. The 'primary committees' in effect functioned as the sounding boards of the means of communication between the leftist leadership and the masses at the grassroots. The leftists were yet to realise the importance of and the urgency for creating local leadership, for generating local initiative. (Gupta 1996: 120)

It was also significant that the decision to start or end a campaign was often taken not on the basis of local circumstances but on the campaign's role in a wider political agenda dictated by totally different interests. What this meant in practice was that the supporters had to do what the leaders prescribed, rather than the latter making decisions based on what their members wanted. The land-poor and landless clientele was therefore encouraged to shout slogans, join marches and attend meetings that had nothing to do with their own predicament. Decisions to act or not were taken on the basis of a short- or long-term strategy in which the rank and file had no say at all. The Kisan Sabha was a broadly based union and tended to focus on peasants who had been dispossessed from land ownership in the recent past – and their interests took priority from beginning to end. Still, given all these obstacles and restrictions, one cannot be but impressed by the army of activists committed to demonstrate the growing assertiveness of the agrarian underclasses. Yagnik and other Kisan Sabha leaders were mobilized by the landless workforce to help them in their struggle against bondage. It was in response to this same pressure that Sardar Patel abolished the *halipratha* system, even though he did it with evident reluctance and in a way that was doomed to failure in advance.

With liberation from colonial domination in sight, there was no change in the state of subjugation at the foot of the agricultural economy. The landless peasants' inability to free themselves from bondage was not a result of lethargy, nor can it be attributed to the shortcomings of the activists who called on the peasants to lose their shackles. If the success was more modest than the agitators claimed, this outcome must above all be ascribed to the obstructive role of the agrarian elite. The ruling class in the countryside had long experience in the brutal repression of demands from below. But this refusal by the main landowners to grant their workforce the right to freedom would have been challenged more fundamentally if this dominating force had not been allowed to retain their privileged position in the nationalist movement. Stakeholders wishing to represent the interests of the land-poor and landless peasantry in the 1930s during a vibrant wave of agitation stood no chance against the alliance Congress had forged with the better-off class of farmers in Bardoli and elsewhere (Gupta 1996: 124; see also Amin 1988: 104). The balance of rural power by and large remained as it had been before. Does this mean that the domination–subordination nexus continued unimpaired? That conclusion would be an overstatement. Certainly there was little scope for manoeuvre, but to suggest that the interaction stayed as it had always been ignores the fact that farmers saw their power challenged while an advance guard among the landless seemed no longer to be shy of expressing impatience with their treatment as underdogs.

Surplus Not of Land but of Labour

The founding fathers of the nation had agreed on a programme of agrarian reforms that would secure land for cultivation in the hands of the actual tiller. In the pathway to Independence a National Planning Committee (NPC), chaired by Jawaharlal Nehru, had decided that the backbone of the agrarian order would be the private farm, equipped with enough land to be classified as an economic holding – a unit large enough to be managed effectively by the members of an average-sized family and to provide sufficient income for their livelihood. By establishing not only a minimum but a maximum limit – the size should not under normal conditions require permanent labour from outside the household – the design planned for the post-colonial era envisaged an agrarian regime essentially consisting of owner-cultivators. With intervention mainly from the top down, a ceiling was fixed for the redistribution of the surplus taken away from landlords among actual cultivators. Landlords were promised compensation for the loss of property rights. It turned out to be much more difficult to agree on the restructuring of the agrarian economy in the lower realms. Opinions differed on the proposal to allocate plots lying waste to collectives or cooperatives in an effort to encourage the land-poor to engage in joint farming. Such schemes were discussed in the context of the awaited transition to a socialist foundation of the state and economy. As for the residual class of landless workers, the working group discussing the agrarian question recommended imposing an immediate ban on debt-bondage still prevalent in various parts of the country. Bonded labourers should be released from debts that were of more than five years' standing. To help their rehabilitation, they would be given parcels of unowned land that was lying to waste to work such plots as self-employed cultivators. However, even in this ambiguous design for a simplified class composition, there would still be room to accommodate a contingent of farm labourers. To protect their welfare the recommendation was to set up unions to bargain and agree on minimum wages, a fixed working day and other terms of decent employment.

The half-hearted promise that the landless would also stand to benefit from the land reforms was not seriously worked out in detail and remained unfulfilled, more so in Gujarat than in a few other states. In his inauguration of Tiller's Day, 1 April 1957, the minister in charge declared that the legislation would especially benefit segments with less or no agrarian property:

It will bring hope to the landless or the partially landless and provide for reasonable means of subsistence ... It gives him (the tenant) a dignity and status which he never possessed before. He will be able to breathe his native air in his own ground. (Shah & Sah 2002: 135)

Tenants from Scheduled Castes and Tribes were often unable to exercise their right to buy the land they worked on. Chances of success were better if the owners did not live in the village and were just rent-seeking moneylenders and traders. The Dublas, now classified as Halpatis, benefitted in no way at all from the land reforms. A handful among them lost the land they had sharecropped under an informal arrangement with the owner. Swami Sahajanand had calculated that half of the landless would become landowners if uncultivated acreage were allotted to them (Hauser 1994: 101). The National Planning Committee had submitted a proposal to this effect, but once again it was not honoured. Waste land, not privately owned, was under the control of the village *panchayat*. Everyone had free access to such common land, including the landless who made use of it to graze their cattle, cut grass, collect firewood and, not least, for defecation. In the decades that followed, however, this access would be increasingly restricted, as a result of a widespread trend to privatization. The transfer of common land into private hands invariably meant that it became the property of the dominant farming castes.

The vulnerability of the rural landless in Gujarat was made more severe by an ideology of inequality that showed no sign of losing ground.

A last chance for the Halpatis to become landowners came with the launch of the land gift movement preached by Acharya Vinobe Bhave. This social reformer, who lived and worked according to the tenets of Gandhi, called on landowners to donate land in excess of their needs to land-poor peasants, voluntarily and without any compensation. The Bhoodan movement spread from the Gaya district in Bihar, where Bhave started his experiment in 1951, wanting to turn the area into Bhoodan's 'Bardoli'. His initiative had already ground to a halt by the end of the decade, due to the unwillingness of farmers to surrender their excess holdings. Where such surplus land was donated it tended to be of inferior quality (Thorner 1976: 70–1; Hardiman 2003: 203–7). Although an outright failure in most parts of the country, the Bhoodan movement was quite popular in Gujarat – particularly in regions such as south Gujarat, where the Gandhian movement had not yet given up on its constructive work programme after the demise of the Mahatma. During my first round of fieldwork in the early 1960s I used to meet these social activists. They would explain why they found the scheme so important, although it was clear that it had had no meaningful results. Halpatis were not eligible to receive Bhoodan land because, as one of them told me, the donating landowners were adamant that they lacked the necessary qualities to be owner-cultivators in their own right. This was a widely shared prejudice:

Yet they are treated with so much contempt that Shri Narayan Desai reported in 1956 a conversation among people of the land-owning class enquiring whether the Dublas at all deserved to be considered fit for being given the gift of Bhudan land. (Shah 1958: 23)

The land reforms were designed and implemented in such a way that groups dispossessed long before, like the Halpatis, were systematically denied access to agrarian property. The most common argument in defence of this strategy was the lack of cultivable land eligible for redistribution. Dominant castes of landowners throughout the subcontinent appropriated the larger part of the surplus that became available. The remaining and lesser part was added to the holdings of the small and marginal famers to make them more viable. They were given priority above the allocation of plots to the landless with the argument that a grant of land with such limited prospects of viability would only reinforce the Halpatis' immobility. Sardar Patel had already said on Hali Liberation Day in 1939 that in order to escape servitude the Halpatis would have to detach themselves from agricultural work and look for a better existence beyond their native village. His opponent Swami Sahajanand made it equally clear that the landless needed to give up their agrarian way of life. Given the lack of employment in the countryside, his solution was that at least half of this huge army would have to go and find work in urban industry after Independence, a scenario similar to the one the National Planning Committee had laid out in its design for the future.

Unfree in a Free Land

The freedom from bondage pledged on the eve of Independence in Bardoli by the Congress high command did not materialized. The *halis* had no other choice than to continue to work under the old regime. The terms of employment and the wages they received were the same as before. As a result of the rise in food prices in the Second World War, they opted for payment in kind rather than in cash. At the end of the day they received the traditional grain ration: 2.5 *seer*[6] of millet or 4 *seer* of paddy. The masters regularly cheated when measuring out the *bhata* and workers received one-tenth to one-quarter less than they were entitled to. Since the expenses the *halis* had to settle in cash also increased, their debt went up accordingly. The 'Grow More Food Campaign' that the colonial government launched in 1944 led to a major contraction in the acreage under non-food crops. To take full advantage of the high price for grain, farmers claimed back the *vavla*, the small plot of land that the *halis* were allowed by their master for growing food for their own subsistence. Many farmers had already abandoned this custom, but it was now discontinued in all villages (Shah 1952: 448–50). A number of daily necessities, including sugar, had become very scarce and were no longer available on the free market. The *halis* in the villages of my fieldwork had to hand over their ration cards to the farmers who, when I questioned them, gave the excuse that the wages of the Halpatis were too low for them to afford such luxuries anyway (Breman 1974a).

By now the Kisan Sabha activists had disappeared from the scene. When they were still around, their more comradely style of interaction made it easier for them to communicate with the Halpatis. The drawback was that they did not stay on but having lodged their protest, left again to continue their agitation elsewhere. The Gandhian ashrams opened in the region had volunteers who usually came from the city and were members of high castes. These *sevaks* (servants) were driven by a moralism that had little empathy for the tribal culture and identity. Their aim was to

[6] A measure of weight, roughly two pounds.

guide communities targeted as backward towards a better way of life and propagate virtues such as abstinence from drinking, while training them in home spinning and the singing of edifying devotional songs. The instruction to desist from eating meat was easier to comply with since this was a luxury that landless labourers could rarely afford. They had to be taught rules for hygiene not only to prevent disease but also to learn to live according to Hindu customs. On the other hand, these social reformers came with the intention of staying and spent their whole life fully committed to their mission of 'upliftment'. The landowners had sharply demarcated the limits within which these 'constructive workers' would be allowed to operate and did not tolerate interference with the terms and conditions of agricultural employment. After the clashes of the 1920s and 1930s, all activity that had the smell of trade unionism – claims for a higher wage, for debt redemption or bargaining with landowners on behalf of the working poor – were not on the Gandhian agenda of social work.

Some issues of a pressing nature were taken up that did not directly disturb the rural power equation. This included plans to build huts for the *halis* on land that did not belong to their masters. To live on on the property of the landowner had been standard practice in most villages of south Gujarat. The landless workforce used to be given permission to build their shelter close to the employer's residence and was also provided straw to thatch the roof of the hut, which was built of mud. As a matter of fact, the master used to insist on having the *hali*'s household close at hand in order to call on him and other members day and night. Moreover, their nearby presence also allowed him maximal control:

The present arrangement in most cases impairs seriously his [the *hali's*] independence. Even at the slightest provocation, the *dhaniyama* will threaten to throw out the *hali* on the roadside. Particularly when it comes to organizing the *hali* for improving his bargaining capacity this arrangement acts as a serious handicap, because the fear of being ejected summarily by the farmer when the *hali* does anything that goes against his interest hangs like the Damocles' sword on the latter's head. (Report of the Hali Labour Enquiry Committee 1948: 18)

The landowners had grown wary of having the landless living on their premises while on the other hand the landless preferred to move to a site of their own. Their separation made the changed character of their interconnection manifest. It was still a master-servant relationship, but had a contractual nature and lacked the former features of patronage, a realignment that expressed increased disjointedness as well as intensified exploitation. The consequence of the relocation of Halpatis in specially designated neighbourhoods was that living now in close proximity with other households of their community promoted interaction and a sense of togetherness and resulted in a much stronger sense of shared identity. Jugatram Dave took the initiative to set up a cooperative housing scheme for Halpatis and asked Morarji Desai, at the time revenue minister in the state of Bombay, to provide the financial means. The government would make the land available – the sites ware invariably at the uncultivated periphery of the village – and a grant of Rs. 500 per house, of which the owner would have to repay Rs. 400 in instalments. The Social Welfare Department of Bombay State sanctioned the scheme and a few of these settlements of huts were built, but enthusiasm for the project waned because the locations selected were far away from the village, had no sanitation, a fresh water well or passable access roads and the uneven terrain made the habitat unfit to live in:

In the case of the Verad colony the village drain which virtually flows into 'Halpati vas' gives out obnoxious smell and is highly injurious to health. In Wankaner, a stream is found to be flowing by the halis' dwellings which perhaps because of its bad layout has been a nuisance to the residents of the colony. (Report of the Hali Labour Enquiry Committee 1948: 18)

The residents were not equipped with a small plot around their self-built hut on which to keep a couple of goats or a cow and grow some vegetables. They also never received the title deeds they were promised for the homestead. Another major obstacle was that the inhabitants of the landless colonies were unable to pay off the loan of Rs. 400. Who had ever thought that they would be able to do so on a wage not even sufficient to meet their basic needs? Nevertheless, compared to the condition in which the landless had previously been forced to live – in the shadow of their master and constantly under his gaze – their relocation to the outskirts of the village turned out to be a blessing in disguise. It was a small step forwards on the long road to emancipation. The government realized that to provide shelter that freed the landless from surveillance by their employers was of great importance, as the minister of social welfare declared in the Bombay assembly in 1948:

Effective steps are being taken by the Government to free the members of the Dubla community in Surat district from serfdom. This could be achieved by providing them with houses and therefore the Government of Bombay has made a provision of seven lakhs in the second plan. (Shah 1959: 57)

The funds made available were no more than a drop in the ocean. Only a small number of hutments could be built with the paltry sum budgeted and the source from which I took the last quotation also observed that 'the policy has lacked continuity and consistency'.

The Gandhian workers claimed the ban imposed on the sale of alcohol as a great success. Prescribed abstinence was first introduced in 1949 in and around Bardoli, a few years later in south Gujarat at large. Prohibition has remained in force to the present, but since its inception the illegal distillation and sale of liquor has remained widespread. This has not prevented the abolitionists from claiming that this sinful habit has been wiped out, leading to material and moral improvement all around, as made believe in sanctimonious accounts:

In pre-prohibition period, a Dubla hamlet at night was but a battleground, crowded with drunkards. Heavily drunk men and women were found making rows, using abusive language and sometimes lying unconscious in a most hideous state. But now the fears of punishment and loss of prestige has considerably disciplined their behaviour. In the same way, the drunken brawls at marriage and such other religious and social occasions caused by excessive drinking are certainly less common. The money spent extravagantly in drinks has been saved to a great extent. (Shah 1958: 218)

The Dublas were principally agricultural labourers and on account of their long addiction to intoxicating drinks, they could never progress far beyond the borders of penury, indebtedness, illiteracy, economic backwardness and peaceful social and domestic life, to say nothing of political consciousness. Today, however, thanks to Prohibition, all that is a thing of the past. They now own part of the land themselves. (Editorial in *The Farmer*, January 1954, vol. 5/1:49)

Propaganda like this also created the impression that the Halpatis were able to earn a tidy sum to supplement their daily income by spinning as 'the charkha [spinning wheel] began to hum in their huts'. The farmers sometimes complained about this side-activity, claiming that it was carried out at the expense of agricultural work. A start was also made towards developing the Halpatis' literacy, with the admission of Halpati children to the ashram schools that had been set up. Education, however, was not yet a must for the landless households and the activity had to be stopped again at the time of the Quit India movement in 1942, when the leadership of the Gandhian movement either went to prison again or was driven underground. The Halpatis faced difficulties in providing for their basic necessities and did not bother sending their children to school (Dave 1946: 43). In my first round of fieldwork, two decades later, near-total illiteracy still prevailed in the landless quarters. The social workers, dedicated though they were, had little insight into the obstacles that prevented the children of the landless from attending school – such as the absence of parents from home during daytime; the need for children to fend for themselves from an early age and hire themselves out on paid work; and, more generally, an inability to invest in the future because priority had to be given to day-to-day survival.

How is it possible that the leadership of a political movement that stirred up the people of the country to fight for their freedom, once it had taken charge of the national destiny could justify the ongoing practice of labour bondage? Just like Sardar Patel before him, Morarji Desai had become a high-ranking Congress stalwart who several times spoke out on the *halipratha* question. He called it an unjust custom with which he – born in the dominant caste-class of a south Gujarat village – was familiar as few others seasoned in politics and governance:

I had not considered Halpati pratha as bad during my childhood but I started thinking about it after I graduated and felt that this unjust tradition must stop. When I joined the civil service and was working as a Deputy Collector in Thane district many Halpatis used to come there to work in the saltpans. Their maliks who were called dhaniyama used to come there to take them away [note: because they had refused their *halis* permission to leave]. Already at that time I made it clear to them that they had no legal authority over these people and I always denied their demands. But I started working against this custom only after I joined Congress in 1930. And after Independence I helped wherever need arose to bring an end to this tradition. (Desai 1972: 13–14)

Morarji Desai would end his distinguished career as prime minister of India (1977–9), but much earlier, as minister in the Congress government of Bombay state, had set up in 1947 a Hali Enquiry Committee to submit proposals for the liberation of bonded labour – to enable members of this agrarian workforce to regain their human dignity. On receipt of the report, this high-profile politician refused to make it public.[7] His insistence that the *halipratha* system had already been abolished referred to another compromise settlement reached between the landowners and Gandhian workers of Bardoli in 1948, one which, like the earlier agreement, was not implemented. An added press note entitled 'No Forced Labour in Surat District' plainly stated that since the system had never been legalized no further enactment was necessary (Shah 1958: 209–11). The argument for not introducing a legal ban does not hold water. It is important to note it was not seen as the business of government to eliminate unfree labour. Rather, as in 1938–9, this task was left to the free interplay of social forces, represented on the one hand by a class of landowners who had strengthened their hegemony in the aftermath of Independence and on the other a large mass of landless workers whose labour power was only required during parts of the year.

---

[7] Alice and Daniel Thorner referred to the report, but were unable to get hold of it (Thorner, A. & D. 1962: 35). Professor M. B. Desai, one of its authors whom I used to meet regularly in the course of my fieldwork, told me that a copy was kept in the collection of the Department of Agricultural Economics of Bombay University and this is where I got access to it.

For many months there was insufficient work in agriculture to keep them all busy. During these slack periods the farmers used to give the *halis* their habitual grain ration but this was seen as an advance on their future availability and added to the worker's debt.

It was clear that both before and after Independence the Congress policy remained committed to prioritizing and serving the vested interests in the agrarian economy. Although pretending, in the Gandhian mood, to be in favour of emancipating the landless – 'the least and the last', as the Father of the Nation called them – from the chains that tied them to the caste-class of dominant farmers, labour attachment was not eradicated, as those in power had always condoned it. Nevertheless, a rationale had to be found to explain why bondage persisted while its abolition had more than once been decreed. Prohibited but going on as before, how could that happen? The answer was given by the 'constructive workers' who had not dared to deprive the landowners of their servants, anxious to keep the class entanglement covered up. In the name of Gandhi-ism, they wanted compromise and conciliation where oppression and exploitation dictated the terms of the relationship. The idea was that the masters had to change their mind and understand that *halis* deserved much better treatment than they got while the latter had to wait until their masters saw the light and meanwhile toil on humbly and dutifully. And, of course, they had to clean up their debased way of life, give up tribal customs that kept them backward, work properly, abstain from drinking, show themselves modest and be frugal in their behaviour. The same shortcomings are evident in the verdict of policy-makers who stated more explicitly why bondage had not become extinct. In their appraisal, the victims were roundly blamed for wanting to keep the system intact. This argument went back to the complaints that employers had consistently made about their *halis'* impropriety. The list of defects also biased the social reformers in their approach to the problem. The widely shared perception was that the landless rather then the landowners should be held accountable for the resilience of *halipratha*:

This system makes the farm labourer free from the worries as to from where tomorrow's meals would come and, consequently the attached servant becomes totally irresponsible and careless and he does much less work than a free labourer. (Parikh 1926: 3 October 1926)

In the case of the Hali, there is one additional reason [note: next to the uneconomical mentality of farmers] why his output is lower than that of the free labourer. It is that, as he is guaranteed every day's food whether he works or not, he becomes irresponsible and indifferent in his work. (Mukhtyar 1930: 169)

At odds with this stigma of the lazy and lethargic farm servant, the HLEC reported that the average length of the working day was eight to nine hours, increasing to twelve to fifteen hours in the peak season. Detailed records submitted by landowners in many villages showed that *halis* might work day in, day out without a break at the end of the week for a long period and then, without prior warning, not turn up. The masters blamed this sudden withdrawal as proof of their servants' indolence and lack of responsibility. The investigating panel's opinion was, however, much more nuanced:

The attendance figures do not mean that the *hali* was intentionally absent for the rest of the days. It is just possible that for some days there was no work on the farm of the dhaniyamo and he was therefore not 'called'. Some absenteeism was due to illness and fatigue. A part of it may be due to festivals. Halis are forced to remain idle during the slack seasons and days of heavy rains. Some of the causes are beyond his control. Sickness and fatigue are the direct outcome of sub-human living standards and the low vitality to which it gives rise. (Report of the Hali Labour Enquiry Committee 1948: 22)

But irrespective of these critical comments on the proverbial laziness of the Halpati, the HLEC report did not at all question what had become the received wisdom: that the landless workforce wanted to hold on to what was now viewed as the security of attachment. But members of this tribal community did not seek reprieve in subjugation. Denied the means to provide for themselves, they became destitute in bondage. It was a state of misery inflicted upon them. Thus, their impoverishment was not the cause but the consequence of servitude.

5   The Gandhian Road to Inclusion in Mainstream Society

The study I made of the *halipratha* system began when I came to south Gujarat at the beginning of the 1960s. My anthropological fieldwork focused on the connection between the polar ends of the village hierarchy: at the top the dominating caste-class of landowners and at the bottom the tribal workforce of landless labourers. The master-servant relationship figured in that polarized interface in a major way, but I realized while doing my rounds in the selected research locations that my immediate findings needed to be contextualized within a longer time span: to make sense of the bondage still going on I would have to trace the practice of servitude back to the colonial setting and perhaps to an even earlier epoch. My Ph.D. thesis described and analysed the political economy at the local level in a historical perspective. I came back to south Gujarat in the summer of 1971 for a second run of research and stayed until the end of 1972. The English translation of my thesis (1974) included an additional final chapter that discussed the changes I found on my return to the sites of my previous enquiries. On the basis of this new spell of fieldwork I concluded that the progressive decline of the *hali* system took the form of an erosion of patronage features in the interaction between the landowners and landless labourers. My opinion on the fading away of the earlier system of bondage was strengthened by taking stock of events in the decade that had passed since my first round of investigations.

I shall elaborate in the next chapter on the dynamics of landowner-landless relationships as they developed in the 1970s and their ramifications for a new form of labour bondage, but some major points need to be brought up in this section. The most drastic changes in the labour market of south Gujarat were undoubtedly that rural labour had become mobile over large distances. Labour migration was one of the main objects of study during my second round of fieldwork, in 1971–2. It meant that agricultural labour could easily be contracted throughout the year, priced at Rs. 1–2 a day, far below subsistence level. Workers continued to be dependent on farmers but without the elements of patronage found in the *hali* system. In this new pattern of employment exploitation of the Halpatis had intensified. Social intercourse with labourers was reduced to an absolute minimum. Considerations of profitability were not the only explanation of why landowners had changed to more capital-intensive agrarian techniques; they also expressed a dislike for personal contact with the workforce they needed, wanting to avoid interaction with them them as much as possible and relied, in addition to mechanized power, on middlemen such as jobbers and foremen instead. I found the landless increasingly marginalized. Pauperization is usually described in economic terms but as in the case of Halpatis the social dimension of life on the margins is hardly less noticeable. The eclipse of vertical ties that formed an integral part of *halipratha* undoubtedly facilitated the slow emergence of a united front in the quarters of the landless community. Spontaneous outbursts of protest to claim higher wages and better terms of employment did occur, but they remained local and incidental in character. Organization is a necessary precondition for any sizeable and durable protest movement to emerge and be successful.

It was clear that state bureaucracy and political parties were not going to introduce policies for the emancipation of the landless workforce. In the course of my new period of fieldwork I had wandered around in the countryside in search of anchor points and spaces for collective action. Were there no initiatives emerging from civil society to develop a sense of agency among 'the least and the last'? Reflecting on the outcome of my investigations, in 1974 I wrote an essay on the Gandhian movement that hegemonized the work of social reform in the countryside of south Gujarat.[1] In the wake of Independence the tribals had been renamed *adivasis*, people supposed to be aboriginal to the often-backward tracts they inhabited. These communities, which included the Halpatis, would henceforth be under the guidance of the Gandhian reform movement. No other concerted activity, politically or non-politically motivated, that wished to cater to the interests of these land-poor or landless peasants could find a foothold in what became the exclusive domain of Gandhian missionaries. From ashrams set up in the tribal belt, they were engaged in constructive work, as shepherds coaching their wily flocks how to live

---

[1] The factual data presented in the essay was gathered in conversations with hundreds of Halpatis and repeated meetings with about 15 of their local leaders in towns and villages, mainly in Bulsar District. Apart from that, I obtained a good deal of information from the regular contacts I maintained with staff of the Halpati Seva Sangh (HSS), teachers in ashram schools and social workers who did not belong to the organization but were active among the Halpatis. This category consisted of more than 25 informants, both in Bulsar and in Surat District. Finally, I interviewed 15 politicians of various parties and an equal number of officials from the district bureaucracy.

properly in the Hindu way. This civilizing mission was interrupted at the start of the 'Quit India' campaign in 1942 when many of these social workers were arrested (Hardiman 1988). As dedicated Congress supporters they had obeyed the call to end colonial rule and taken part in civil disobedience activity. In this period patriotism took priority over efforts to emancipate the deprived social classes of south Gujarat.

As early as 1942, an association called Halpati Mahajan was set up with the aim of uplifting this landless community (I. I. Desai 1971: 170). Most likely it was a hub through which the social reformers of ashrams in and around Bardoli collaborated on a common goal. The participants registered the network in 1946 as a formal organization and agreed to base their activities on the Gandhian principles of 'truth, non-violence and arbitration'. The earlier name 'Mahajan' was a direct reference to the trade union Gandhi had set up for the workforce in the textile mills of Ahmedabad in 1920. This trade union, the Majoor Mahajan Sangh, endeavoured not merely to achieve improvements in the material conditions of its members but also to imbue discipline in an urban proletariat said to lack the traits required for civil self-constraint (Breman 2004). The ashram workers in south Gujarat were not held accountable to the targets of their mission in the countryside, but were supposed to coach the Halpatis along the road to a better future by showing them how to behave as respectable members of society. The landless community had no say at all in what the agenda of constructive work should entail or the manner in which the association born our of Gandhian activism, the Halpati Seva Sangh, was run. From the very beginning, the driving principle was 'for them, but not by them'.

Obstacles on the Path to Self-Mobilization

The introductory part of my essay on the Gandhian social reform movement attempted to throw light on the marginality in which agricultural labour was kept and the prospects for their progress guided along by well-meaning outsiders who had committed themselves to redeem the Halpatis from their subhuman existence. My critical assessment of the Gandhian approach led me to conclude that that the civilizing mission not only failed to achieve the stated objective but was even counterproductive to the goal of emancipation. The more radical agitation that had been going on in the area for land rights and freedom from *halipratha* had evidently left little trace. As a matter of fact, my account incorrectly said in so many words that a genuine kisan movement had never cropped up in the region. Although the landless underclass were mobilized in the slipstream of land-poor tribals who had managed to hang on to their fields as sharecroppers or tenants, those communities – Dhodhias, Chodharis, Gamits, Naikas, Bhils – had at least retained their communal identity as self-reliant peasant cultivators. Interesting also was that the Gandhian movement operating from ashrams had made more inroads in this milieu than among the Halpatis, even though for the latter community a separate organization had come into existence. Since my essay was meant to convey the gist of the agrarian question at the time and my digest of it, I thought it might be appropriate to republish in this treatise what I wrote up in the early 1970s since the contents do fit the period that will next come up for discussion. It is a chronicle of past events but in the following account – which runs through to the end of this chapter – I have adhered to the present tense and the verbatim text as it was published in *Economic and Political Weekly* (1974) in order to maintain the spirit of the moment, even then a not very hopeful one.

The impression that one is left with after talks with Halpatis in their peripherally situated village quarters is one of utter defencelessness in all respects. Their inability to find a way out of the misery and insecurity of their daily life leaves most of them no scope at all for any ulterior purpose or action. In the present frame of the agrarian economy there are simply not enough means of existence for the rapidly growing number of Halpatis. In the rural districts the labour supply far exceeds the demand; nor do the Halpatis easily find employment outside agriculture. They cannot be absorbed by the urban economy of the region. In the rivalry for the slowly expanding employment opportunities outside agriculture the urban Halpatis barely come into the picture. As an unskilled category they are only considered for the lowest paid, least valued and most irregular work, and most of them lead lives nearly as forlorn as those of their fellow caste members in the villages. In a never-ending cycle a major part of the surplus is thrown out of the rural system. After the rainy season, around October, men, women and children migrate in large numbers – in the Bulsar villages more than half of all Halpatis may go – to the brickyards and salt-pans near Bombay, to return home only at the end of May, before the beginning of the monsoon. Year after year this seasonal migration is repeated. The splitting up of households – some members stay behind, the others are put under contract by one or different jobbers – fits well into the picture of pauperization. The yearly exodus does not really enhance the employment opportunities for those who stay at home. In the slack season the agrarian labour market remains saturated, partly on account of the influx of migrants from the nearby hinterland looking for work.

The Halpatis have become redundant in society. Many of them are drifting around and have all but lost their roots in both village and family life. A coalition with tribal castes of petty cultivators – notably Kolis, Dhodhias and Chaudharis – might invalidate the marginality in which the Halpatis live, but it is not likely to occur. In a very general sense the land reforms have stabilized the position of the small landowners and most of them have few interests in common with the Halpatis. Although many smallholders have not profited much from the Green Revolution – if their position has not deteriorated – the social, economic and political advantages attendant on caste membership operate against their identification with the predicament of the landless proletariat. That the demoralizing situation, in which the Halpatis are placed, manifests itself in political inertia is only natural. Their need of security and protection, essential to the former *hali* system, is not met by the government. The huts of the Halpatis used to be spread out on the land of the landowners, but in many villages they are congregated together in separate quarters. They have usually been allotted the worst parts of the terrain, difficult of access and far from the village centre (*gamtal*), where they live as untouchables. Compulsory education has been introduced, but very few Halpati children attend school. About nine in ten caste members are illiterate, the highest proportion in the central plain of south Gujarat. In the second half of 1972, after years of delay, the legal minimum daily wage for agricultural labourers was at last fixed at Rs. 3. Effective control is lacking, however, and in practice employers do not abide by the law. But if they did, the amount would still not be enough for the Halpatis to meet the sharply rising cost of living.

The majority of Halpatis believe the only thing they owe the government is obedience, and try to avoid all further contact with its officials. The benefits put at the disposal of Scheduled Tribes do not reach them. 'For that you need influence', they say resignedly. The time is past that the votes of the agricultural labourers were returned through their masters, but that does not mean they are now politically emancipated. They lack the awareness that, collectively, they generate power. During the campaign for the state elections in 1972 I found that many Halpatis were not registered in voting lists. Often they had no idea of the differences between the parties. But then such differences were scarcely relevant if seen from their position. Their votes were for sale at a few rupees, and especially among the higher castes colourful tales were told about it. An often-heard opinion among members of the upper social layer, who feared the strength of their number, is that only literates should be allowed to vote. The Halpatis' passivity is closely bound up with their ignorance. They often turn out to be only vaguely, if at all, aware of slogans such as *garibi hatao* (get rid of poverty) although these were raised in their name. Illiteracy deprives them of a great deal of information. The combination of indifference and ignorance, both indissolubly bound up with penury, underlines their exclusion from society.

Those among them who have some notion of what is going on have the greatest trouble to explain their point of view. These drawbacks are partly due to the fact that the members of castes of landless labourers are not accustomed to function within frameworks that stress collective aims. Their experience with joint activity is very limited. The traditional caste *panch* at the village operates only incidentally, and then it is a question of one or more persons (*patels*) meeting to settle divorce or other disputes among or within households. Probably more important as a new organizational form are the *bhajan mandlis* which, stimulated by workers from the ashrams, have been set up in the past few years. These are groups that gather one evening a week to sing devotional and Gandhian songs. Finally, group experience is gained by working in gangs, initially contracted for semi-industrial work, but now increasingly also for agricultural operations. The Halpatis themselves explain their backwardness from a lack of leaders. It is true that there are no figures among them who are known and prominent in the region as is the case with most other tribal castes in the plain of south Gujarat. Even at the village level there is very often no leader recognized by all Halpatis. Influence seems to be exerted by individuals only within their own hamlet and jealousy is a complaint often heard on every part. Outsiders, experienced social workers, also assert that Halpatis are not capable of collaborating with one another, It should, however, be borne in mind that landless labourers do not form a homogeneous mass as such. The interests of farm servants, casual wage-earners, gang labourers, piece-rated workers and seasonal migrants do not necessarily coincide. Moreover, all of them are to varying extents dependent on landowners and jobbers, their principal employers. The competition for the few favours to be had in a situation of continuous scarcity in each and every respect invalidates any strengthening of horizontal solidarity.

Dependence has, finally, been internalized by the Halpatis. In the households of the high castes, one Halpati said, our women are daily injected with poison. In conversations with Halpatis, references to their own backwardness are not at all uncommon. Those few that have been educated may speak bitterly of their fellow caste members' lack of culture, but many of the others have a low opinion of themselves, too. What other caste, they wonder, lends itself to cleaning the stables and performing the dirty housework for the landowners?

Does the above suffice as an explanation of the passivity among agricultural labourers? Apathy, ignorance and feelings of inferiority fit too well into theories of a culture of poverty to be altogether acceptable as the sole or even the main reason. The Halpatis are certainly aware of the structural conditions that obstruct the betterment of their lot. They show a deep grudge against the high castes in general, and the Anavil Brahmans and Kanbi Patels in particular: 'They are the ones who oppose us; not only in the villages, but also in the government offices, where they have to put their signatures and stamps on papers that are important for us.' Agricultural labourers used to be able to count on the intercession of their masters, but now they often meet with opposition on the masters' part, inspired by vexation over their labourers' insufficient work performance. To prevent the Halpatis from becoming too independent, the landowners may use their influence with the district officials against them. They often succeed.

The Halpatis have their dependence rubbed into them in more direct ways. As I said above, the agricultural labourers especially are wide open to the range of sanctions that the rural elite has at its disposal, particularly that of demoralizing their potential leaders, those who testify to an insight into their own situation and adopt militant attitudes. The police, too, are an instrument of oppression. Although the days of individual violence are gone, when every landlord felt entitled to give his farm servant a good thrashing for 'misconduct', other kinds of arbitrary behaviour are still common. Accusations of drinking or crop theft, false or not, are an effective way to call Halpatis to order, and maltreatment of the accused by the local police force, the hated 'brown dogs', is not exceptional. In the circumstances prevailing, submissiveness and avoidance is an obvious reaction. A group of agricultural labourers who had been granted permission to build their huts in a village on government land concurred with a petition, drafted by the large landowners who were afraid to lose their grip on them, in which they cancelled their request. Examples such as this are the order of the day. Their fear of risking the anger of the landlords is evident, and this explains why only the somewhat better-off among them who enjoy a measure of autonomy and security emerge as leaders in the Halpati neighbourhoods. Yet even these self-styled representatives of their own caste are not altogether to be trusted. All too often they have turned out to be agents for outside interests.

The investigator's contacts with Halpatis do not run smoothly. Questions asked are answered obliquely, evasively or not at all. The informants are fully alive to their own vulnerability and have learned to put no trust at all in outsiders. They pretend to lead an extremely atomized existence. A striking number of Halpatis denied having friends or maintaining social contact with neighbours or others in their hutments. To some extent this is true, no doubt, but at the same time statements like these indicate the defensive attitude they have adopted. It is the contacts in their own neighbourhood that enable them to form closer mutual ties. And in fact they sit together in groups in front of their huts at night, and thrash out among themselves the forms and degrees of exploitation they suffer at the hands of landlords, shopkeepers, government officials, police and social workers. The cumulative weight of economic, political and social dependence invalidates the view that class feelings do not occur among pauperized categories. For them to show any such feelings is imprudent; to act accordingly, impossible. My conclusion is that this combination of structural and cultural conditions, intra-caste and inter-caste contradictions is at the bottom of the Halpatis' inability to mobilize themselves. I hope to show below that not every outside attempt to mobilize them is successful, either.

Organized Action: Gandhian Approach

The role played by the Gandhian movement in the disappearance of the *hali* system has been touched upon above. In the early 1920s, some of Gandhi's close collaborators made themselves leaders of a reform programme that was to bring about the emancipation of the adivasis in south Gujarat. But the activities undertaken by these people, working from the Swaraj ashram in Bardoli and one of its branches in Vedchhi, both in Surat district, were mainly directed at the tribal castes whose members led a semi-independent existence as petty cultivators. Already then there were a few ashramites who took interest in the Halpatis, but under pressure from the local landlords they gave up their attempts to run night classes for the agricultural labourers in a number of villages. Serious work among the Halpatis only started after Independence, partly inspired by the report written about them by Jugatram Dave, the oldest and most prominent protagonist of the movement. The ashrams, most of which have also become educational institutions, function as action centres that aim at changing the rural system in a Gandhian direction.

Apart from this, Gandhi's ideas have penetrated among the population of south Gujarat in a more direct way. In many villages there are persons who perform social work on an individual basis in accordance with the doctrines of Gandhi. They advocate social reforms such as the material and cultural improvement of the tribal castes, abolition of untouchability, prohibition, women's emancipation or village uplift in a general sense. For the ashrams these social workers are key figures, through whom they maintain their contacts with the local population. The chief task of these social workers is mediation. Their aim is to promote neglected interests and to speak for deprived categories. They try to gain access to those who take decisions or have favours to distribute in the government offices. Most of these voluntary workers are inspired by a mixture of social awareness and political ambition. Their influence on the regional level is needed to gain advantages for the people under their care, whilst on the other hand they are attractive to political parties owing to the votes they can control.

The older social workers are mostly members of higher castes and, if only for that reason, not acceptable to the Halpatis as agents of good-will, even if they are apt to describe themselves as such. In the last few years, increasing numbers of young adivasis, trained in ashrams, have succeeded in establishing themselves as social workers. They are prac-tically all Dhodhias or Chaudaris, that is, members of tribal castes owning some land that form the majority of the population in their constituencies. They see to it that the benefits distributed on behalf of the Scheduled Tribes in the way of employment, education, agriculture and so on, go to their fellow caste members. The landless and illiterate Halpatis are given the go-by. The Halpatis live scattered over a large area in which they form a minority and, as I said above, they have no supra-local leaders of any importance. More than half the taluka seats for the state assembly in Ahmedabad have been reserved for tribal candidates, but not one of these seats is occupied by a Halpati, nor does the weight carried by Halpatis in the district councils correspond in any way with their proportion in the total population. In Bulsar District, for instance, no member of the important Social Welfare Committee through which the benefits for 'backward communities' are channelled, belongs to this largest tribal caste but one of the region. The Dhodhias, on the other hand, who are only slightly more numer-ous, command an absolute majority on this committee. Whereas some decades ago the voluntary social workers in the villages followed Gandhi in stressing their spiritual guidance, since Independence they have narrowed their role to that of local-level politicians. In a slightly differ-ent way the Gandhian movement itself has undergone professionaliza-tion. I. P. Desai is the author of a very interesting study (I. P. Desai 1969) in which he described this process of change and its implications. Commenting on the ashram cadre of today, he says, 'The social worker is likely to be a paid worker and organiser, committed to fixed, assigned duties, rather than the Gandhian missionary type, which is becoming a historical type.' The transition outlined by him from movement to organization is very noticeable in the case of social work among the Halpatis.

Halpati Seva Sangh: Its Organization, Programme and Impact

For many years Jugatram Dave continued to act as chairman of the Halpati Seva Sangh, albeit in an honorary capacity. Although the tie with the ashrams was preserved after 1961, that year saw the beginning of a new phase. In Bardoli a head office was established, in which an ever-growing administrative staff now coordinates all activities among the Halpatis of south Gujarat. During the years that followed, twenty local branches were founded in *talukas* where Halpatis form a substantial part of the population. The survey published on the occasion of the organization's tenth anniversary[2] claimed that in 1972 almost 20,000 Halpatis were registered with HSS; they theoretically pay a subscription of 10 *paiysa* a year. Apart from the nearly 500 paid staff members, the organization comprises about 2,000 unpaid helpers and contributors, for the most part non-Halpatis. There are *taluka* and district boards, composed of members of these branches to discuss the activities once a year. The subscription fees are, of course, negligible as a source of income. The broadly conceived programme, aimed at the upliftment of the caste of agricultural labourers in south Gujarat, is practically wholly financed by the government. The most important HSS activities are:

- Mediation in the allocation of land to Halpatis to build their huts on, so that they depend less on the landlords, the striking of wells or pumps in the new quarters, the establishment of co-operative housing societies to enable them to build better huts. The government has not gone beyond granting subsidies for this purpose since the great floods of 1968, and until now on a limited scale.
- Foundation of schools of their own, to make up for backwardness in education. In the new village quarters, over a hundred kindergartens have been opened. Distributed over the districts, there are also five primary residential schools and four secondary schools. In spite of the provision of free books, clothing, food and accommodation, the schools do not generally attract many Halpati pupils. To avoid losing the government subsidies they therefore accept children from other tribal castes, who in some schools account for more than half the total number of pupils. This also applies to the seven hostels that accommodate boys and girls who attend the ordinary village schools.
- Employment opportunities. A limited number of young males and females are enabled to be trained as artisans. After completion of their

---

[2] Halpati Seva Sangh, Bardolini Pravuttini Jhamki. Bardoli 1971.

training they are given a modest tool kit needed to practise their skills. The *khadi* household industry, much less propagated now than it used to be, has failed to take root among the Halpatis. The establishment, after years of preparation, of eighty-five agricultural labour coopera-tivcs seems to be more promising, but none of these has as yet developed into a going concern.

– A wide range of socio-cultural activities. Propaganda is carried out for prohibition, till now without much success. It is encouraged indirectly by *bhajan mandlis*, which spread Hindu values. Young people's clubs campaign to attract pupils for the schools. Women's groups are formed, which apply themselves to learning *garba* and other high-caste dances at festivals. To prevent crippling expenditure for marriage festivities – often the beginning of increasing indebtedness – garlands are presented to couples in substitute marriage ceremonies. In case of illness, Halpatis are entitled to either medicines or the cost of medi-cines. Agricultural labourers who are in serious conflict with the police or their landlord can count on legal aid. A few times a year, *sibhirs* are held, meetings of one or more days, to which Halpatis with leadership qualities are invited. To widen their horizon, they occasionally go on tours to other parts of south Gujarat.

Although on paper this looks impressive enough, various components of the programme are only moderately successful. It is, however, not at any shortcomings in the implementation that our criticism should be directed, but at the ideology underlying the programme and the policy of the organization. To begin with, the HSS has become the executive body for all provisions and regulations intended to benefit Halpatis. Besides the activities enumerated above, the salaries of the staff members and other overhead costs are paid by the government. This means that the organization is an extension of the bureaucratic appar-atus without, however, possessing its authority. In the circumstances, any real consideration of Halpatis' interests is an illusion. The HSS is a semi-government body and cannot act as a pressure group, which is a *sine qua non* for winning the confidence of the people whom the workers are supposed to represent. Secondly, the work of the HSS has aggra-vated the isolation of the agricultural labourers rather than relieved it. According to the law they cannot be evicted from the land on which they have built their huts. Instead of supporting the valid claims of the Halpatis in this respect, the organization promotes their removal to separate village quarters. In remote and often badly drained neighbour-hoods, deprived of the most elementary public facilities, the Halpatis live together with a stain of untouchability. Separate educational provisions contribute to their apartheid. Young people who have been educated in these schools complain that the Gandhian bias in the curriculum damages their chances, which are weak to begin with, in the labour market. Thirdly, the HSS is above all a welfare organization. Most of its activities are ameliorative in character. They are aimed at relieving the worst distress, and at the same time, at educating the Halpatis to be better Hindus. This, especially, seems to be the nature of the emancipation the HSS promotes.

Political Leadership

The HSS advocated higher wages for the landless proletariat. But when agricultural labourers go on strike somewhere to reinforce their claims, the social workers intervene in order to prevent rising tensions and to reach a compromise. Self-respect and class consciousness are not taught, on the contrary. The organization does not aim at making the Halpatis able to stand up for themselves, aware of their exploitation and oppression, but envisages their adjustment to mainstream caste society without any fundamental change in their dependence. It is true that the rural elite does not take very kindly to the existence of the HSS, even if no threat to the *status quo* emanates from it. But, says the present leader meaningfully, it is due to the absence of communist influences among the Halpatis that the organization is assured of support by the government and does not meet with more obstruction on the part of the landlords. The mobilisation of the labourers is non-antagonistic in nature. The Gandhian principles of arbitration, compromise and avoidance of open clashes between the parties concerned form the basis of this policy. In the Gandhian ideology, the class struggle is not so much strategically unjustified but rejected as immoral. In the very conservative climate of south Gujarat, to speak of an unbridgeable cleft between rich and poor is nearly viewed as sinful. In the strongly harmonious Gandhian view of the social order, the landlords are placed as guardians of rural welfare, ideal patrons, who are expected to take good care of their subordinates. There are, of course, stark contrasts dividing rich and poor, but these should be neutralized by persuasion and reconciliation. Capital and labour should co-operate. In spite of disappointing past experience, the HSS persists in this approach. But in the prevailing socio-economically sharply polarized system, such an ideology plays the game of the landlords. Attempts to persuade them to treat their labourers better are to no avail. Yet the labourers are invariably urged to be patient and moderate in their demands. The HSS, in short, is a movement of accommodation rather than emancipation.

Ever since its foundation, the HSS has been a stronghold of the Congress Party. As early as 1963 I attended a meeting at which Morarji Desai, a man from the region, announced that times were changing for the Halpatis. Now that, after the disappearance of the hali system, the labourers' votes can no longer be controlled through their employers, the existence of the HSS makes it possible for a party that serves the interests of the landlords to acquire the support of the labourers. The 1969 split in the Congress Party seemed to initiate a more radical course. The majority of the HSS top brass and most of the voluntary social workers fairly soon declared themselves for Indira Gandhi's party, while the regional government was still solidly in the hands of Morarji Desai's supporters. Promptly the subsidies to the HSS were stopped. But the time of adversity did not last long, for in 1972 the Congress (Renewed) came to power in the region, and the interests of the HSS and the ruling party ran parallel again. The split has further strengthened the tendency towards polarization. The HSS leaders became very prominent in the Congress (R) of South Gujarat. Fearing that the Halpatis would take the *garibi hatao* slogan seriously and follow Indira Gandhi's supporters in a body, members of the Congress (Old) founded a new organization, the Halpati Vikas Sangh. They put forward a number of discontented Halis as figureheads. One of them, whom they suspected of having political aspirations of his own, was sent home before the election; the others were dimissed afterwards. In none of the talukas of Bulsar and Surat districts were locally influential Halpatis put forward as candidates. They were only required for canvassing among their fellow caste members.

The HSS is an organization for the Halpatis, but not of them. The leadership is solidly in the hands of members of high castes. Among a delegation visiting Indira Gandhi early in 1972 to request her to allocate more money for the work among the Halpatis, only six of the thirty members belonged to this tribal caste themselves. The hierarchical order is also evident at the meetings that are held in the districts. The senior social workers sit in the front rows with the local notables. They address the agricultural labourers, who are standing at some distance. The social workers from the higher castes attach great importance to excessive drinking, lack of self-discipline, etc., as explanations for the Halpatis' poverty. In fact they agree with the translation of the Halpatis' former name of Dublas as weaklings. As one of them remarked, 'You can always see which of them are bastards of the landlords: they have more courage and intelligence.' The Gandhian veteran Jugatram Dave has entrusted the daily management of the HSS to Arvind Desai. The transition from semi-religious to political leadership could not be better illustrated. The aged spiritual leader is held in great veneration. Those who meet him derive moral inspiration from the contact. He is far above the parties. The contrary is true of Arvind Desai, a 'boss' if ever there was one, who leads the organization with a strong hand. His word is law, and he leaves no doubt about it. His attitude is recognizably that of a member of the dominant Anavil caste. Not afraid to evoke the wrath of the landlords, he is paternalistic in his behaviour towards the labourers. He acts like a *rajah* in his domain. When, for instance, the rendering of the song of welcome by the pupils in honour of our visit to a Halpati school was not wholly perfect, he gave vent to his displeasure in no uncertain terms.

The HSS cadre – the local staff members and school teachers – consists for the most part of Halpatis. They are generally young people who have been educated at secondary schools, some of them even at the Gandhian Vidyapith College in Ahmedabad. The organization is strongly centralistic, keyed to one-head leadership. The staff members at the local level are not authorized to take decisions on their own; they have to refer for the smallest details to the directives issued by the Bardoli head office, where policies are determined. Those who act on their own authority run the risk of being instantly dismissed. The lack of security – in the lower echelons, the staff members do not hold permanent appointments – virtually enforces submissiveness and unconditional obedience. One of these workers described the HSS succinctly as *halipratha* with Arvind Desai in the role of *dhaniamo*. They have to take second place, and regard this as a conspiracy of the high castes, of which they are able to quote many examples. They are not always right, but figments of the imagination may be quite as illustrative of the prevailing social relationship as facts. These staff members dream of taking over the leadership of the organization, or discuss plans to form groups in secret, in order to offer resistance to the established interests inside and outside the HSS. There were vague references to the Naxalist movement and – very topical at the time of my fieldwork – the Mukti Bahini fighting groups in Bangladesh. But most of the staff members in the lower echelons have resigned themselves to powerlessness and dependence, are under no illusion as to the power of their number and also show little compassion for the miserable lives led by their fellow caste members. They cling to their jobs in the certainty that they cannot find any other employment.

Interaction with Halpatis

The local workers represent the HSS in the villages. The contacts with the agricultural labourers are indirect, that is to say, through those who have come to the fore as leaders in one or more neighbourhoods (*falias*). They are visited in the villages or asked to come to the small office of the local branch in the taluka for consultation. As I said above, this informal leadership can only be fulfilled by Halpatis who are not directly dependent on the landlords. Another condition is that they must have enough time to maintain their contacts. A Halpati is not recognized as a leader either inside or outside his village until he proves that he is functional on both levels. Since communication is nearly completely verbal, he has to move around most of the time, keeping up with the news, maintaining and extending his channels of information. Some basic ability to read is a real asset, and he must at least be able to put his signature. Finally, all my informants asserted that a certain amount of 'culture' was required: a leader must know how to behave in his contacts with outsiders. The leadership in question is of a different kind from that exerted by the *panch patel* (member of the communal council) and the *bhagat* (tribal priest-cum-medicine man). Their roles have traditionally been attuned to the needs of the Halpatis themselves, whereas the mediation of the leaders in the village quarters is primarily a question of liaising with outside parties. They themselves have none of the scarce resources at their disposal, but they know how to get access to them. Their intervention is badly needed, especially since the landlords have come to refuse to promote the interests of their subordinates. Through these intermediaries the isolation of the landless labourers is somewhat mitigated.

The leading position of the local influentials finds recognition by and through the HSS. They are invited to meetings at which social workers of a higher level lecture on the abuses of alcohol or propagate education. All those present are asked to introduce themselves and tell something about their own background. In this way they get acquainted with each other, and a loosely structured network of supra-local relationships grows. The HSS staff keeps them posted on the various activities; the distribution of possible benefits – allocation of land for huts, issue of scholarships, the striking of wells – takes place through their mediation. These local leaders form the backbone of the HSS. In the latest election campaign they functioned as the real mobilizers of the Halpatis. But as it turned out, their political preference was inspired by very pragmatic considerations: they selected the candidate who stood the best chance of winning. There was no question of any ideologically motivated choice. Most of them were inclined to regard the differences within and between the parties as conflicts between persons and factions of the elite. Being aware of the fluctuating course of coalitions, these Halpatis tried to behave politically as neutrally as they could.

Are they recognized by the Halpatis as their spokesmen? They are, as I said above, the only channel through which the labourers can obtain benefits. But very clearly they have their own interests, and these do not always run parallel to those of the labourers. They are often blamed for being agents of those in authority. It would, therefore, be incorrect to believe that the Halpati who have placed themselves at the forefront enjoy the confidence of their fellow caste members. This is even more the case for the workers of the HSS, who are in fact identified with the government officials and scornfully called *chamchas* (lackeys) of the high castes. The local staff members also behave like minor officials. Dressed in terylene trousers, shoes, socks and shirts, and armed with plastic brief-cases and with fountain-pens in their breast-pockets, they address the Halpatis on their rounds through the villages – reprimandingly, because they do not send their children to school, or encouragingly when it is a question of a *bhajan mandli* to be formed, but always as their betters. Their audience is silent, smiles diffidently, or shows signs of muted consent. Behind their backs the Halpatis – those at least that know about the existence of the HSS – complain of the carelessness, arrogance, and also the corruption of the cadre. The Halpatis are as wary of them as they are themselves of voluntary social workers and politicians from the higher castes.

The Halpatis have not much cause to regard the HSS as an organization that fights for their interests. For them it is an obscure body, affiliated with the government and representing external interests. It is therefore doubtful whether the HSS may be called an emancipation movement at all. Its aims and methods rather seem to prevent mobilization to assertiveness. With the above, the HSS would seem to stand condemned, but any such judgement should be modified by an appraisal of possible alternatives. First of all, the situation of pauperism as such prevents the agricultural labourers from reaching solidarity on a class basis. In a situation of such extreme scarcity, how could we expect them to mobilize on their own? To be sure, dissatisfaction among them is clearly growing. But it still expresses itself in disconnected incidents, particularly in strikes that flare up suddenly but remain limited to one village and soon fall flat when the landlords engage labourers from elsewhere. There is further, little likelihood that the bargaining power of agricultural labourers will be strengthened by their joining forces, on their own initiative, with castes of small landowners. Their economic interests differ too much for that, and their social distance is too great.

What possibilities of organized social action other than by the HSS are there? The political Left has barely found a foothold in south Gujarat. The Praja Socialist Party is as good as liquidated. The cadre of this party had collectively gone over to the Congress Party in the early 1960s, in exchange for the promise that the large grassland area in the south of Bulsar District, which was in the hands of big landowners, would be distributed among the petty cultivators of tribal castes mobilized for the Pardi Grassland Movement. The Communist movement, which had always been weak in the region, lost even more power after the split in Congress. Its most prominent leaders joined the party of Indira Gandhi, taking part of the rank and file with them, and they adjusted themselves without difficulty. Only in the cities of Surat and Bilimora there are small nuclei of the Communist Party of India (CPI) left. The section in Bulsar district has less than a hundred members. They are practically all urban factory workers, an exceedingly privileged category in comparison with the landless paupers. In the rural regions the CPI is not very active. Bulsar and Surat districts have never known a strong kisan movement.[3] A handful of members in a few villages of Chikhli taluka – the red flags fluttering from long poles over their huts does not make them difficult to trace – led the illegal occupation of some fields belonging to big landowners at the time of the Land Grab Movement which took place all over the country in the autumn of 1970. Hundreds of Halpatis joined in the short-lived, badly prepared action. The HSS staff received orders from the head-office not to support them, nor were they allowed to aid the victims of the feared police raids. Rumour has it that the recent murder of a CPI cadre member in this region was staged as a drunken brawl. The CPI leader of the Bulsar District stated that the factory workers are much less militant than the landless Halpatis for fear of losing their jobs. In explanation of the lack of political awareness among the peasant population in the area he exclaimed, echoing the words of a national party leader, that Gujarat was the Taiwan of India!

Nor will Halpatis join the tribal movement, which reached a peak towards the end of the 1960s. The chances of following one of the religious sects based on simple Hindu doctrines, however, are much greater. Literate Halpatis feel strongly attracted to the popular devotional tracts that are distributed on a large scale. The rise of sectarian movements – for which the *bhajan mandlis*, too, prepare the way – is to be explained as a protest to counter social discrimination against the Halpatis, but also as an escape from the misery of daily life. It does not look as if the situation of the landless proletariat will soon improve. What are the perspectives for betterment envisaged by the Halpatis themselves? They are not expressed collectively. In any case they should not be measured by those of the HSS. It is believed that pauperized categories tend to hark back nostalgically to the past, and to some extent they do. They claim that they are entitled to the security that was inherent in the

---

[3] This was before I came to know about the Kisan Sabha struggle that had its heyday in the late 1930s and on which I have elaborated in Chapter 4.

hali system. Does this mean that they long for the old order to be restored? Not at all. They value the security of having enough work at a wage that enables them to keep alive, but are certainly adverse to a return to the dependence and bondage that formed the basis of the relationships of former times. Landlords show boundless irritation over the fact that agricultural labourers no longer know their place – that is, no longer wish to behave obsequiously. It would seem that the hopeless situation in which the Halpatis now find themselves enhances their militancy. But mobilizing agricultural labourers requires more than that. An increased capability to organize themselves is crucial, and this is done, albeit with other ends in view, by the HSS. The establishment of agricultural labourers' co-operatives, and the leadership training courses for Halpatis who, owing to the efforts of the HSS, have been elected village headmen, widens the organizational expertise of a growing number of Halpatis. It is an experience that may in the future be used in a way that leads to real progress.

From this point of view, the growing impatience of a number of social workers inside and outside the HSS is equally promising. Disappointed in the landlords' unwillingness to offer the Halpatis a decent existence, they are inclined, in imitation of some movements based on Gandhian ideology elsewhere in India, to set a different and more radical course. It is the course of so-called non-violent direct action in which, if necessary, a confrontation with the landlords is not avoided. The supporters of this view may succeed in adapting, in this way, the Gandhian strategy to the actual situation, that of a polarized rural system. An important fact in this connection is the organized radicalization of the rural elite. Their representation in the political arena was until now mainly based on caste, but their dominant position is gradually changing in quality. They are increasingly manifesting themselves as a class, and the emergence of economic-interest organizations – such as the rapidly growing Khedut Samaj (farmers' union) in Surat district – confirms this tendency. The landlords are strongly opposed to any movement, however moderate, that aims at improving the condition of the agricultural labourers. The aggression of the large farmers is heightened by the organized pressure they exercise nowadays, and this in turn leads to a further escalation of conflicts. The situation is ripe for an explosion; in fact, it has been ripe for a long time. Yet none has taken place until now. This is not because things can be worse still: there are limits to the absorption capacity of a demoralized proletariat. Organization of the latent unrest is the lacking factor. It will probably be after the event that we will know at what moment the optimal combination of factors came into being. But it would be frivolous to assume that, on account of their pauperism combined with Gandhian conditioning, the Halpatis cannot be mobilized in a more antagonistic way. How this will come to pass and what will be the outcome is difficult to predict. In view of the present situation in India, however, there is little reason to be optimistic about an early emancipation of the agricultural labourers.

Part III

The Political Economy of Boundless Dispossession

6   The Agrarian Question Posed as the Social Question

In my account of the system of labour bondage as it operated in south Gujarat in the past and present, I reported in the early 1970s that *halipratha*, which had already shown signs of disintegration in the preceding decades, was now on the verge of collapse. My sustained interest in the changing configuration of the political economy and how it played out at the local level focused on queries that immediately came up in the light of this conclusion. In the first place, how to explain the erosion of the master-servant relationship in agriculture? The second question focused on the pattern of employment that replaced labour attachment in the prime sector of the economy, and the third one meant to deal with the changed fabric of interaction between the main landowners and the landless workforce. I set out to answer these questions through new spells of fieldwork in the same region, the central plain of south Gujarat. These rural investigations were carried out between the early 1970s and the early 1990s in two villages that had been my previous fieldwork sites in what was now demarcated as Valsad district and, in order to widen the scope of my enquiries, in one more village near Bardoli situated in the restructured territory of Surat district. This chapter discusses my findings over the reported periods.[1]

The Demise of *Halipratha*

Since I have elaborated on the first question in earlier parts of this book, I shall only reflect on it in summary here. I attribute the fading of labour bondage as it used to be practised to the penetration of capitalism in the agrarian-rural economy during the late-colonial era. From the second half of the nineteenth century onwards, cultivated crops were increasingly produced for distant... destinations. Commercialization went together with monetization of exchange transactions. The sale of food as well as

---

[1] The research was consolidated in two major books: Breman (1985) and Breman (1993).

non-food crops for cash instead of mostly localized barter for other com-modities or services ultimately also led to wages being settled in cash rather than in kind, although this change occurred at a much slower pace. The custom of handing out a food ration to agricultural labourers at the end of the workday and providing other emoluments in kind took much longer to phase out and endured until the beginning of my fieldwork in south Gujarat in the early 1960s. A steady expansion in the amount of land under cultivation and an increase in crop density resulted in growing agricultural production. Trade grew in size, scale and value, spurred on by better connectivity between the countryside and urban locations. The construction of all-weather roads and a railway network facilitated transport and access to distant markets. This ongoing process led to a switch from inward-looking, parochial and predominantly localized inter-actions to a growing involvement in outwardly bound business. This new commercial activity was less open to control by local stakeholders.

The dominant class-caste of landowners initiated the change to a form of farming that in the course of time became capitalist in nature and from which they stood to benefit first and foremost. The restructuring was the outcome of a gradual shift from a more diversified and mainly food-based pattern of production low on capital outlay and productivity to a crop schedule of more valuable production meant for market sale and driven by the prospect of gaining a higher money income. Cotton had already become a major cash crop that occupied a large part of the cultivated acreage in the northern part of south Gujarat during the late nineteenth century. In the villages of my fieldwork fruit orchards and somewhat later on sugar-cane were the major money-spinners in the second half of the twentieth century. The new agrarian cycle had an uneven spread over the year, more sharply defined by peaks and slacks, and resulted in a pattern of employment different from the one it replaced. It is debatable whether the seasonal rhythm of ups and downs diminished the demand for farm servants. The profits realized from the cultivation of cotton had created a middle class of farmers much better off than before. Improvement in their material conditions enabled them to withdraw from working in the fields alongside their labourers and to engage domestic help – the *hali* and his wife – to do household or other chores (such as tending the cattle) that were considered demeaning. But the growing wealth of the agrarian class of substantial landowners was no longer spent on the maintenance of a retinue, as it had been in the past mode of production.

For the rural elite conspicuous consumption and leisure remained important goals but were not now expressed through clientelism. Culti-vation for cash gave rise to an altogether different lifestyle, one in which the income earned was spent on conspicuous leisure and consumption

reflecting the material comfort and social standing attained by the pro-
ducer's household. A new set of values and preferences had emerged that
demonstrated the growing separation between top and bottom of the
rural class hierarchy. The ranking was based, as previously, on the use of
property and the exercise of power but now rearranged to promote the
maximization of profit and accumulation of capital in a market-directed
economy. The steady rise in income allowed for a consumption pattern
that expressed the affluence of the spenders. The household was run on a
more lavish footing, demonstrated in food of better quality to which
items bought in shops were added. The substantial landowner no longer
sat down in the field with workers to share food brought from his kitchen
and his wife gave up binding up the sari between their legs and now wore
a blouse piece. *Bidis* were replaced by cigarettes. Cheap wear was discarded and a taste developed for more stylish attire and expensive ornaments worn by women on festive occasions. Accommodation was
upgraded – which meant brick-built housing, tiled floors and plastered
walls, the installation of a bathroom-cum-toilet inside or outside, the
addition of another floor of rooms in which to spend the night and, to
begin with, the removal of cattle to a nearby shed. Over time the house
turned into a spacious, well-furnished, decorated building equipped with
modern gadgets for cooking, cleaning, washing, etc. Electricity, tap-
water and motorized transport contributed to a life of leisure. But these
amenities, of course, were only at the disposal of the top segment. The
desire to elevate one's social standing in a capitalist society led to lavish
marriage celebrations that functioned as a display of wealth. For the same
reason, people began to attach a new priority to articulating the religious
identity of household members, leading them to spend money and time
on rituals at home, temple worship, participation in festivals and pilgrim-
age to gain the level of honour and respectability that their affluence
merited.

Education at primary and secondary level and later on also going to
college in the nearby town was looked upon as the pathway to the future,
a must for life outside agriculture. Whereas in 1921 785 out of 1,000
males from the dominant class-caste in the region were still classified as
landlords, this ratio dropped significantly in the next few decades. Commenting on this trend among the members of his own community, I. P.
Desai wrote in a portrait of the village in which he was born and bred.

In their evaluation of occupation, "service" comes first and probably agriculture
has no place. Now it is fixed from the day the boy goes to school that he has to be
a salaried employee and they think of what he has to be and think of what they call
the "line" for the boy. Education is becoming a normal necessity and so much so
that they are sending their girls also to the secondary school. Some girls every day

walk four miles to the school and back to the village. Even for a girl matriculation is becoming the minimum requirement. (Desai 1964: 81)

Farming was no longer the main occupation within the dominant class-caste. Life in the village was cheaper than settling down in a town or city. But even without surrendering their residence in the countryside, many lost interest in the business of farming. They might have decided to stay on in their place of birth, but indifference to the work and life of a farmer made a sizeable section live effectively as absentee landowners. Working in the field was beneath their dignity but farm management did not appeal to them any more, either. They diversified their capital away from agriculture but wanted to keep the inherited family property in the village.

The main landowners consolidated their hegemonic control at the local level and further reinforced their hold in a regional setting. They extended their reach beyond the village by establishing agricultural co-operatives, on the board of which they had a commanding say. Their overrepresentation was equally strong in the management of schools, hospitals and other institutions – often set up by them and operating within a wider spatial grid. With the devolution of governance to the district, these vested interests had a strong footprint at this level of public administration. Funds and facilities provided by the government were channelled through the district and sub-district council. Access to benefits distributed in the corridors of power was restricted to local people of influence who could show proof of their credibility and success. The dominant caste's heavy weight was also apparent in politics. The drift from the Congress Party was in a more conservative direction, first leaning towards Jan Sangh followed by a lukewarm affinity with Janata and in recent decades giving vent to strong sympathy for the BJP and its Hindutva programme. Finally, a class-based organization catered to the interests of capitalist farming. The *Khedut Samaj* (farmers' union) became a powerful lobbying group and campaigned to keep the cost of inputs low, to increase the price of crops and to reject the claims of the landless class for a better deal, to begin with, a higher wage. An agrarian elite with ample economic, social and political clout was able to take orchestrated action to secure its privileged position.

The landowners separated themselves physically and socially from their workforce. They adopted a lifestyle that set them at a distance from the landless households. Employment in agriculture became thoroughly commodified. Farmers no longer felt bound to provide a livelihood for their workforce, to protect and keep secure the people they hired to cultivate their fields and perform chores in and around the house. They continued to engage farm servants because they required one or more hands on a permanent basis to do manual work. Having them around full-time was driven by economic utility, the assumption that the cost of the servant was in the end less than the value of the labour power extracted from him. The agricultural labourers' right to employment was no longer recognized, their social security no longer guaranteed. The transition to capitalism required that profit be viewed in cash terms as gains derived from a monetized economy. In the relentless drive for higher income, the effort to reduce cost played an important role. This was why landowners became increasingly wary of attaching labour to their farming business by the provision of 'loans' in advance. The risk of not getting the expected return on the amount invested increased with labour having become more mobile than ever before. No legal sanctions enforced the repayment of advance wages through labour power at the proper time and in the agreed quantity. Accordingly, landowners tried to minimize the handing out of loans to secure labour for their future needs.

Wages had never been granted out of charitable generosity, let alone because of compassion for the plight of the underdog. A minimum level of sustenance had to be provided to ensure a workforce numerous and strong enough to meet the demand for labour at the high point of the agrarian cycle. Farmers preferred employing local labourers because it made sense to have them close at hand and readily available. But there was no longer a need to cover against a possible shortage in the peak season: with the construction of paved roads, the motorization of transport and the introduction of modern systems of communication, the countryside was better connected to the wider economy. It was less time-consuming and costly to cover distance, meaning workers could search for employment beyond their immediate locality. But mobility also had the opposite effect, in facilitating an influx of labourers from outside the local area. It is a subject on which I shall elaborate later on. The enlargement in the scale of the rural labour market had major repercussions for changing the pattern of agricultural employment in south Gujarat. In the context of this chapter it is important to emphasize that labour beyond the village was or could be made easily available at short notice. This increased the reluctance of the main landowners to offer better terms and conditions of engagement to the local landless. In their experience labourers coming from elsewhere were cheaper and much less demanding to handle than workers from their own village. These outsiders came when called for and went away again when dismissed.

Deepened Exploitation due to Loss of Patronage

A clear indication of the end of the relationship binding landless to landowners from generation to generation was the removal of more than half of all Halpati households to the outskirts of the village. Their departure had already taken place in Chikhligam a few years before my arrival in the early 1960s and occurred in Gandevigam in the aftermath of a major flood in 1968. In Bardoligam, which I selected as my third site of fieldwork, the relocation of an equal proportion of the landless out of the village centre happened around the same time. Their removal from the village centre was partly at the behest of the dominant caste, who were eager to clear their property of subordinate households. But the latter did not resist the move because they found that being resettled in their own colonies beyond the reach of the landlords they were able to make their own choice what to do and for whom to work. As mentioned above, the substantial farmers still engaged a small core of *kayem majoor* or regular farmhands who were invariably recruited from landless households that stayed behind in *gamtal*. But it would be a misconception to portray them as *halis*, Uma Kothari rightly noted in the account of her investigations in south Gujarat:

Men who work as *kayem majoor* for a landholding household tend to be those whose parents worked for the same household. Although they are not bonded and are no longer part of a relationship with farmers based on coercion, subjugation and dominance, which was characteristic of the *halipratha* system, they have some "obligations" through household ties to work for the same household. (Kothari 1990: 162–3)

Curtailed freedom of manoeuvre and infringements on unlimited latitude in deciding how to spend a workday did not necessarily apply only or primarily to the man or woman with whom the farmer entered into an agreement. The arrangement could involve more than one member of the landless household and might lack personal specificity:

M is one of the few Halpatis in Gandevigam who has been granted a rice field on a sharecropping basis. The owner has also given M permission to cut grass for his two cows. The milk that they yield is sent to the dairy co-operative and, together with the rice harvest, provides a yearly income, which is substantially higher than that of an average agricultural labourer. Cultivating the land and looking after the cattle takes up the greater part of M's time, and the farmer seldom calls upon him for work. Only when questioned further does it emerge that two of M's sons are employed as farm servants in the benefactor's household. (Breman 1993: 312)

One can speak of accumulated dependency when the farmhand's wife was also required to work in the farmer's house on a continual or rotating

basis. Although my data shows that this linkage was no longer as auto-
matic as in the past, the combination of farmhand and maid servant had
nevertheless remained fairly common. The term *gharni Dubli*, formerly in
usage, meant literally a Halpati female who belonged to the employer's
household. It was an arrogation that arose from payment of the money
needed by her husband and/or his father at the time of marriage. In my
fieldwork villages the provision of money for a wedding became more
exceptional, but a Halpati in regular employment might require his wife
and daughter to work as a domestic help in the household of his boss and,
at times, to work on the land as well. In fact, calling on the labour power
of other members of the landless household remained common practice.
It was one of the considerations for landowners in deciding whether to
take one or more Halpatis into regular employment. A submissive attitude was another requirement. Farmers rejected Halpatis known to be
'troublesome' or 'obstinate'. Such features indicated that some of the
mechanisms that were inherent to the operation of the *hali* system
lingered on.

By and large dominant landowners stopped providing loans as a means
of securing the Halpatis' labour. This was mainly because farmhands did
not hesitate in walking out when a request for an advance was curtly
refused or if they could strike a better deal somewhere else. In both
instances they left without bothering to work off the accumulated debt.
Farmhands were paid at a lower rate because they enjoyed more days of
employment. Their regular wage was barely enough for daily sustenance
and to cover the deficit they were forced to bargain for loans to meet the
cost of life-cycle events – marriage in particular, and house repair or
construction, as well as failing health in their household. Saving up for
these major expenses from their regular pay was out of the question. It
meant that the boss had to arrange for some means of adding to farmhands' income that did not entail higher cash expenditure on his part.
Loyal farmhands in Gandevigam were sometimes permitted to grow
plantains in a new orchard, a useful crop to give shade to the young
growth of mango saplings. Once the trees reached maturity the farmer
became less inclined to continue the practice. The custom of granting
cows on a sharecropping basis that I came across in both Gandevigam
and Chikhligam also fell into disuse once landowners began to find the
keeping of cattle too cumbersome. But Halpatis still tended a cow or a
buffalo bought with the aid of loans from the regional dairy co-operative.
Only by selling every litre was the landless owner of a healthy and
productive milch animal certain of a reasonable return. Even then, the
Halpati could not really manage without the farmer's consent – for
example, permission to cut grass on his land. Only regular workers were

allowed free access to their employer's fields or orchards. It is paradoxical that, while the Halpati felt more secure when he owned one or two head of cattle, he remained dependent on the farmer's leniency to care properly for these animals. There was no question of benefiting from the cow for the purpose of consumption; the use value had to be converted into cash with which to meet the cost of a wedding or any other major household event, so that the animal really functioned as a savings bank.

Time and again landowners would tell me that the reason they were willing to grant only very small advances was the lack of good faith on the part of the recipients. The latter always claimed inability to repay but, according to their creditors, never meant what they promised. But why, I asked a landowner in Gandevigam, didn't he pay a little bit more each day and so spare himself the recurrent appeal for more credit? He replied that although it meant a lot of trouble, in the end it was the cheapest way out. In his experience farmhands did not resent being paid a lower wage daily so much as being deprived of the small loans that they every now and then needed for sudden and unexpected expenses. The lesson that he had drawn from this experience was to pay the lowest wage of all landowners in Gandevigam but, on the other hand, to be a little bit more generous than his caste fellows with giving a petty 'advance' once in a while – and never to ask for repayment. Landowners's unwillingness to grant a request for advance payment, particularly when the amount was a modest one, aroused ill-will among the Halpatis that they were not at all reluctant to express. In contrast to older males who hoped to benefit from the security of working as *kayem majoor*, young Halpati men tended to detest employment as regular farmhands. The higher daily wage for casual labour was not the only reason for them to avoid engaging themselves permanently. A thorough dislike of being bossed around by the high-caste landowner was more important. As long as they were able to find enough work to make do, although their earnings were low and did not cover much more than their basic daily needs, their preference was for casual employment. The problem they faced was where to get the 'loans' that would enable them to spend on life-cycle events or meet the cost of illness and other recurrent crises in their household. They had to apply, then, for advances from one or more employers for whom they worked on and off. But a series of small loans inevitably added up to a sizeable amount that restricted their mobility in the labour market. They could not go for the best deal available since their creditors claimed the right of first call on them. In the end no alternative was left but to settle for more regular work with one of the landowners. It was an outcome that did nothing to solve their incapacity to make ends meet, of course.

The loss of benefits that the master was supposed to have bestowed on his *halis* went together with their deepened exploitation as a disposable commodity. Disease, injury, disability and other health handicaps impaired the ability of these households to earn their livelihood and demonstrated their increased vulnerability. Whatever value could be squeezed out of them at the lowest possible cost added to the profit of the employer and the resulting depreciation implied early debilitation and a shorter working life.

In the decades under discussion the demand for agricultural labour did not go up. The area under irrigation expanded and crop density intensified with the so-called 'green revolution', which was meant to boost agricultural production and productivity in the late 1960s, but this development did not result in much higher employment. Mechanized equipment – tractors for field operations and transport as well as the installation of electrical pumps – made draught cattle redundant and ended the need for farmhands to take care of these animals. The main landowners diversified their interest away from agriculture and their reduced zest for farm management was one more reason why the absorption of the landless in agriculture stagnated while the number of their households increased. There was simply not enough work in the prime sector of the economy to provide a livelihood for a growing workforce that had been deprived of the means of production for many generations. The Halpatis lost their former label of agricultural labour. They should be viewed as rural labour at large, still working in agriculture and whenever the occasion arose involved in other gainful activity.

Doing what? Within the village occupational diversity for the landless proletariat hardly existed. Depending on the season, they might do anything unskilled that came up: digging, fetching and hauling in construction; head-loaders in transport; peripatetic vendors and hawkers; collectors of rejected goods; scavengers along the highway – a succession of odd jobs for whoever wanted to engage them for a short period of time. A second-hand bicycle widened their operational reach. On this vehicle they roamed around the wider area, found their way to the nearby town, visited the weekly markets throughout the sub-district and returned home at day's end with the lean yield of their petty endeavours and forays.

The most dramatic change in the pattern of employment was undoubtedly the mobilization of labour for agricultural or non-agricultural work across considerable distances. The landless and land-poor from many villages in south Gujarat had already become accustomed two generations previously to migrate to the salt-pans and brickyards close to

Figure 6.1 Mechanized transport has enlarged the scale of the rural labour market

Bombay after the monsoon was over. The growing scarcity of work and income forced the exodus of a much larger army of seasonal migrants from the 1970s onward. The loss of livelihood for the local landless was, however, aggravated by the influx into south Gujarat of huge numbers of labour nomads from outside the central plain. I shall come back to this seasonal influx in more detail, but my immediate question was to find out why Halpatis did not try to escape and find work in the expanding urban economy? After all, in the last few decades urbanization had begun to accelerate, above all in booming Gujarat. Construction of paved roads and highways and motorized transport facilitated departure from the countryside. However, throughout my five decades of fieldwork in the countryside departure from their rural habitat for more than a fleeting halt in urban destinations has not become frequent occurrence in the quarters of the landless. A handful of men and women have been able to benefit from the reservation policy and to find a job in the public sector. After completion of secondary school education, they have shifted to urban locations: these fortunate ones do not return to the village often. The overwhelming majority of Halpatis have remained unskilled and their eventual presence in towns or cities is restricted to single males who arrive early in the morning on foot or bicycle in search of casual work and at the end of the work stint leave again. Only rarely have these daily commuters managed to establish a foothold in town or city. When they do find employment, the wages are higher than in the countryside, but the cost of commuting reduces the difference significantly. For this floating workforce to take up urban residence with their household is out of the question because of the high cost of urban housing and livelihood and the outright refusal of employers to pay a family wage that includes the maintenance cost of dependents. While members of this tribal caste may add up to one-third or even more of the village population in many sub-districts of the central plain, they are low in number in the main towns and cities of the region. It comes as no surprise to the high-caste landowners that few Halpatis are able to find regular work outside agriculture, even though earnings are higher. Their former 'benefactors' attribute this to the fact that these landless tribals are physically as well as mentally not fit for any other work than what they have done from generation to generation: tilling the fields that don't belong to them. Hidden away at the village margins, not equipped with skills that would pay them a higher wage and also without a network of contacts to facilitate their access to employment in the urban economy, the rural underclass has little scope to move up and move out. The majority of migrants from this background who come to the city are and remain unable to settle down in regular work and life.

The slow erosion of labour bondage that had been prevalent until the late-colonial era meant that men and women of the landless caste-class gradually reached a stage where they were able to exercise their own choice in deciding to whom to sell their labour power. At the same time, however, they lost the basic subsistence security that earlier generations had enjoyed: a daily pittance even when there was no work to be done. In other words, lacking any means of their own, they forfeited the meagre support that was so essential if they were to survive the recurrent crises in their lives, and also the credit that enabled them to bridge the gap in their means of existence. That deficiency was due to a wage far below the amount needed to remain independent. The possibility and even necessity for landless people to 'live in freedom' in future brought an end to existing relations of patronage. Under the new laws of the capitalist mode of production, redemption from bondage reduced agrarian labour to the status of a commodity, for which the demand was and remained limited. The disappearance of the elements of patronage that had helped to conceal the earlier abundant supply of rural labour put an end to the state of unfreedom in which this class used to live, but not to the stark and precarious conditions that accompanied it.

Remnants of former servitude can be seen above all in the attitude of dominant landowners to their regular workers. As I have pointed out Halpatis who have stayed where they lived before are less militant than their caste mates who resettled in the newly built colonies on the village outskirts. My impression is that at the time the move took place, those landless who continued to live in their old habitat felt more empathy with the landowners with whom they kept their relations intact. On the other hand, the households who left seem to have become more detached from their former patrons, stressing the impersonal nature of the tie with farmers for whom they work on and off. In so far as the landless living in these new settlements continue to work in the fields, they do so because work outside agriculture and beyond the village does not yield so much more money that it is worth the trouble and expense of seeking it. They combine agricultural labour with other chores in the wider area. But however difficult it is to find employment, they try to avoid attachment as farm servants to a landowner. In their opinion, the security of more days of work cannot compensate for the restricted freedom of movement that is the lot of the successor to the *hali*. In this context it is relevant to compare the empirical study conducted by Max Weber. His treatise discussed the demise of agrarian labour bondage in the late nineteenth century in eastern Germany. In a similar way the Prussian *Junker* had replaced their bonded farm servants with swarms of seasonal migrants imported from Poland. Weber noted that the German landless were not passive victims of their declared redundancy in agriculture. They deserted their masters to become independent even when that escape from servitude for casual work did not bring immediate redemption from poverty. But, as he observed, man does not live by bread alone. It was in his words the psychological magic of freedom that was of crucial importance (Weber 1892: 797–8). A fundamental difference, however, continued to exist that brings out the worse plight the erstwhile *halis* and their successors faced in Gujarat from the second half of the twentieth century onwards. In Germany the process of industrialization enabled the dismissed agrarian workforce to leave the countryside and settle down with their families in the rapidly growing urban economy for regular and better paid jobs in industry. Contrary to the widely shared prognosis at the time of Independence such alternative forms of employment on a massive scale have failed to materialize in India.

Falling Apart

The main landowners and the landless workforce grew apart once the close personal relationship which *halipratha* implied ceased to exist. The divide is a break with their former work and life in nearby proximity to each other and can be demonstrated both in the pattern of agrarian employment and in the spatial separation of their habitat. Having gone back to the villages of my first fieldwork for a full-scale reexamination in the mid-1980s and in order to get a quantitative basis for my comparison over a twenty-five-year period, I conducted a survey in the quarters of the landless. Casualization stood out as a progressive trend in both villages. In Chikhligam, the proportion of Halpati males working on a daily basis for various landowners had risen from 45 to 60 per cent, and in Gandevigam from 20 to 58 per cent. The casual wage earners in the two villages combined doubled in number and while in 1962–3 farm servants numbered two-thirds of all agricultural labourers, their share had dropped to 40 per cent in 1986–7. The casual wage earners not only worked in the fields but were also engaged in other activities inside and outside the village. They had multiple unskilled or self-skilled occupations now. They might work for one employer for some unstipulated time, but neither side felt obliged to continue the relationship from one day to the next. The loosened employment tie was also apparent in the fast-spreading tendency to give out work on contract (*udhad*). Self-selected gangs made up of young Halpati males undertook to carry out a specific amount of work at a pre-arranged and piece-rated wage for harvesting paddy, cutting grass or picking fruits. The landowner agreed the collective arrangement with the gang leader who distributed the earnings among the members of his team. Such gangs, which usually excluded elderly and others lacking the stamina to work long hours, were not permanent but broke up again when the contracted job ended. Another way landowners found to keep their relations with the landless workforce as distant and businesslike as possible was to delegate the task of supervision to intermediaries. The big farmers appointed overseers or foremen, charged farm servants with the handling of casual labourers or dealt exclusively with gang leaders or labour contractors who brought in migrant workers.

Farmhands were split up into two categories. The *rojio* was employed by a farmer who had the first right of call on his labour power. This worker had to report each morning and might be given work or not, depending on the need of the moment. No wage was paid on workless days and though the employer had the right of first refusal, he was not at liberty to replace these regular hands with temporary substitutes. Conversely, the labourer was only allowed to seek other work on days when the boss had no need of him. The *rojios* did not qualify for the somewhat higher wage paid in the peak period of the crop cycle. On the other hand, they enjoyed a higher number of work days than daily wage earners. The second type of farm hand was the true successor to the former *hali*. He had a closer personal tie with the landowner, being charged with tasks other than field operations. His working day was longer, starting earlier in the morning and going on after the casual workers had gone home. Even on slack days he did all kinds of odd jobs in the farmer's house or courtyard, including some unpaid chores. He was responsible for irrigating the fields, as well as collecting, returning and maintaining farm equipment – and often transmitted the boss's orders to the casual workers. He did not receive a higher wage for his longer workday but was rewarded with some perquisites: a meal or at least a cup of tea, some fruits fallen from the trees during the picking season, standing permission to cut grass and collect firewood on the property of the boss. He also stood a higher chance of securing an additional loan when the employer might turn down a similar request made by a *rojio*. The farmhand's female equivalent was the domestic maid (*vasiduvali*), a Halpati girl or woman employed in the landowner's household. She invariably worked in the morning for between two and four hours, dependent on the chores she was expected to do, such as tidying the house and its premises, cleaning pots and pans, doing the laundry, fetching water, preparing food for cooking and in general being helpful to the mistress of the house. She could take away a midday meal from the leftovers in the landowner's house as part-settlement of her abysmally low monthly wage paid in cash.

An agricultural labourer in daily contact with a single employer could bring more pressure to bear when in need of money over and above his wage. This was why Halpatis opted for a labour agreement that restricted their freedom of bargaining and mobility. At the same time, these restrictions were precisely the reason why a majority among them preferred the more risky but less inhibited life of a casual wage earner. It was certainly the landowners' ploy to manoeuvre the landless into a situation of dependency. They still needed to grant cash credit every now and then, though in small amounts, in order to have sufficient leverage over the regular workers. Such tactics had only partial success since even Halpatis engaged as farm servants refused to behave as if they were debt-bonded. In effect, the petty loans the employers considered an advance on later wage settlement were seen by their subordinates as compensation for the shortfall in earnings they needed to survive. Employers looked upon the cash advance as a claim on future services, while workers considered this money to be their due for underpaid labour rendered in the past:

During my stay in Gandevigam, I experienced at close quarters the escalation of an argument when an Anavil refused to give a servant the sum of 50 rupees for which he had asked. The Halpati responded by not turning up for work next morning. I found him in his hut, still grumbling. The farmer also refused to give in and had to make temporary use of a casual worker . . . When I returned to the village during the 1991 rainy season I asked how the conflict had ended. According to the farmer, the Halpati's mother had asked him not to give her son any credit because he wasted these petty loans on buying alcohol. The man stayed away even when his employer ordered him back to work. After working as a casual labourer for some time, he entered the service of another landowner in the village. A short while ago these two also quarreled and now, after two years, the man is working for his former boss again. Peace has been restored between them, but from what the Halpati told me it seems that a new argument is not inconceivable. The money that he had asked for was needed to pay for medicine for his wife. To whom else could he have turned? Another time he will do just the same. (Breman 1993: 306)

In the wake of the Abolition of Bonded Labour Act, promulgated in 1976, the Government of Gujarat commissioned a series of local-level surveys to report on what all had of a sudden become a politically sensitive issue: the condition of agricultural labour. The reports on Surat District concluded that Halpatis led an extremely miserable existence but found no evidence of labour bondage (Lal 1977; Shah 1978). However, the team entrusted with these investigations in Valsad District decided that there was indeed evidence of bonded labour (Gupte & Charan 1978). Based on my own research in both regions of south Gujarat, I was certain that these contrasting opinions could not be explained by any drastic difference in employment modalities. In my view the divergent appraisals were caused by a different interpretation of labour bondage. The maximalists argued that the hegemonic power exercised by the dominant caste-class of landowners over their landless workforce was reason enough to speak of bondage. The arguments most frequently mentioned in the report on Valsad District were: permanent employment without a prior time limit; low remuneration in combination with indebtedness; occasionally, also, residence in a hut on the farmer's land; employment of various members of the landless family by one and the same landowners; and illiteracy. This profile indeed resembled the lives led by the farm servants. But my dissenting contention was that the features listed had more to do with exploitation and did not confirm that the erstwhile *halipratha* system still existed (see also Breman 1985: 306–13).

Although the dominant landowners insisted on their own respectability, dignity and elevated ranking in the status hierarchy, they were not prepared to accept any attendant responsibility for the well-being of the Halpatis dependent on them for livelihood. On the contrary, in order to maximize their profit in capitalist terms, they tried to lower the cost by specifying their obligations and reducing them as much as possible. In other words, these farmers no longer behaved as patrons, but insisted on the unswerving commitment and loyalty of the workers they employed. They became more demanding with the increase of their subordinates' dependency. All agricultural labourers among the landless were at their behest, but dependency was particularly inescapable for the farm servants among them. While the latter were supposed to make themselves max-imally available, they did not receive the security and protection that an earlier generation could hypothetically claim. In reaction to the sense of loss experienced, these farm servants tried to confine themselves as much as possible to a fixed workload and to keep their obligations specific instead of diffuse. Whenever possible, they sabotaged any claim the farmer made in excess of this quantity. It meant that both parties appeared to have unbound expectations and both equally tried to get away with lesser compliance. It comes as no surprise that in the end the landowners, by virtue of their dominance, succeeded better at this than the landless.

A Mutual Distancing

The heightened tension between landowners and landless was expressed on both sides in a language of antagonism. The farmers stigmatized the Halpatis as *kamchor*, thieves of labour time who came late in the morn-ing, already had left before the fall of evening – and also took time off in between to rest. It is the classic complaint about the landless, that they fail in their duty to work diligently: according to the landowners, com-mitment and dedication have given way to indifference and carelessness. As the rural economy acquired a more explicitly capitalist character, the demands on labour as a factor of production became more onerous. While the shirking and loitering behaviour of the landless was a source of boundless annoyance for the farmers, the grievances of the badly exploited and underpaid workers were equally expressed in abusive language. Crucially, in contrast to the past the rural proletariat had lost its fear of speaking up in protest against the demeaning treatment meted out to them. No one among them was willing to praise his employer as benefactor. The aversion and animosity felt on both sides showed in an eagerness to avoid each other's company as much as possible. What also played a role was the way agricultural work was denigrated as an occupa-tion. The landowners, who used to go the fields alongside his servants, now kept aloof from taking part in all work of cultivation. In freeing themselves from such undignified employment the farmers made the landless workforce more aware of their humble position. Attachment to a landowning household had always meant remaining stuck in a position of economic vulnerability but in addition it came to be regarded as dishonourable – if not shameful.

This stigma applied to both male and female servants. A Halpati girl would not want to marry an agricultural labourer and a *kayem majoor* even less so because apart from facing a life of poverty she ran the additional risk of the need to work as a domestic maid. To be attached to a landowner's household and be forced to do all kinds of menial chores was considered more than ever before degrading (Kothari 1990: 184). Kothari does not mention the molestation of landless women and girls by their employers. This must have happened far more frequently in the days when Halpatis lived dispersed from one another in huts built on the property of their masters, as was still the case in the following account by another researcher, Neera Desai:

Manjula Gulab, a young daughter of a Halpati, mentioned that she, her sister and sister-in-law were alone on occasions when her father and brother went out for work. Their hut is in the *wadi* [garden], which could be easily approached by Bhathela boys [sons of the landowners]. On those days, she says, "each night brings with it new fears and we have to plan to cope with them. We usually sleep bundled together right here on the porch, it is very warm inside the house and also difficult to run if you are trapped. Huddled together we feel quite confident that nobody would dare to take us on all at the same time." (Desai 1990: 81–2)

Reluctance to rely on the local landless to grow crops and do all the work necessary to extract profit from their farming business has prompted the landowners to bypass the detested Halpati workforce in their own midst. One way to do this is to sell the standing crop in advance to a trader who stations a few guards at the site and brings his own work gangs when the harvest is due. Landowners engaged in other business or occupations outside the village have in this way contracted out their fruit orchards and the handling of labour required for it. But the majority of substantial landowners for whom management of their farm is still the first priority are also no longer dependent on local labour in the exploitation of their agrarian property. They prefer to make use of swarms of migrants coming in and going off again in a rhythm attuned to the annual cycle of peaks and slacks. The circular migration consists of two different streams. The first is organized by prior recruitment of the required workforce, as in the case of sugar-cane cultivation, which has been the main cash crop all over the central plain for more than half a century. All field operations from planting to harvesting have been taken over by co-operative sugar mills. This outsourcing of farm management to agro-industry has turned a sizeable contingent of the dominant caste-class in the rural economy of south Gujarat into a new kind of absentee land-owners on their own property, imbued with proper capitalist spirit but in rentier fashion. The recruitment and deployment of the workforce is a large-scale operation that lasts throughout the dry spell for a period of six or seven months. The work contract is shaped in what I have called neo-bondage and the mobilization of labour in this state of immobility will be dealt with in Chapter 7.

Characteristic of the second stream of seasonal migration is a more spontaneous pattern of mobility, self-regulated and broken up in sorties that tend to be spasmodic and short-term in nature. These are land-poor peasants who have no means of existence after the rainy season in their home area, the eastern *talukas* bordering on Maharashtra. In the busy months of the year the agrarian workforce in the villages of my fieldwork would increase by one-fifth to one-quarter. They come in small batches of ten to fifteen men and women to harvest the standing crops in order, as they themselves say, to meet their need for cash. Food rations are brought along for the duration of their stay. They can be met along the roadside, walking in single file. The adults carry pots and food supplies on their heads, tools in their hands and sometimes a child on the arm. Their movements should not be seen as aimless drifting through the rural landscape. They go straight to the locations where they have been before and are directed to new employers through established contacts. Neither do they migrate for an indeterminate time but for no longer than a few weeks, until the grain supplies brought with them have run out. They then go back home by bus or train before making a new sortie with the same or another gang. Arrangements are sometimes made long in advance and sometimes cemented with a down payment that the gang leader comes to collect in advance. Coming and going is in an irregular flow that determines this kind of labour nomadism. The farmers in Gandevigam readily admitted that the migrants coming from the eastern hill tract were easy to handle. In other words, they were more pliable and satisfied with what they were given. They did not complain if they were occasionally or rather frequently required to do more than the standard work load, even without extra payment. At the same time their behaviour was unpredictable. Quite often they would leave without giving notice in advance and without apparent reason. 'You can't really depend on them,' was an opinion frequently voiced by farmers, meaning in effect that they had a much better hold over the local landless. Although they were always finding fault with the Halpatis, their employers also seemed to accept that in the end they could not manage without the help of the bottom segment in the village. The movement in both directions of people in search of work and income they cannot find at home was a major theme during my bouts of fieldwork in the 1980s, in Bardoligam in particular (Breman 1985: 225–59). For the moment I just want to point out that the much-enlarged scale of spatial mobility has had a depressive impact on wages and employment for the workforce hovering at or close to the bottom of the rural economy in my fieldwork localities.

Exploited and Excluded

The Halpatis are no longer subjected to the *halipratha* system in which the dominant caste-class held them captive until the middle of the last century. How does the current generation look back on that time? The answer is: with resentment at the bondage practised by their former masters. But they express the same feelings at the treatment meted out to them since then. They do not really feel they have been emancipated. Farmers are aware of these sentiments, as one of them told me. 'When you came here for the first time, his father [pointing to a worker] spoke about my *wadi* [garden], my paddy, my buffalo, as though they were his own. Nowadays his son thinks about me as a man who has grown rich by our sweat' (Breman 1993: 313). The worker referred to was a farm servant whose work and life in *gamtal* has remained under his boss's close scrutiny. But he is no longer admitted to the intimacy of his master's household, no longer comes to know about family matters and the exploits of children, is no longer a person with with whom news on coming events are shared. Similarly, the other way around, the master does not keep himself informed about the strokes of good luck or bad luck in his servant's household. The commodified *hali* is kept at arm's length and in turn tends to avoid coming near his master. The prevalent mood of animosity is even more pronounced in the colonies on the outskirts of the village, where the Halpatis who are casually employed have congregated. The influx of seasonal migrants means that their labour power remains underutilized by the main landowners in the village, which forces them to wander around in the area in search of work. It is a non-transparent and fluid labour market, with which the landless find it difficult to come to terms. How far should they travel on foot or bike, when, in which direction, for what and with whom? It explains why, when I ask them how they find work, many Halpatis reply: 'We remain sitting at home and wait until we are called.' The lack of sufficient and somewhat regular alternative employment means that they depend on labour contractors to take them away to remote destinations for many months of the year. The household becomes multi-locational, with the dependent members staying behind while those who qualify for waged work – adolescents and adult men in particular – moving off. Because of their long, recurrent periods of absence the ties of the house-hold in this local setting add up to a bricolage of many features and have contributed to a social fabric marked by hybridity and marginality all around.

The Halpatis share their membership of the same caste. This primordial loyalty is expressed in the fact that they live together in the same settlement and restrict their choice of marriage partner to those who belong to the same community. The landless have remained detached from the institutional framework on which mainstream society is built, but they also lead their lives rather independently of each other. The colonies that are their inferior habitat seem infested and squalid to an outsider, equipped with few amenities for the common good. The stark deprivation is a source of segregation rather than solidarity. At the end of the day, while the women prepare the evening meal, the men sit outside. But they often sit apart, in silence, not talking about anything at all. Drink makes them more sociable, but it does not really make them more relaxed and, with the consumption of low-quality alcohol in large quantities, their exuberance can easily erupt in irritation and quarrels – another reason to avoid one's neighbours rather than seek their company. In serious emergencies – such as when a financial contribution is needed if someone dies or is admitted to hospital – they cannot refuse to chip in a small amount since doing so might jeopardize one's own chances of support in similar circumstances. These incidental cases apart, reliance on mutuality is minimal. In a situation of substantial and chronic scarcity, households are less willing to share what little they have and tend to live separately from each other rather than as a community.

Defending their joint interest does not mean that the members of a household always pull together. Parents have little control over what their children do, men take little notice of what women want and vice versa. Wives have often no clue where their husbands go for work, what it is they are busy at and how much they earn. Conversely women decide themselves whether to work as domestic maids and how to spend the trivial cash paid monthly. Adolescent boys evade parental authority and thereby postpone joining the labour process. Daughters are kept on a tighter rein and marry younger than their brothers. Getting married often but not always means a breakaway from the parental home. Not catering to the interests of other household members can lead to serious conflicts and disintegration of the unit of cohabitation.

Broken families are not exceptional in the landless neighbourhoods: men who desert the household, women who return to their own village, children who run away at young age. The Halpatis strive for equality and dignity not only in their work but also how they live their lives. They no longer baptize their children after the days of the week or give them demeaning names such as *bhangiya, kachara*, etc., to protect them from

Figure 6.2 Escaped from parental control, vagrant children team up with each other

harm. I have seen their dress code change from generation to generation. At the time of my first fieldwork farm servants went barefoot or wore an old pair of shoes discarded by their master. Their women would wear their simple sari tied up between the legs and small children went naked or only clothed in underpants. Nowadays the young men wear a shirt and long trousers, while the girls are dressed in saris of synthetic silk, are adorned with bangles and other ornaments and on festive occasions some may even have facial make-up. Some of the boys have a baseball cap and sunglasses. Bidis have been replaced by cheap cigarette brands and the local shops that have sprung up sell soft drinks and snacks, shampoo and other toiletries.

Consumerism has made inroads into the milieu of the landless. Among the somewhat better-off, the interior of the house may have some wall decoration – the photo of a relative, the portrait of a Hindu god or goddess – and the sleeping mat has been replaced by a cot; there will be a few plastic chairs for guests and a cupboard to store garments. Durable goods such as a fan, a TV set and a mobile phone are often second-hand, bought on instalment, received as wedding presents or given away as junk by an employer. Poverty, of course, is an obstacle to the desire for a more dignified lifestyle and girls are for that reason keen not to select a partner who is an agricultural labourer – and a farm servant least of all. Halpatis are not accustomed to practise religion in their daily life. Most of them never go to a temple and have no space in their house for rituals. 'My god is here', a farm labourer told me, pointing to the bottle of drink in his hand, when I asked him if he was a follower of one of the sectarian movements. Addiction to drinking and gambling is common but much more for men than women. In the past the dominant class-caste farmers, who used to have extramarital affairs with the wives and daughters of their *halis,* boasted that their semen was crucial to upgrade the inferior genetic quality of the landless. Such licentiousness has become rare but not totally extinct and also does not necessarily take the form of vicious molestation. Abuse is no longer subjected to sanctions from the community. The caste *panch* that used to settle marital problems, solve disputes and punish antisocial behaviour has become defunct with the evaporation of communal control at the local level. Although wife-beating is quite common, the gender balance in the Halpati household is less unequal than in the castes, which have domesticated women in accordance with the Hindu rule of patriarchy. Dire poverty does not allow the landless to leave the labour power of females unused. They have to work in the fields and the contribution they make to the household income sets them free from the kind of gendered restraint to which their better-off sisters higher up in the ranking are subdued. There is still sexual contact over the caste line, but the difference now is that coercion is rarer than it used to be in the past. The difference is one of degree only, because it is extreme poverty that may women force to bargain with their body – more likely if they live alone or are widowed or divorced. Commodification has also led extramarital intercourse to become monetized.

The amount can vary from Rs. 30 to 100 and, if it becomes a frequent occurrence, she also expects presents and other favours. Her husband usually says nothing, even if he is aware of the affair. This may be because when you are living in chronic poverty, any additional income is welcome, or perhaps because extramarital affairs are also very common in the landless neighbourhoods. In such cases, the women do not demand payment for their favours. It is a choice they make, which reflects the freedom the women allow themselves. (Breman 2007a: 113)

Do the Halpatis have little choice other than to accept their subaltern status? Due to their social isolation, the landless require the mediation of one of the village bosses to get things done outside their caste and locality: to find a job or a house, apply for support or a BPL (below poverty line) card, admission to the corridors of authority and power, etc. The need for a link to where benefits and licenses are dispensed indicates acceptance of dependency. An attitude of antagonism is incompatible with the need to show oneself worthy of consideration by behaving 'well'. Mediation is a favour that is not bestowed generously and a request may or may not be granted, free of charge or at a price. Having no social capital of their own makes the landless suspicious of the goodwill of the facilitators to whom they have to turn for help. The acute distrust they conveyed during my first round of field-work is as relevant now as it was then:

Not only has the landlords' traditional help and protection disappeared, but they do their utmost to obstruct any direct contact of their former clients with external sources of power. By taking advantage of the ignorance and powerlessness of the Dublas, some Anavils use their influence and their familiarity with laws and regulations to prevent outside support for Dublas. The Dublas in both villages complain of the opposition they encounter in their attempts to qualify for the facilities which the government expressly make available to the tribal castes. Anavils and members of other high castes, they say bitterly, bar the way for us everywhere. (Breman 1974a: 256)

As already discussed, the members of the dominant caste-class complain endlessly about the disobedience and insolence of the Halpatis, who refuse to do work assigned to them, commit sabotage, or lie and deceive their employers. Why should they behave as benevolent patrons if they are blamed for exploiting them? The farmers express their grudge and annoy-ance by saying: *kamchor, dhanchor* – since they cheat us in work, it is only natural that we rob them of money. In this argument the inability of the rural underclass to live decently is seen as the consequence of manifold deficiencies. Sheer indolence keeps the landless in a state of deprivation and stops them from making any effort to improve their lives. In line with this mentality, the landowners professed that India cannot afford a polit-ical democracy based on universal suffrage. They never tired of telling me that this useless class of people are surplus to requirement, simply too defective to apply the principle of equality for the structure of society. It means that the exclusion of the Halpatis is not merely the outcome of the economic and social policies followed. Indicative of the mindset quite prevalent among the well-to-do is the claim that the people made surplus should be firmly kept beyond the pale of inclusion. Discarded and stigma-tized, they constitute and are dealt with as a new kind of Untouchables.

The behaviour of the landless is characteristic of a proletarian identity, but clearly not one in which social consciousness is fuelled by a sense of a common destiny or solidarity. In addition to the fact that they often have to change jobs, the rural proletarians are unable to take a common stand because they are often engaged in multiple jobs in quick succession, or even at the same time. Furthermore, Halpatis meet each other as members of the same caste but in the diverse terrain of casual work, they encounter many others who also promote their own primordial loyalties rather than class-based concerns. Self-interest is defined and articulated in a way that takes account of the similar predicament of other people but without resulting in collective action. The defiance should not be under-rated. The majority of Halpati women refuse to become maidservants in the households of large landowners, work that yields little more than a pittance and exposes them to constant humiliation if not sexual abuse. Not only are employers unwilling to provide bonuses in kind in addition to the monetary wage, but farmworkers and maidservants no longer welcome such extras. They decline 'generous' gifts, for example food scraps or waste such as used tea-leaves or worn clothes, that are meant to compensate for unpaid labour chores. But the impudence only incidentally solidifies into concerted clamor. Strikes do occur, as a matter of fact much more often than the public might suppose. These signals of discontent with the going wage, uproar about maltreatment, protest against inhumane work conditions, etc. do not catch the public eye. Such resistance, although widely prevalent, goes unnoticed because outbursts are not organized and planned in advance but spontaneous and sudden eruptions which, moreover, remain localized to a particular work site instead of spreading out and last only a few days due to lack of wherewithal. If someone hesitates whether to accept an offer of work, another person is always willing to take his or her place, as I was told time and again. The Halpatis are aware of their isolation and attribute it to a lack of leaders in their midst who dare to stand up against the village magnates.

In this milieu the confidence in politics is extremely low. The Congress Party has not fulfilled its promises, repeated again and again, to take resolute steps to tackle poverty. If most Halpati voters have remained loyal to Congress, it is not out of innate trust but because the dominant caste-class vehemently rejects Congress policies. The dispossessed poor have not followed intermediate castes such as Kolis, which have also defected to the BJP. At election time, politicians come to the Halpati neighbourhoods and canvass for votes by distributing money and promises. Local inhabitants are willing to mediate between the candidates or their touts and the names registered on the voting lists. They negotiate the price of a vote and are paid for it but they make similar arrangements with the representatives of other parties taking part in the campaign. The Halpatis do not consider themselves bound by these deals and do not vote as a block. 'Whosoever gives us money for drink on the evening before the election has the greatest chance of getting our votes,' one of them told me laughingly.

The successive governments of Gujarat – Congress in command from Independence until close to the end of the twentieth century, followed by the BJP for the subsequent two decades – have shown minimal commitment to the needs and problems of the rural landless. When dire poverty turns into pauperization, the introduction of basic social provisions for the down and out could offer some relief, but this intervention of state benevolence has by and large failed to materialize. Such sparse attempts as are made are met with lack of goodwill or even ill will from official quarters, right from the village level up to the higher corridors of the bureaucracy. The unproductive poor are encouraged to fend for themselves. For the old-aged, the chronically ill and disabled, this is clearly not an option and the assumption of family support was not borne out by my findings in the Halpati settlements. The large-scale national scheme of rural public works has a record in south Gujarat that is equally dismal (Kannan & Breman 2013: 321–8). It has reinforced the facile policy opinion that self-help best delivers social security and protection. The alleviation of poverty no longer seems to be a major political issue, not even in terms of lip service being paid to this objective. The lack of attention given to the deplorable situation in which the lower echelons of the workforce have to live follows from the dictates of neoliberalism. Labour in the informal economy is underpaid and casualized, hired and fired according to the need of the moment. After Independence a Committee on Fair Wages was set up and recommended that setting a minimum wage should comprise more than fixing it at a rate sufficient for reproduction; the stipulated amount should also take account of the human quality of labour. In essence it was a prescription, which Mahatma Gandhi had likewise proposed, to harness or at least moderate the capitalist drive towards commodification:

We believe that the minimum wages should be such as to ensure that the worker can not only maintain himself, but can secure enough to enable him to keep up his efficiency [note: female workers were, if not beyond the mandate, then certainly beyond the horizon of this panel of experts]. For this purpose minimum wage should satisfy to some extent the need for education, medical aid and other conveniences. (Government of India. Report of the Committee on Fair Wages 1948: para 10)

Not until 1972 did the Government of Gujarat finally enact a minimum wage for agricultural labour. However, it set it at a level that did not allow for much more than bare survival; and even that floor rate was never properly implemented. Large-scale evasion of the statutory ordinances in the decades that followed took place in an atmosphere of unbridled corruption in which the government labour inspectors collected money from farmers in exchange for not prosecuting them.

The engagement of civil society with the rural proletariat has continued to be localized, and the performance of the social movement that took the lead in emancipating the Halpatis was perhaps even counterproductive. This critical assessment does not become more positive if we look at the role played by trade unions. It is widely known that organized and sustainable collective action is uncommon in the opaque and fragmented landscape of the informal economy. Yet it is remarkable that the interests of the largest working class in India – the huge mass of agricultural-to-rural labour – have remained by and large unrepresented in the political and economic arena in the wake of Independence. The policy of informalization has effectively undermined the infrequent and weak attempts to mobilize the lower echelons of the workforce for collective action. What, then, are the prospects for a better future? The politics and policies of 'growth and development' pursued in Gujarat have been flagged as a model that should be followed by the nation at large. This announcement was part of the Hindutva agenda that Narendra Modi, chief minister from 2001, brought to Delhi on his inauguration as prime minister in 2014. The state is noted for its above-average rate of growth in past decades, which has resulted in a significant leap in wealth for the already better-off segments of the population. The wide divide that already existed between this privileged upper layer and the majority of people hovering on or below the poverty line has steadily increased. The suggestion that making the middle class better off and prioritizing their interests will eventually also benefit the multitude stuck at the foot of economy and society is, although repeated again and again, incorrect. The persistent poverty of those who lag behind is the outcome of the leap forward made by those higher up in the class structure. The existence of contingents such as the Halpatis is necessary to meet the need for cheap labour, overworked if hired and redundant to demand when laid off. Underpayment has ceased to be looked upon as a problem. It is an effective means for the generation of a higher surplus and an incentive for economic growth. That it takes the form of downright exploitation and discrimination is no reason to change direction. In the age of neoliberalism, social practice and its ideological underpinning are founded on the notion that an underclass incapable of contributing adequately to the production of wealth and to virtuous social order should be classified as paupers and dealt with as the undeserving poor. It is the upshot of the new paradigm of inequality that has become so visibly manifest in south Gujarat.

7   Labour Migration: Going Off and Coming Back

The Shape and Pace of Mobility

The exodus from agriculture and the countryside is a worldwide phenomenon. In South Asia capitalism made slow but steady inroads into the peasant economy from the late nineteenth century onwards, giving rise to a process of dispossession in which people with little or no means of production who are unable to find sufficient employment have come to constitute a huge reserve army of labour. For most rural households agriculture is no longer the mainstay of their work and income. Households stuck in poverty cannot afford to become and remain unemployed. Road construction and motorized transport have opened up the countryside and a reduction in the cost of travelling long distances has speeded up work-driven migration on a larger scale than ever before. But any attempt by these newly mobile masses to settle down where they have gone for work is frustrated by the informalization of both rural and urban employment. Those who belong to these floating armies remain outsiders at the sites to which they have been recruited on a temporary basis, where they are treated as transients by those who make occasional use of their labour power. Informality and circulation together allow us to define these people as perpetual footloose. It means that instead of finding proper jobs they are contracted on a hire-fire basis that does not allow them to establish a permanent foothold where they have arrived. Thus, migrant labour has remained thoroughly casualized and is subjected to continual circulation rather than to permanent resettlement elsewhere.

After a phase in which jobless numbers rose in the 1990s the National Sample Survey Office (NSSO) reported in 2004–5 that employment in rural India had started to pick up again. However, this upswing happened to coincide with a looming agrarian malaise that led to higher rural indebtedness. The higher number of people in gainful employment may well have been triggered by a cutback in household budgets, as Vinoj Abraham has argued:

Under conditions of distress, when income levels fall below sustenance, then the normally non-working population is forced to enter the labour market to supplement household income. The decline of the agricultural sector has also probably created forced sectoral and regional mobility of the working population, with the non-working population complementing them. (Abraham 2009: 97)

His conclusion was backed up by an editorial note on jobless growth in the *Economic and Political Weekly*, which commented on the outcome of the sixty-fourth NSSO round (2007–8), showing a paltry increase in waged work in the preceding years, but far too low to keep pace with population growth. While the generation of employment in this period slowed considerably in urban areas, it actually declined in rural areas. In both the rural and urban economy it was mainly women who were hit by job loss (Editorial note 2010: 7–8).

The rise in labourers' footloose mobility appears to have been driven by distress and the reason for this is amply substantiated by the findings of the official Socio-Economic Caste Census 2011, belatedly made available in mid-2015 on the website (https://secc.gov.in/welcome). Data on caste distribution were not made public, no doubt because of the political sensitivity of these statistics. But the information provided on poverty and destitution in the countryside should be equally disconcerting – more so because many of the households steeped in dire indigence have not been properly listed. It is now on public record that half of all rural households are landless, have to survive on casual labour that is locally often not available and therefore live in stark deprivation. Drawing attention to a systematic oversight of registration, one commentator on the census made the following caustic comment:

Either the definitions of deprivations are deliberately kept narrow so as to exclude a large number of people or enumerators have lived up to their past reputation of collusion with the rich. In the process a large number of poor would be denied access to targeted programmes. Government has not been able to eliminate poverty, but it has certainly succeeded in eliminating the poor from its radar. (Saxena 2015)

In my opinion, the main bias in the data made available is the lack of information on intra-rural as well rural–to-urban labour circulation and the impact of that mobility on the socio-economic status of the households investigated. The door-to-door census referred to above, which is supposed to have covered each and every locality in the country, tells a story of widespread and staggering rural misery. The widely discussed agrarian crisis tends to focus on the frequent cases of farmer suicide, in several states. Taking note of this is quite right, but such suicides are also a frequent occurrence – though much less noticed – among the landless.

In my fieldwork I have come across such cases of ultimate despair – in the absence of sufficient employment and income, people driven to self-willed demise by their inability to keep the household going and to meet the cost of life-cycle events. In the case of debilitating ill health and old age among a growing number of the dispossessed, death by starvation tends to be a common way out of life (Breman 2013b). The agrarian crisis is a structural one that derives from the growing reluctance or outright unwillingness of all classes of the peasantry, although for very diverse reasons, to remain engaged in the production of food and non-food crops.

Opinions differ as to the magnitude, scale and spread of circular migration; the underlying causes of people leaving home for rural or urban destinations; the migrants' socio-economic status; what they get out of their employment elsewhere; and the duration and impact the spatial and sectoral shift has on the economy and social fabric. The range is too broad to deal with this issue in much detail; my focus is on the flight of the land-poor and landless classes away from their habitat in the countryside and their attempts to gain access to a variety of rural and urban opportunities of waged work away from their habitat. In its 1991 report the National Commission on Rural Labour (NCRL) wrote that about 10 million rural workers left their place of origin in search of employment (Government of India, Ministry of Labour 1991 vol. II: K-17). The actual figure was already much higher than accounted for in official statistics or census reports. In the years that followed the number of labour migrants rose sharply and at the beginning of the twenty-first century the size of this floating workforce was supposed to be hovering around 30 million for the whole of India (Srivastava and Sasikumar 2003). Among these, short-duration migration – going off for up to six months for employment, but without including short-distance daily commuting – accounted for 15.6 million according to the NSSO 2007–8 survey. This figure suggested that seasonal migrants were only a minor segment among the workforce leaving for other destinations. It was again a huge underestimate of the vast and rapidly increasing scale of short-duration migration for work. Srivastava put the number in this category for the same year to be *at least* 40 million (Srivastava 2011a: 375). The report submitted by the National Commission for Enterprises in the Unorganised Sector (NCEUS) confirmed that the number of such migrants who stay away for up to one year is much higher than conceded in official sources (National Commission for Enterprises in the Unorganised Sector 2008: 96). My own 'guesstimate' was that 50 million were taking part in what I called circular migration by the end of the first decade of the new century. In support of this tally, which I consider to be conservative, I argued that official statistics did not cover the matter adequately due not only to a lack of investigative zeal and definitional rigour (for example, a clear line between where commuting stops and migration starts) but also because of a politically inspired unwillingness to find out what was going on in the lower echelons of economy and society (Breman 2010b: 7). It is therefore not surprising that other publications suggest an even higher volume of temporary migrants, an army of not less than 100 million at drift (Deshingkar & Farrington 2009: 16). The government now acknowledges that labour migration is much higher than earlier reported and in its latest count considers a multitude of 140 million, or more than one-quarter of the total workforce, to have become footloose (Government of India, Ministry of Finance 2018). But this estimate is mere speculation, a wild guess not substantiated by concrete evidence.

Labour migration has to a large extent remained the prerogative or predicament or men. They are increasingly prone to leave the village for shorter or longer bouts of absence in order to access waged work they cannot get at home. They are pushed out to bring back badly needed income for their household. However, going off also enables these members of and Scheduled Caste (SC) and Scheduled Tribe (ST) communities to break away from the caste-based domination that condemns them to subordinate behaviour at home. While the men escape local discrimination and derogation, the inferior status of their households at the bottom of the village hierarchy implies that the women who stay behind continue to be exposed to a combination of class and caste exploitation. They are made to comply with what the substantial farmers order them to do. This is what Ishita Mehrotra found when she conducted fieldwork in Uttar Pradesh:

. . . these Dalit women cannot decline work like tending to livestock or making cowdung cakes – dirty and lowly work that these women do in their households only. They have to seek permission of the creditor household before taking up wage labour for any other household, especially during the peak season time, and they cannot work for any household whose relations with their creditor household are strained. When they are hired as part of a labour party, for wage labour in the creditor household's fields, they have to accept lower wages paid much after the others have been paid. These labour relations are sustained by the relations of domination and subjugation that are in-built in capitalism and not by physical force. (Mehrotra 2017: 250)

The quotation illustrates the caste-class angle and also shows that the distinction between free and unfree cannot always be sharply drawn and needs to be viewed in context, that is, in terms of the type of work done and the compensation for it. The divide is gradual in terms of rigidity (running from extremely harsh to less oppressive forms of subjugation), length (shorter, longer or indefinite) and selectivity (social identity, also gender-

and age-wise). The literature on debt bondage both in the present and the past has strikingly understated the gendered features of this ordeal.

Men, much more than women, have been portrayed as victims of such forms of dispossession as well as of disempowerment. Yet while entrapment in bondage may be brutal for men, the severe hardship faced by similarly trapped women has not been highlighted in equal detail. Women not only lack control over their labour power but also over their body (Anandhi 2017; Still 2017). Working-class women live under threat of rape all the time and wherever they are, but are even more likely to become a rape victim when they are outside their own habitat. Like the men, they are subjected to exploitation of their labour power, but unlike men female migrants and children have to deal with the additional risk of sexual abuse when at work away from home. In the villages of my fieldwork women from land-poor households withdrew from the circular migration to the brick-kilns whenever that opportunity arose. The explanation usually given is that they need to look after their small plot of land, tend to their few head of cattle and send their children to school. Women from landless households are not able to opt out and had a good deal to complain about when I met them wherever they had gone to. Apart from the gruelling pace of work and the extra household chores they have to do, they are anxious about sexual molestation at the hands of employer, jobber, foremen and male workers. The combination of fatigue and stress make the annual trek to a distant and unfamiliar work site a hateful experience – but many cannot escape it. On the other hand, however, going off in search of work can also be seen as an attempt to escape social control and dependency, as well as abuse, in both age- and gender-specific behaviour (Shah 2006; Picherit 2018).

Figure 7.1 A short break after a long night's work and six more hours to go

The great majority of the men, women and children involved in labour circulation comes from households belonging to the lower castes-classes in the rural economy. Their growing livelihood deficit in the village makes them migration-prone, but being illiterate and lacking social capital they mainly qualify for labour that is unskilled or at best skilled-on-the-job when away from home. As I have already pointed out, the more vulnerable migrants' social and economic status is in their place of origin, the fewer and more precarious options they have wherever they go (Breman 1996). A recurrent finding is that migration tends to replicate and intensify the class differentiation as it exists in the countryside, leading to a further widening of inequalities between the various categories made mobile in the overall occupational hierarchy. In his appraisal of the outcome of labour migration, Srivastava contrasts two broad segments of migrant workers, the second subdivided into two categories. The first segment comprises permanent migrants, with physical and human capital, who are better placed in the job market; the second segment consists of the poor semi-permanent migrants, who have few assets and mainly work in the urban informal sector, and the short-duration seasonal and circulatory migrants, who are principally employed as casual workers (Srivastava 2011a: 378). His conclusion that nearly half of the total migrant workforce in India should be characterized as vulnerable concurs with my findings and is the point of departure in this chapter. Srivastava suggests there is an urgent need to improve the conditions of the vulnerable segment and this should be made a high policy priority. However, my contention is that government interference in the landscape of labour circulation tends to aggravate rather than improve the terms and conditions of this footloose workforce. More elaboration is required on the current shape of urbanization, the social identity of the migrants, the role of government in the shifting balance between town and countryside, the employment modalities in the various economic sectors and the absence rather than presence of the state in the regulation of labour practices.

Labour Circulation

Recruitment of labour for no more than one season is in line with the time-bound nature of most open-air operations in the rural economy: harvesting crops, quarrying stone, moulding bricks or manufacturing sea salt are activities that can be carried out only during the dry months of the year. The same goes for other industries, such as rural or urban construction, which depend on fair-weather conditions and come to an end before the onset of the rains. The sixty-fourth NSSO Round (2007–8) reported that nearly two-thirds of labour migration is rural-to-urban while intra-rural mobility accounts for a little less than one-third. I believe that the unequal divide is less stark than official counts suggest. However, mainly because of misconceived policies for the agrarian-rural economy the swelling numbers of casualized footloose labourers have indeed gravitated of late more to urban localities. Labour circulation facilitates the informalization of economic activity; at the same time the informal economy puts a premium on labour mobility. Circular migration does not mean that the whole household moves out. Dependents usually remain behind, although that status is flexible and does not always apply to young children and the old-aged, many of whom are forced to participate in the hunt for wages. With one or more members going off and others staying behind, the household becomes multi-locational. The non-economic features of living apart are seldom discussed in the literature but the cost implied is higher than a split budget and creates frustration and tension on both sides.

Figure 7.2 Power-loom workers rotate in twelve-hour shifts on and off work

The circulating migrants often have to make do without decent accommodation. This goes for the power-loom workers in Surat who sleep in a packed room in the company of workmates, construction workers who arrange a sort of bivouac at the building site, brickmakers or salt-pan workers who erect a makeshift shelter, gangs of paddy harvesters allowed to cook their food and pass the night in the farmer's courtyard and the army of sugar-cane cutters who camp along the roadside or in the open field in a tent of tarpaulin sheets. For the duration of the working season all of them have to make do without drinking water and toilet facilities. One cane cutter had the courage to tell a group of senior officials that had come to find out about the way they were treated by the mill management that 'even dogs are better off' (Breman 1994). This was more than twenty years ago but the anger with which these roaming workers react to their exploitation and oppression shows that they are not only in search of employment far away from home but also deprived of an existence that allows for a modicum of decency and dignity. One wonders what the prospects are of their realizing the deeply felt ambition for a better quality of life.

Construction has become a booming industry in both urban and rural Gujarat. Although in this sector, too, the use of new materials for building, road-laying and irrigation works and the changeover to more mechanized technologies have made the industry much more capital-intensive, the sector still has a huge army of skilled and unskilled labour at its disposal, hired and fired under informal terms and conditions. The modality of employment takes two forms. The first entails the recruitment of work gangs by a jobber in the villages of origin. The jobber comes from the same milieu as the labourers he contracts, usually accompanies the gang to the building site and acts as foreman to supervise the work. He is responsible for everything going as planned on the site. The real estate developer, a builder or contractor himself, has no direct contact with the workers hired for the season and leaves it up to his agent to distribute an advance before they leave their homes in the countryside and settle their remaining wages monthly or at the end of the dry season. The jobber is at the pinnacle of circular migration, a type of mobility that is well organized from the workfloor right up to the commanding heights of corporate capitalism. The contracting of labour has become a big business in the informalized economy and relies on a long chain of mediation incorporating contractors and subcontractors. The focus in this study is on the local-level boss of work gangs engaged in the recruitment of men, women and children and the supervision of his catch in the labour process. In the case of the brick-kiln workers and sugar-cane harvesters discussed below he is the link between the ultimate employer and the members of his gang for the duration of the season. He contacts the migrants at home, brings them to the worksite, takes care of their requirements for the duration of the season (shelter, food and water), supervises his gang at work, keeps track of the daily output and, eventually, makes arrangements for their return home – which includes settling their wages. Employers hold him liable for the quantity and quality of the work done by his gang and, the other way around, the workers have to rely on the jobber's word that the employer can be trusted. Good faith on both sides is one of this middleman's major worries. In their area of recruitment the jobbers, who have usually come up from the ranks, are known to interact with each other in discussing the terms and conditions they have on offer for their catch and to avoid undue competition and friction in their midst.

In a different mode of recruitment, workers turn up on their own initiative to hire themselves out for a day or longer at one of the early-morning markets, mostly to contractors or builders carrying out reno-vation work or smaller-scale construction projects. These labour markets, known as *naka* or *chowk*, can be found in large cities and small towns throughout the country. Those seeking employment gather at road junctions, near markets or at bus or train stations. Supply and demand interconnect at these crowded meeting points to negotiate payment for the work to be done and other conditions. The workers who offer themselves for hire are mostly migrants and are also engaged to do a number of other jobs like pulling or pushing freight, loading and unloading trucks or earth-moving in preparation for con-struction – land levelling, digging trenches, laying sewage pipes and cables, road paving and so on. Of this huge workforce employed in the building industry three out of four are seasonal migrants and they invariably belong to socially and economically deprived communities – Scheduled Castes, Scheduled Tribes and Other Backward Classes, without much or any land at all to cultivate. They have no kind of portable shelter and lack any form of protection along the roadside, on the city pavement or at the work site. When they go off to work in the morning, they tie up what they have brought along (some clothes, pots and pans and a cover for the night) in a plastic sheet, which they leave behind. This bundle (*potalum*) is unpacked again on their return in the evening. They light a fire, cook a meal using utensils from the bundle, then roll out a mat or some clothes to sleep on. Although they may have been squatters for many years, they are not able to put up even a partly durable shack – the moment they try to do that, people from the buildings around chase them off or pay the police or *goonda*s (hired thugs) to remove them.

In this chapter I confine myself to studying the forced departure of the unskilled and low-paid workforce from the countryside, and their return after a short or longer period as a result of their failure to establish a permanent foothold wherever they travelled for employment. In previous publications, I have criticized the lack of research on rural-to-rural labour mobility. The suggestion that outside labour is recruited to make up for local shortages seems to have lost little of its currency, despite an abundance of evidence to the contrary. Unlike the stereotypical premise that supply and demand are mediated by the market, I have emphasized that employers prefer labour from elsewhere because migrants – often attached in a state of neo-bondage – are not only cheaper to recruit and maintain but also easier to discipline. Recent case studies in Gujarat – of, amongst others, salt-pan workers, the army of labour employed to cut sugar-cane, nomads from far-off regions who come to Alang on the coast to break ships, the cruel subjugation of almost one *lakh* (100,000) children (girls and boys) from Rajasthan as cotton pickers, and the employment of men, women and children in many hundreds of brickworks – show the massive scale of the migration in search of work throughout the country. The sites of their temporary employment, for which they are mobilized in separate circuits of recruitment, cross state borders and are not covered by official statistics. They are not on record thanks to a deliberate attempt to cover up the footloose character of the workforce at the bottom of the economy. The swarms of time-bound migrants recruited from all over India to work in the Special Economic Zones (SEZs) contracted out to corporate business are also beyond critical scrutiny. These large-scale enclaves, set apart from from the public domain, are growth poles established within the state but cut off from its territory and gifted to private enterprise operating with national or international capital. As part of the neoliberal policy regime, the SEZs have become a favoured brand of economic activity kickstarted with government subsidy, tax exemption and other generous facilities. Gujarat has more of these zones than any other state, privatized domains in which labour laws and regulations do not apply and mandatory environmental protections are not enforced. Any effort to gain access to these cordoned-off bastions of crony capitalism invariably ends in failure (Breman 2016: 156).

The government's labour inspection machinery is conspicuous by its absence throughout the economy. It is declared policy not to implement statutory laws for the security and protection of members of this footloose workforce trying to force their way into the urban economy. In the official mindset, these hordes of nomads are an intolerable hindrance and should be dealt with as trespassers against municipal law and order. On enquiring at the highest municipal level in Ahmedabad, I was given to understand that rural migrants are free to come and work in the city on condition that they arrange for their own shelter. If employers are unwilling to provide accommodation or pay for the costs involved, and that rarely occurs, the migrants have no choice but to camp under the open sky on whatever unoccupied plots they can find. However, squatting on such sites is not allowed. When their presence is considered a nuisance, they have to clear out and, if they fail to do so, they run the risk of being forcibly removed. This has happened to many of them, not once but repeatedly. Sometimes they have to pay protection money to a local gang to avoid being harassed or bribe an official to avoid eviction. My conclusion is not that the government is absent in the regimentation of labour in the informal economy. The authorities are present, but their interventions are not intended to enhance protection and security for the migrant workers – rather to maintain or even further exacerbate the excessively weak bargaining position of this footloose workforce. The standing policy is to defuse collective action and to label brave deeds of resistance against exploitation and oppression subversive, as incompatible with the maintenance of peace and order. It is not the migrants who break the law, but public servants – up to the highest level.

Neo-bondage

Labour migration has been a recurrent topic of my empirical research in Gujarat since the 1970s. The reason I discuss the influx or exodus of land-poor or landless labour in the villages of my fieldwork in this chapter is to highlight the return of debt bondage as a major feature in the mobilization of many of these workers. Receiving a monetary advance at the low point of the agrarian cycle, they contract themselves for employment under duress in an agreement that forces them to leave home at the command of a jobber. Acting as an agent of the ultimate employer, the jobber takes his catch of men, women and children away to a remote destination, where postponed wage payment means the workers are constrained until their labour power is no longer required. It is a modality of attachment that I term neo-bondage. The gist of what this form of an unfree labour contract entails, why and when it begins and how it ends (or not) is elaborated upon in the text below. The point that needs to be emphasized is that the commodification and bondage of labour are shown to be not mutually exclusive. The workers are engaged for production that is organized along capitalist lines. My first case study is of the landless workers I traced from the start of my first round of fieldwork in their exodus from village to brick-kilns. The second case discusses the influx of a huge wave of migrants for harvesting sugar-cane throughout the central plain, also in the villages of my fieldwork. Although recruited and paid as agricultural labourers, their pace of work as well as the management of this massive army of harvesters is agro-industrial in character, highlighted in my account as cooperative capitalism.

The text that now follows is the reproduced verbatim version of a summing-up article on circular migration published in *International Labor and Working-Class History* (Breman 2010a). While my basic argument is that the type of bondage that used to exist has disappeared, in my ongoing empirical investigations in Gujarat in subsequent decades I often found practices at the bottom of both the rural and urban informal-sector economies that restrict labour's freedom of movement. Indebtedness is invariably what causes labourers to comply with a condition of employment that keeps them entrapped at the worksite. Employers use the payment of advance wages ('earnest money') as a mechanism of attachment. The recipient has to repay the provider in labour if and when desired, for a price lower than the going market rate. The account that follows does not refer to sources other than my own writings, but the relationships I describe are, of course, also reported in many other publications that discuss ongoing practices of unfree labour in South Asia more generally. Employers who recruit migrant workers for an entire season are accustomed to hold labour captive in a relationship of indebtedness. A wide variety of economic activities that take place in the open air make use of such 'footloose labour' tied down in a cycle of production that begins at the start of the dry season and ends before the first rainfall about half a year later. The seasonal migration of labour has been a worldwide phenomenon for quite some time. The transition to a capitalist mode of production put a premium on mobility, resulting in an increase in both the scale of migration and the distances covered. However, as the transformation of Western economies progressed in the late nineteenth century, the widely practised earlier circulation of labour tapered off. On the one hand, increased and more regular employment reduced the pressure to migrate temporarily to work elsewhere, while on the other hand the impetus of industrialization made it possible for rural migrants to settle down in towns and cities. The mobility of labour in India, both rural-to-urban and intra-rural, started to gather momentum in the second half of the twentieth century. The annual trek from village to distant worksites and back has resulted in labourers being permanently afloat. It is the exception rather than the rule for migrants to settle down elsewhere – and in particular to establish a household and take up residence there –because most remain alien to where they have gone.

But likewise back home their bouts of absence contribute to a growing hybridity of these footloose workers, facing marginality both in the household and in the locality. The circulation of labour is going on with no end in sight, as described in two case studies relating to the villages of my recurrent fieldwork in south Gujarat.

The Annual Trek to the Brick-kilns

In the vicinity of Chikhligam, labour from far away is mobilized for a variety of activities, including the sugar-cane harvest, road-building, sand-digging and working in stone quarries. But large groups of labourers from south Gujarat go in search of work elsewhere, mostly in brick-kilns. For many years, middlemen acting on behalf of brick manufacturers have recruited members of the land-poor and landless castes from Chikhligam. I have defined the modality of employment to which they are recruited as neo-bondage. Let me first explain why I see this arrangement as a form of labour bondage. During the monsoon, when the subsistence deficit in the landless neighbourhoods is at its most urgent because of lack of work and income, the recruiting agent arrives to hand out earnest money that commits the recipient to leave the village two or three months later to go work in the brick-fields. When the migrants arrive at the worksite, the jobber or labour recruiter (*mukadam*) becomes the foreman of the gang he has contracted. The manner of recruitment is the same as that of the earlier *hali*, who was not forced to become a farm servant but offered his services 'voluntarily' to a master who was prepared to pay him an advance, usually to enable him to marry. The bondage relationship usually started with a debt, which is also true of the labourer nowadays, who surrenders his freedom of movement at the moment he accepts an advance from the jobber. Just like the *hali* – the bonded farm servant who had to work for his master until the debt was paid off – the seasonal worker cannot leave the brick-kiln until he has worked off the advance payment. Once the debt has been cleared, he should be free to leave, but his wage is then held back after a deduction of a weekly amount to cover his daily requirements, and paid in a lump sum when he returns home at the end of the season. If he leaves the kiln prematurely, he loses the net balance of seven months' work. He can ask for a new cash advance in between but if he does, too often he may have very little left at the end, perhaps just enough to pay for the journey home. Sometimes the migrant may even leave the kiln with a debt if he has received a large advance from the owner or the *mukadam* – for example, to arrange for his own wedding or that of another family member – an amount that cannot be paid off with one season's work.

I refer to this situation of indebtedness as neo-bondage because despite its resemblance to the previous practice of *halipratha*, there are significant differences. Both situations lead to loss of freedom of movement, but in the case of the seasonal migrants, the advance they receive binds them only for the season. The agreement is not, as with the *halis*, the start of a relationship that often lasts for life or is even kept intact from generation to generation. Secondly, it applies only to the labourer, whereas when a *hali* was employed, his wife and children were usually in the master's service, too. That is not necessarily the case for the brickmakers. The jobber pays earnest money for the wives and children, depending on their productive capacity. Sometimes members of the same family even hire themselves out to different *mukadams* so that they can obtain a higher advance payment. Lastly, seasonal migrants are hired purely on the basis of a labour contract. The non-economic aspects of patronage that were so characteristic of *halipratha*, the *halis*' function as an indicator of their masters' power and prestige, play no part in the kiln owners' decision to hire labour. They are not feudal patrons who surround themselves with clients but capitalist entrepreneurs who satisfy their time-bound demand for labour by recruiting workers in the rural hinterland. They do this with the aid of jobbers and in such a way that the army of migrant men, women and children is immobilized as long as their presence is needed and sent back to where they come from when the season is over. If they lose their productive capacity, they are a burden to the employer. Their temporary employment entitles them to no additional benefits. While the *halis*' masters were willing to provide support in cases of illness or old age, the kiln owners resolutely refuse to provide any guarantee of survival for their employees.

It is certainly not my intention to exaggerate the extent to which *halis* could solicit support and protection under the old system of patronage, but the seasonal migrants are not better off under a labour regime in which they are treated as commodities. Being unable to work affects not only those suffering from illness but also the other members of the team because the work is based on the active participation of men, women and children in the production process. One evening, I was taken to a brick-kiln that had been opened in Chikhligam – which, of course, used labour from elsewhere – to see a young girl of about fifteen who had symptoms of malaria. I found her lying on the ground under a couple of jute sacks, shivering with fever. Her younger sister came now and again and shook her gently, trying to get her to go to work because she was unable to carry all the bricks away from the base plate by herself. The labour power of her sick sister was needed to eliminate the backlog. When she had done this, she could lie down again, although for no longer than ten minutes (Breman 1996: 135).

Figure 7.3 Men, women and children are engaged in brickmaking day and night

The relationship between the jobbers and the labourers is contractual, but they are relatively close to each other. There is no great difference in social identity, such as that between the *dhaniyamo* and the *hali*. The labour contractors come from the same background as the migrants. They are part of the footloose army for many years until the kiln owner asks them to act as intermediaries and gives them a sum of money to recruit labour. To be eligible for the position of jobber, they must have experience with the work, possess the qualities required to act as an intermediary and have a certain amount of property that can be used as security in the event that the agreed number of migrants do not show up. This set of criteria explain why outsiders cannot be middlemen. How completely wrong things can go is shown by the case of D., an Anavil Brahmin and former village head of Chikhligam, who saw labour contracting as an attractive source of additional income. For many years he had witnessed the departure of seasonal migrants to the brickworks, whose owners regularly visited the village to gain information from him about the reputation of recruiters and workers. D. reckoned that he was better qualified than anybody else to streamline this demand for temporary labour according to the requirements of modern times. After all, members of the low castes in the village trusted him, and a man of his social background would find it easy to convince distant employers of his integrity and intelligence. D. took up matters in a big way and, according to him, entered into contracts to supply some thousands of workers to the brickmaking industry of Bombay and south Gujarat from Chikhligam and adjacent villages. He even accompanied the first contingent of some hundreds to Bombay. However, the factory owners there, who had indeed provided him in good faith with a large amount of credit, were dissatisfied with the poor quality of the workers with whom he arrived. When these bosses continued to refuse payment of the commission he had been promised on deliverance of the gangs, D. loaded all his workers into lorries one night and took them to other brickyards in Surat. My landless informants burst out in laughter as they told me about this adventure (Breman 1996: 99).

Nearly all jobbers are Dhodhias, a tribal caste of land-poor peasants, who have first worked in the kilns themselves. They are therefore thoroughly familiar with the situation in the kilns, know what work to give to whom and how to make sure it gets done properly. They are appointed as middlemen because of their good service record and their willingness in preceding years to act as an agent in the village for their own jobber. They give him information on suitable candidates, who will come with their wives and children for recruitment and act as witnesses when the earnest money is paid out. In this way, they show their suitability to act as jobbers themselves and are eventually promoted. The Dhodhias have the advantage of owning some property – land and cattle – that they can offer as security against the debt the seasonal migrants have entered into. That is why very few jobbers are Halpatis, a tribal caste of agricultural labourers. In Chikhligam, L. succeeded in being promoted to the position of jobber, but he was unable to sustain it. At the time I noted the following:

L. is again working as brickmaker having acted as jobber and gang boss for two years. He was ruined by a couple of migrants who had agreed to go with him at the start of the second season but failed to show up at the time of departure. At that late date, he was unable to find replacements, according to him due to lack of solidarity of Dhodhia *mukadams* in the village. They are prepared to help one another, but they spread a rumour about L. that the brickworks' owner had no faith in his ability as a gang boss. The patron was angry when L. arrived with fewer workers than he had promised and deducted the advances given in the monsoon to the missing workers from his commission. But this was not all the damage. Two members of his gang returned home early due to illness with the result that the output of the others was reduced. The upshot was that at the end of the second year he was indebted to the owner of the brickworks. According to the calculations of the latter at least, with the result he had to return to the village without a penny in his pocket. (Breman 1996: 97–8)

Jobbers are the guardians of the routes leading from the village to the outside world. They know how to deal with employers and to make sure the members of their gang do the work they have agreed to do, to pay out the weekly living allowance, to keep production going until the end of the season and to mete out punishment in the knowledge that they will be backed up by their principals. The debt the migrants enter into commits them to obedience and a show of deference in the same way that the *halis* had to respect their *dhaniyamo*. The migrant workers, however, have much more opportunity to escape the grips of the jobber/gang boss, and this is perhaps the greatest difference between traditional bondage and neo-bondage. Often they are cheated by one or the other. They are not able to check the balance of pay they take home with them at the end of the season. Protesting against maltreatment or underpayment when they leave is ineffective. All they can do is choose a different jobber the next season and go to work at a different kiln.

The reserve army of underpaid and underemployed labour has to stand by in the hinterland until the time comes to leave, but this does not mean these workers behave as a docile and helpless mass who, having received their advance, have no other choice than to accept their bondage from the moment they leave the village to the day they are sent home again at the end of the season. The jobbers have to keep a constant eye on them to ensure that they actually stick to the agreement to leave when the time comes. Some labourers accept earnest money from more than one jobber. The jobbers protect themselves against such deceit or disloyalty by keeping in contact with each other and drawing up a blacklist of clients who do not honor their contracts. When I came back to Chikhli in 1986, I was foolish enough to accept a ride in a jeep. Vehicles rarely enter the isolated landless neighborhood, and when the inhabitants saw the dust cloud announcing my arrival they fled into the fields, thinking that it was the *mukadam* who had come, together with the brick-kiln owner, to pick up those who had not turned up when the migrants left for the kiln a couple of weeks earlier. Complaints of ill health are not accepted as a good excuse for not turning up. The least these no-show cases could expect was a beating, and if they still refused to go, they would have to find a replacement. There is no point in demanding repayment of the advance, since the landless have hardly any property that can be confiscated in place of payment. What is often presented as deceit on the part of the migrants, however, can be fraud by the jobber, who has kept back some of the credit for himself rather than paying it out as an advance. The employers are aware of such practices and replace the *mukadam* if the scale of 'bad debts' becomes too high.

The jobber is a necessary evil but needs to be kept under close surveillance, according to a kiln owner with whom I have remained in contact for many years and met again during the 1986 monsoon when he was staying with the manager of a petrol pump sited on the main road from Chikhli to Valsad. Here he meets the migrants recruited for him by a new gang boss. In exchange for placing their thumbprint on a paper, they are given the first instalment of the promised cash advance. But the *sheth* has armed himself against the deceit by which he had formerly been victimized. He takes a photo of each contracted worker. The flash that accompanies the making of the portrait is not really necessary, but its use dramatically stresses the importance of the proceedings. In a loud voice he then says that this evidence will be a great help to the police if the workers try to defraud him. In an aside, he tells me that he turns down anyone who refuses to follow his order to look straight into the camera when he is taking the photograph (Breman 1996: 107). But the seasonal migrants do not allow themselves to be intimidated by these threats. Both parties are fully aware that trying to get compensation from them for failing to keep their part of the agreement is doomed in advance. The workers toe the line as long as it is in their own interests but do not hesitate to back out if that suits them better. Nor do they let their indebtedness stand in the way.

Harvesting Sugar-Cane

For many years, the Bardoli sugar co-operative mill recruited the majority of its cane cutters from Khandesh in the neighboring state of Maharasthra. During the monsoon, a staff member of the co-operative management was stationed in Dhulia town to recruit cutting teams from the surrounding villages. He did that by taking on jobbers, who each received a sum of money for putting together a gang of work teams and contracting them by giving them an advance. This earnest money was paid in several instalments and came at a time when the village economy offered little work or income for the majority of land-poor farmers and landless labourers. This desperate situation was even worse in years when there was insufficient rainfall and going into debt was the only way that these households were able to survive. The jobbers had to sign a printed form that they had to follow to the letter: to depart with his gang when told to, to be at the designated locations with their gangs from the beginning to the end of the harvest campaign and to supervise the work and ensure that it went as instructed. There were two kinds of teams. The *gadavalas* [cart owners] took an ox cart with them to transport the cane to the factory themselves. Four or five workers were needed for each cart:

two to take the fully laden cart to the factory, while the other members made sure there was a new load of cane ready to be transported when the cart came back. Much more numerous were the *koytavalas*. *Koytas* were the machetes used to cut the cane. The long knives were owned by the factory, issued at the start of the campaign and collected again at the end. If one broke or was lost, the user had to pay for a replacement. Each cutting team consisted minimally of two members, usually a husband and wife. Children from the age of eight would also often take part in the work. The teams were clubbed together into gangs which did not transport the cane themselves but loaded it onto carts, tractors and lorries sent by the factory. The *gadavalas* received higher advances than the *koytavalas*, but both groups were forced to sell their labour in advance to enable them to survive the slack season.

The army of harvesters increased in size from the 1960s onwards, when the expansion of irrigated land allowed the agro industry to spread all over the central plain. New co-operatives were set up in neighboring sub-districts. They built their own factories and modelled their activities on the formula that had proved so successful in Bardoli. They, too, chose not to employ local landless labour and recruited work gangs from the far-off hinterland, using the routes that the pioneers from Bardoli had opened up. The intermediaries who form the link between the co-operatives and the migrants are crucial to the recruitment process. They come from the same background as the cane cutters, have worked as cutters themselves for many years and therefore know what is expected of them as a jobber: they must be sufficiently creditworthy; know when, how and whom to recruit; direct the work during the campaign; and settle wages with their gang. Being too accommodating to either side can get the *mukadams* into trouble but being unwilling to take risks or refusing to pay out more earnest money than the factory agent is willing to supply can also be costly. The labour brokers are in competition with one another and often have to take out high-interest loans from private moneylenders to make sure their teams are complete. But this does not mean that they have no sanctions at their disposal to see to it that the seasonal migrants do as they say. These are applied with customary brutality when making up a gang of cutting teams. It is found wholly in order even by their victims that the *mukadams* should demand and eventually force their rights. The factories discharge the recruitment risks onto the labour brokers, who consequently shift these further down onto the actual workers. The cane cutters have no means of defending themselves against unjust or unreasonable claims and resign themselves to their fate or are at least not in a position to come out in open protest against it (Breman 1994: 192).

Upon arrival on the central plain, the army of thousands of cane cutters is immediately split up among the various zones demarcated by the co-operative, an area within a radius of 12–18 miles (20–30 km) of the factory. The *gadavalas* teams are sent to locations up to a distance of 6 miles (10 km), while the *koytavalas* work in the fields further away. For their tent-like shelters, the migrants are issued a few bamboo poles and three mats or sheets of blue tarpaulin. They erect these less than a yard from each other, leaving no room for the cutters to retreat in a niche of their own or to sleep in the intimacy of their family. After the evening meal they sit together around the fire on which the food is prepared. In the winter months they warm themselves against the cold evening air. These compact camps, ranging from a few dozen to several hundred men, women and children, are set up in open spaces on the roadside or at the edges of villages. They are temporary settlements, which take no more than a couple of hours to erect and can just as quickly be dismantled when all the fields in the immediate vicinity have been harvested. The removal to a new location takes place as quickly as possible, so that the cutters do not lose a working day. There are usually several gangs in each camp. The teams are clustered around their *mukadam* for protection and to ensure that they are always at his disposal. They lack even the most basic facilities, such as a latrine, and often have no drinking water. The migrants have to wash themselves and their clothes in the irrigation channels, which are badly polluted as a result of the excessive use of fertilizers and pesticides. The impossibility of observing even the most elementary rules of sanitation means that diseases are widespread, especially dysentery, diarrhea, malaria and all kinds of infections. The camps are a filthy habitat that leaves no room for human dignity. From a short but continuous stay in two camps– of ten days and a week, respectively – it was chiefly the tiredness and dreariness of the migratory existence that impressed me most strongly. People live packed very close to one another in extremely primitive conditions, often outside the regular family attachments and with an overrepresentation of young men and women. All sorts of social conventions and control mechanisms that apply back in their own village lose their significance and efficacy in this alien and harsh milieu. The mood in the camp is often tetchy, and small and unimportant differences of opinion easily blow up into fierce fights. The inhuman treatment that the cane cutters meet is unloosened between them in rancour and aggression (Breman 1994: 163).

The working day starts early and the men leave the camp first. The women come a little later, as they first have to prepare the food they take to the fields. The gang boss assigns each cutting team several rows of cane, which the men have to cut off close to the ground. The women

Figure 7.4 Sugar-Cane cutting is arduous work, made worse by lack of protective gear

follow on behind, cutting the cane stalks into smaller pieces and removing the leaves on the sides. If there is a child in the team, he or she makes the cut cane into bundles, tying it together with leaves. The work is heavy and has to be done quickly, with no protection for the bare feet against the stubble and no covering on arms and hands to prevent cuts from the sharp leaves. The midday break is short, just long enough to eat the meal. Water is fetched from an irrigation channel to drink and to wash the sweat off. The average daily yield is 1,325–1,750 lb (600–800 kg) of cane, the equivalent of a ten-hour working day cutting cane. Some teams finish before others, depending on their experience or the number of helpers for each cutter. The faster teams will sometimes help the slower ones, but if they are not closely related, they will come to some compensatory arrangement. At the end of the day, the gang members return to the camp. They walk back in a long, straggling procession, all arriving by the time darkness has fallen. My daily presence in both the camps and the fields made me realize the burden that the women have to bear. I quote from my field notes:

Although the cutting-knife is wielded mostly by the men, their helpers, usually women, sometimes take over so that the men may rest. The cleaning, breaking and bundling of the cane-stalks, all very demanding tasks, are handled by the women. While the men drink some water or lie down exhausted during the short break, the women have to attend to infants they may have brought to the fields with them, the youngest not yet weaned. On returning to the camp at the end of the day, it is the women again who carry a bundle of wood for the cooking fire on their head, and back in the camp they have many chores to attend to. (Breman 1994: 259)

The working day continues through the night. Milling the cane is an industrial process that continues without interruption, and the same applies to the transport of the cane cut during the day. The transport has to be spread out so that the roads to the factory and its premises do not become congested with lorries, tractors and ox carts unable to unload their cargo. The daily processing of large quantities of cane is a logistical operation that is worked out in great detail far in advance. The planning starts with the planting of the seed and goes through to the end of the growth cycles, fourteen to eighteen months later. On the phased harvest timetable, the fields in which the cane is ripe for cutting are grouped in clusters. The members of the co-operative therefore know when the cutters will be working on their land. Until that time, they have to follow the instructions of management to the letter. The cut cane has to be milled within eight hours or the sugar content will fall. This means that the *koytavalas* are picked up during the evening or at night to be taken by tractor or lorry from the camp to the field in which they were working during the day. The men never know when this is going to be, but they have to be ready to leave immediately to drag the bundles of cane to the roadside and load them onto the vehicles. That takes an hour to an hour and a half, after which they return to the camp, only to start the new working day a few hours later. The *gadavalas* are no better off. They take the cane to the factory themselves but have to wait their turn when they get there. Tractors and lorries have priority, and the ox carts have to wait for hours before they are unloaded. They form a buffer the factory can use to compensate for the uneven rhythm of the motorized vehicles, which may experience delays as the result of problems with loading or hold-ups en route. The frenzy not only continues throughout the day and night, but also there is no weekly free day, not even for religious festivals.

The *mukadam* tolerates absence in the event of illness. Leave to return home for a short time is only granted on very rare occasions, for example the death of a close relative. If the cane cutters do not turn up for work, they do not get paid, and that is the last thing they can afford. On the other hand, the cutters are not paid if production comes to a standstill because a machine at the mill needs to be repaired for the fortnightly cleaning operation. And if the factory compound is too congested to continue unloading, or if a lorry has broken down on the road, this is radioed to the supervisers in the fields, and cutting is suspended for a few hours. Sometimes teams are instructed to cut more cane and to keep working for longer hours. In such cases, the factory management is not prepared to accept responsibility for any risk whatsoever, or to pay the extra costs. I concluded from all this that the army of cutters is entirely at the mercy of the sugar factory for around seven months, without even a minimum of labour rights. This means that the workers have no set times for eating, sleeping or resting. These and other activities can only be managed if the gangs of harvesters are not on duty. But they are always expected to be so. For work, everything else must give way. Even several basic social habits in their way of life – for instance, that women eat after their husbands, that baths are taken or at least the mouth is rinsed early in the morning on rising – cannot be followed. For the duration of the harvest, everything turns on keeping the factory constantly supplied; yet this does not imply that there is any fixed rhythm. Every change that occurs – stoppage of the cutting, changes in the transport schedule, sudden orders (also) to cut double the quantity – has to be endured by the workers. The working day is long, knows no specific hours and, moreover, is in part not paid for (Breman 1994: 166). Labour is a factor of production without human value. That became clear to me when I tried to calculate how many workers were involved in the cutting, how long they worked and what they earned. My questions remained unanswered by the factory administration. Only the *mukadam* knew how many members each gang contained and how the work was divided up among them. His job was to make sure the migrants did what they had been contracted to do: cut enough cane and make sure it got to the factory on time. I summarized this complete subordination of the army of harvesters to the labour regime in the title I gave to my fieldwork report: 'The Crushing of Cane and of Labour by the Co-operative Sugar Industry of Bardoli.'

What wages do the cane cutters receive, and when are they paid out? Each cutting team consisting of at least two members is required to harvest around a ton of cane a day, but the average throughout the campaign is around two-thirds to three-quarters of that, 1,325–1,550 lb (600–750 kg) per day. One indicator of the level of productivity is that the size of the army of harvesters is 30–40 per cent larger than the volume of cane produced by the factory in tons per day. Wages are fixed on the basis of piecework. The rate of pay per ton is set every year, but the cutters are only told what it is at the end of the campaign and not beforehand. The factory management wants to know first what price it can get for the sugar. The financial administration draws up an account twice a month of how much cane each gang has cut on the basis of the slips written out by the slip-boys for each load of cane transported from the field. On arrival at the mill, the load is weighed and the exact quantity recorded.

The *mukadam* comes to the mill every fortnight but does not receive the full pay his gang has earned. First, the advance he paid to the teams when they were recruited is deducted. Until the debt is paid off, the gang members receive only a grain allowance to meet their basic needs. The sacks of millet are delivered to the camp every fortnight. In addition to the allowance, the *mukadam* gives the head of each team a small amount of money to buy vegetables, dried fish, red pepper and salt. Most of the men, however, use this pocket money to play dice or to buy tobacco and drink. Alongside the formal accounts, the *mukadam* keeps his own accounts to keep track of the money he has paid to the cutters, both the earnest money paid out at the start and anything else he has given them before departure or during the campaign. Once the cane cutters have worked off their debt, the mill still does not start to pay their full wages. Payment is postponed until the end of the campaign on the pretext that this is in the best interest of the workers themselves. On the last payday, the factory cashiers give the *mukadams* the balance of what their teams have earned. How the money is then distributed in the camps is no longer the responsibility of the mill management. And, of course, these inter-mediaries between the cooperative and the cutters find all kinds of ways to cheat the migrants. The latter have neither the knowledge nor the power to claim the amount they are actually due. The only weapon they have against fraudulent practices is to go and work for another *mukadam* the following season. But that is no guarantee that they will not be cheated again.

I have used the term neo-bondage to describe this labour contract, which commits the cane cutters to the regime imposed by the sugar factory from the start to the end of the harvest campaign. By accepting the advance, the migrants commit themselves to work to pay off the debt. But the state of bondage continues after the debt has been paid off because they only receive the wages they are due after they have harvested all the fields. In this way, the factory makes sure the migrants do not just pack up and go home before the season ends. Their bondage is therefore founded not only on the fact that they receive a payment in advance, but also by the holding back of their wages until the work has been com-pleted. This 'custom', as the employers call it, is an effective means of preempting opposition to the abominable working conditions. The workers withhold protest against the long working days, the pace of the work, the great distance to the fields, the continual moving from place to place, the low grain ration and so on, for fear of incurring the displeasure of the employer. I was actually staying in a *koytavala* camp on an important Maratha feast day that normally would have been celebrated. However, the order came down from the field manager that work had to go on as usual. Nevertheless, some of the gangs in a nearby camp did not turn up that day. The grain allowance to the cutters involved was imme-diately stopped for a week as penalty, and a work ban was put on them for the same period. The *mukadams* of the gangs concerned hurried to the factory to apologize – initially in vain. A day or two later they presented the managing director with a written statement in his office. In the most abject manner and words, they again acknowledged their disobedience, requested forgiveness and promised never again to transgress the regulations. With ill grace and many stern words, the manager finally relented. He made a great show of filing their petition, gave permission for the ration of grain to be handed out and rescinded the work ban (Breman 1994: 175). In addition, the combination of advanced and postponed payment means that the labourers are at the mercy of the untrustworthy practices of the intermediaries, who provide credit at an exorbitant rate of interest. It would be incorrect to calculate the wages the labourers actually receive on the basis of the mill records. Although these show how little the cane cutters are paid for the heavy work they perform – much less than the minimum wage – the real extent to which they are underpaid is concealed by the machinations of the *mukadam*.

The nature of the seasonal migrants' bondage is different from that between the erstwhile *hali* and master. Firstly, the cane cutters only commit themselves for a limited period of time, which in theory does not exceed the duration of the harvest campaign. It also lacks any of the elements of patronage that committed master and servant to an all-embracing relationship with each other and that was automatically passed down from generation to generation. The *mukadam* stakes a claim to the labour power of the members of his gang and pays them a wage in return. The agreement is more specific by nature, is purely economic and has nothing to do with the acquisition of power and status as an aim in itself. The middleman is after all a broker who works on commission and at his own risk and expense. He acts as an agent in finding workers, setting them to work and paying them off at the end of the campaign. In theory, the migrants are free to offer their services to a different gang boss every year. In reality, however, they have learned that it often pays to stay with the same one. His gang consists of a fixed core of workers who remain loyal to him and who can rely on a wide range of favours. And they can ask him for credit for exceptional expenses, like a wedding or paying for a house. Such loans often take longer than one campaign to repay, which means that the contract is automatically extended for the following year. Jobbers with a bad name find it more difficult to recruit enough workers, but it also happens that they refuse to employ candidates who cannot work to full capacity or who have a reputation for being difficult. The gang boss supervises the daily work and is an indispensable link between the management and the workers. The company's office and field staff have no direct contact with the cane cutters, and the cutters fall completely under the authority of the gang boss. His word is law in the camp. He takes charge of setting up and dismantling the tents, collects the fortnightly ration from the factory and divides it up among the teams (they all receive the same amount, irrespective of the number of members in each team, and with deductions for days they have not worked through illness or for other reasons) and settles arguments between or even within teams. There is a small shop in the camp where the migrants can buy small items for their daily use. This is often run by the gang boss's wife or another family member, and customers can buy on credit, but up to a limit set by the gang boss. The far-reaching authority of the jobber-cum-gang-boss-cum-camp-leader becomes apparent when he is absent. Outsiders who speak directly to the cane cutters receive no answers to their questions but are referred to the *mukadam*. His authority expresses itself in his resolute treatment of those who are dependent on him, while his attitude to his superiors is typified by a moderated servitude and an ability to interact with them. *Mukadams* normally have little trouble in disciplining their workers, and even when this is done with the use of some force, they know that they can depend on the covert or even overt support of factory management. Intimidation can give rise to heated reaction, however, particularly when physical rather than verbal force is used. It would be quite inaccurate to picture the cane-cutting army as a docile mass of people whose spirit has been broken. *Mukadams* who handle their workers too drastically are likely to encounter some who are not afraid to show forcible resistance and beat him up (Breman 1994: 146).

The low profile that the cane cutters adopt is not founded on a natural docility but on their awareness that they are in an alien environment and a fear of getting into trouble through ignorance of the appropriate code of conduct. The migrants rarely or never have contact with the local people in the area in which they spend more than half the year. This marginality is only part of the story. Their tendency to hide behind the *mukadam* for protection and their dependence on him reinforces the impression that the large army of harvest workers do not live in freedom. The final clause of the contract that the *mukadam* is made to sign with the mill commits him to leave the region with his gang as soon as the campaign is over. The case studies reported above are based on practices I found in earlier rounds of my fieldwork. Is neo-bondage a phenomenon of the past that does not exist any longer or at least has gone down in magnitude? No. At the bottom of the informalized economy of India, neo-bondage is indeed rampant because the workforce suffers from lack of sufficient employment. Workers are hired and fired according to the need of the moment and receive for their labour power wages that are too low to live on.

Consequently, the members of this huge reserve army have no alternative but to sell their labour power in advance and are thus entrapped in a state of indebtedness that takes away their freedom of movement. In a 2009 report, the International Labour Organization identified debt bondage as a form of unfree labour to which poor peasants and indigenous peoples in Asia and Latin America fall victim (International Labour Organization 2009). In an edited volume, Isabelle Guérin, Aseem Prakash and I have highlighted the linkage between past and present forms of labour bondage in the Indian subcontinent (Breman et al. 2009).

It is not only because they are unable to find sufficient employment and livelihood opportunities in and around their own locality that vulnerable segments of the workforce are being driven out of their ancestral homes. Development-induced displacement – infrastructural works such as large-scale irrigation projects and road construction, but also the ill-advised mining of minerals, which has a devastating impact on both environment and inhabitants – has led to the forced relocation of an estimated 70 million people in India since 1950 (Padovani 2016). Due to lack of proper resettlement legislation compounded by callous follow-up policies, the majority of these victims of underdevelopment have been left to fend for themselves and, in their new sites of precarious residence, are even poorer than they were before.

Relentless Dispossession

Indebtedness has been the operational device of labour bondage in India both past and present. This apparent continuity should, however, be unpicked to drive home my main point: dispossession leading to attachment in debt dependency can be framed in a variety of contexts, and this study is focused on its role in the restructuring from a pre-capitalist to a capitalist setting. The erstwhile *hali* system has been shown to operate in a subsistence-oriented peasant order that endeavoured to maximize profit in non-economic terms. Patrons satisfied their desire to increase their social status and political power by attaching a dependent clientele to their households. The inequality the patrons aimed for was made manifest in the assumed acceptance of servility by the dispossessed who were rewarded for their deference and allegiance with the provision of a livelihood allowance. Agricultural production was mainly geared to satisfy local demand, exchanged for other goods and services but also shared with the attached clients who sought to be assured, not always successfully, of minimal means for their social reproduction. Payment made in kind did not bear the character of cost. Rather than being viewed as an expense that lowered income, it was administered as an investment in further accumulation, an outlay required to raise the standing and leverage of the 'benefactor'. The surplus value extracted from bonded servants was not measured in their capacity to increase production and make agriculture more profitable but in the extent to which the size of the master's entourage met his prime objective – to demonstrate power and prestige. Crucial for the size of his retinue was not how many *halis* he needed but how many he could afford to maintain.

In the slow but steady intrusion of capitalism in the peasant landscape during the late-colonial era, the master-servant tie was progressively reduced to a labour arrangement that attached a landless worker to a substantial landowner. Cultivation lost its subsistence-driven and local character and the increased monetization that accompanied the market-directed process of commercialization implied the replacement of wage payment in kind by settlement in money, a few coins as a matter of fact. This conversion, which signalled the increasingly capitalist nature of agriculture, did not happen overnight but was drawn out over a long period. It saw the gradual substitution of food and other allowances in kind for remuneration in cash. The conversion went together with the detachment of the labouring household from living in the shadow of the master. The daily allowance provided for the regular farmhands' sustenance was now defined as the lowest possible expenditure to realize a maximal profit from the sale of the crops produced. Already under colonial rule debt bondage had been reclassified from working in an explicit state of unfreedom to a labour contract based on voluntary engagement. The tie of attachment stipulated the obligation of the farm servant to render an indefinite amount of labour power until the employer-creditor considered the debt to be redeemed. It basically meant that in a commodified format *halipratha* continued to exist, shorn of its earlier features of patronage but as bonded as before and, if only for this reason, more exploitative than it had been in the past. The surplus valued extracted from the worker was forthwith only his or her sweat and toil, no longer moderated by the promise of a livelihood guarantee, however whimsically delivered.

A prolonged and timeworn process of dispossession, the original stages of which date back to an unrecorded past, forced the tribal caste-class of landless workers from generation to generation to sell their labour in advance and thereby place themselves in bondage. Their commodification in the transition to capitalism cannot be identified as the final point in a trajectory that deprived them of all bargaining power in securing their livelihood. Redundant to demand is how I have characterized the current fate of this rural underclass in south Gujarat. Dispossession has progressed to the displacement of the local landless by outsiders. A migrant workforce willing to come and go in tune with the flow of agrarian production, put to work at an even lower wage rate and endlessly pliable to manage, has made workers born and bred in the village even more vulnerable. Following up on my first round of fieldwork I traced the Halpatis who are left with no other option than to move out when the occasion arises, to hunt far away from home for casual employment and get whatever wage they can in the informal economy for as long as possible in order to keep their household going. Dispossessed, they have gone via displacement to dislocation in a mode of engagement that keeps them trapped in bondage – although quite differently shaped to the former one from which they were 'liberated'.

Their dispossession has also been aggravated by the changing mode of wage payment. When wages were still paid in kind, they tended to consist of the same commodities that were consumed or used in the master's own household. No doubt, the relationship between master and servant was one of superior and inferior, but this had minor impact on the relative difference in their material conditions. The most important wage item was the daily grain ration and the staple food was similar for both. The master actually used to share the noon meal brought from his house with the labourers in the field. A bonus or other perquisites were often crumbs from the master's table, an assortment of leftover dishes or ingredients (such as *chas* or skimmed milk collected early in the morning from the master's house) and castoff clothing or footwear and other hand-me-down items discarded by him or other members of his family. It makes sense to think of the master's household as a corporate body and the *hali*, his wife and children as part of it. A favoured image saw the old-time *hali* and *harekwali* as strongly identifying themselves with what the boss owned. They would talk about his property as if it were their belongings – 'my *wadi*, my paddy, my buffalo' – and from their humble position took pride and shared in the master's splendour. Monetization put paid to all that. It marked the beginning of an ever-growing distance in livelihood and lifestyle between the polar ends of the village hierarchy, which under the weight of capitalism was restructured into an antagon-istic class divide.

When I first came to the villages of my fieldwork in the early 1960s a cash wage had become customary – eight *annas* for a farm servant and twelve *annas*[1] for a casual worker – but perquisites were still provided in kind at the discretion of the landowner. Over the years, payment went up but remained consistently far below the level prescribed as the legal minimum for meeting the basic needs of the household. The cash amount was fixed at a rate so low that it did not even allow for the purchase of bare daily necessities for the Halpati household. In addition to what I myself observed and reported, I. P. Desai – who as an insider belonged to the village scene he described – wrote at the time of my first round of fieldwork in a reference to his native place in south Gujarat on the condition of agricultural labourers: 'they live from day-to day and even by any standard, starvation is general, even in 1963, in spite of the five-year plans' (Desai 1964: 140). In the presentation of my findings in past publications I have also elaborated on when, why and how the going wage rate increased in a covert way through strictly localized bargaining:

---

[1] Equal to respectively half and three-quarters of one rupee.

some frontrunners among the casual workforce took the lead while farm servants invariably lagged behind in daring and imploring their employers, all substantial landowners, to follow suit. During my last village stay, in 2013–14, the daily pay for agricultural labour in my sites had increased to Rs. 100 and I am informed that now (late 2018) the going wage has further risen to Rs. 150. This seems like an enormous leap forward in a period of a little over five decades, from less than R.1 to an astronomical figure that came close to the total annual income of a landless worker half a century ago. But such a conclusion would be incorrect because the cost of daily livelihood has increased in equal proportion to the cash payment earned by what was and has firmly remained the bottom class of the workforce.

Throughout the years the real wage rate for agricultural labour has barely kept up with the rate of inflation. Each time the daily pittance went up a little it was because farmers understood that the going wage no longer enabled their dispossessed workers to buy the daily food ration the family needed to survive and reluctantly decided to give in to mounting pressure from the landless in their employment for an equivalent raise. My argument is not that Halpatis have become poorer than they were when I first met them in the early 1960s – because a plight worse than that of the commodified *hali* is beyond imagination. But their degraded status as an underclass has kept the majority of them firmly stuck at the bottom of the pile both within and outside the agricultural sector. Meanwhile the castes-classes above them have been able to improve their economic standing, by a good deal in the case of the dominant caste-class and a moderate amount in the case of the segments lower in the rural hierarchy who are equipped with a few means of production. My more than five decades of fieldwork in south Gujarat clearly show that capitalist growth has widened the class divide from top to bottom. The switch in wage payment from kind to cash that followed when capitalism began to make deeper inroads into the rural economy has made the underclasses more vulnerable than they already were. This point of view is confirmed by a similar argument made by John Harriss many years ago:

An extremely important but very little recognized fact about poverty in India is that poor people are *not* primarily 'small farmers' but those dependent upon irregular and unreliable incomes – and who are thus exposed to the hazard of sudden deterioration in their exchange entitlements in circumstances of inflation. (Harriss 1992: 199)

As discussed in earlier chapters, the features of patronage found in the *halipratha* system disappeared in the transition to treating the agrarian landless as workers only. Provision of social security (a basic subsistence allowance) and protection against adversity (bouts of being out of work) or loss of labour power (due to illness, disability or old age) were exempted from the terms of the oral labour contract in the transition to capitalism. The reduction of labourers to the status of a mere commodity contributed significantly to the extreme fragility of the landless existence – particularly since after Independence the post-colonial state did not step in to compensate the landless for what their employers refused to offer: the guarantee of the most basic of livelihoods.

In the light of what I have already documented, little elaboration is needed to illustrate the many ways in which the agrarian-rural proletariat in south Gujarat has been persistently deprived of state support and protection. To sum up the most critical issues: this long-dispossessed section of the population was excluded from reforms that at the dawn of Independence promised to hand over land to the tiller; a minimum wage for agricultural labour was fixed only belatedly and then was not enforced; the landless poor were excluded from many civic amenities and facilities that were haltingly introduced in the public domain, such as in housing, health and education; public works were not carried out in good time and sufficient quantity for the un- and underemployed; the overwhelmingy majority of the landless poor were denied the social benefits that the state eventually but haphazardly began to provide. Attempts to alleviate poverty under Congress rule failed miserably to achieve their stated objective: *garibi hatao*. Congress leadership actually owned up to the fact that of every rupee spent in tackling poverty at best 15 *paisa* reached the targeted beneficiaries: the labouring and non-labouring poor. A rider has to be added to this evidence of negligence. The spectrum of failures – from blatant discrimination to total disregard – does not apply all over the country. The prospects for inclusion of the lower castes-classes in the southern states of India are reportedly much better than I found to be the case in the region of my fieldwork research. A ready explanation for this contrast is that there is more effective collective action by the poor and dispossessed in states such as Kerala and Tamilnad. But 'the Gujarat model of growth and development' has become the policy recipe for the whole nation since 2014. In many comments on the power shift from the Congress-led coalition to Prime Minister Modi's BJP drive for monetarism and hegemony, BJP rule is seen as more exclusionary than that of Congress. This observation can be backed up in many respects and for Gujarat above all. However, what tends to be seen as a major rupture should actually be understood as a progression from less and covert exclusion (under Congress rule) to undiluted and overt exclusion (under the BJP) both

of minority creeds and of all groups of all communities that fall under
the label of the forsaken poor.

The Notion of a Built-in Depressor

When addressing the social question academics and activists tend to turn
to the state, which they expect to redress a distorted balance – understandably so, since in the age of neoliberalism politics and governance,
which together embody the state, are complicit in promoting the interests
of owners and managers of capital while only paying lip service to the
need to consider the interests of labour – or not even bothering about
these at all. But this was not how Daniel Thorner, an economic historian
who sought refuge in India from the Cold War in the United States,
analyzed the agrarian economy he studied. According to Thorner the
root cause of the hideous and disgraceful misery he encountered on field
trips around India in the 1950s and 1960s was a stultified mode of
production that continued to block development. He came to this conclusion on the basis of hit-and-run raids into the countryside. In the first
of five lectures on land reform delivered at the Delhi School of Economics in 1955, Thorner clarified the lack of dynamism he regarded as
symptomatic of an outdated rural-agrarian regime stifled in stagnation:

This complex of legal, economic and social relations uniquely typical of the
Indian countryside served to produce an effect which I should like to call that
of a built-in 'depressor.' Through the operation of this multi-faceted 'depressor,'
Indian agriculture continued to be characterized by low capital intensity and
antiquated methods. (Thorner 1976: 16)[2]

In his opinion India's unique agrarian structure derived from the fact that
it lacked capitalist producers who, in line with the received wisdom, were
set on paving the way to economic growth and development. Thorner
identified three major classes as stakeholders in agriculture. The *maliks*
or proprietors comprised the first and smallest class, though they owned
most of the land. The *kisans* or peasants were the petty owners of
smallholdings that they themselves cultivated. Labourers or *mazdur*
made their livelihood from tilling the land of others. This three-tier class
composition was congruent with the caste hierarchy, with the main
proprietors at the top; the peasants in the middle – but most of them at
risk of sliding downwards; and the labourers at the backward bottom.
The layering of rights to land was such that the multi-graded class of

---

[2] The republished edition of 1976 contained an introduction in which he adjusted his
earlier opinion in the light of new findings a decade later.

major landowners appropriated a substantial part of the output under share-cropping, tenancy and other outsourcing arrangements that established a creditor-debtor relationship. It meant that the cultivating *kisan* was left with no surplus to invest in better tools, improved seed or fertilizer. For the landless *mazdur* there was even less point in trying to improve his efficiency. In addition, the dominating class-caste of proprietors had little incentive to increase production and productivity. In Thorner's observation they were interested in agriculture only to the extent that they might continue to draw their incomes from it without tilling the land themselves:

Clearly it was not worth their while to invest capital in agricultural operations so long as these operations were to be left in the hands of the most backward and ill-educated villagers. On the other hand, as members of high castes, they preferred not to think in terms of undertaking the 'degrading' field work themselves. The primary aim of all classes in the agrarian structure has been not to increase their income by more efficient methods, but to rise in social prestige by abstaining in so far as possible from physical labour. (Thorner 1976: 16)

Although in overall agreement with this analysis, I would like to express my difference of opinion with Thorner in so far as his conclusion is concerned: the regrettable absence of capitalism. He is right to point out that those higher up in the agrarian hierarchy are since long accustomed to avoiding manual work, and tilling the land in particular. However, a preference for ostentatious leisure does not necessarily signify the absence of qualities conducive to the emergence of capitalism.

I refer to my earlier publications to back up this view. The main landowners in south Gujarat transformed themselves into capitalist farmers without surrendering a lifestyle in which they had substituted the labour power of the landless Halpatis for their own and thereby were free to indulge in conspicuous leisure and consumption. Among this dominant caste-class of Anavil Brahmans, the lower section of Bhathelas imitated the example of the more illustrious Desais by employing landless adults and children not only to work on the land but also to perform a variety of chores in and around their household. When their prosperity began to increase once they began to grow cash crops (cotton at first), the Kanbi Patidars, who were middle-class peasants at best, followed suit and in similar fashion increased their sense of their own decency and dignity by giving up working in the fields. The fact that they employed landless labourers therefore confirmed rather than denied their capitalist mentality; they chose a lifestyle that combined their accumulating acumen with ostentatious leisure and conspicuous consumption. Different to the past, however, was the way in which the farm servants were no longer an expression of their masters' aspirations for power and prestige – the upwardly mobile peasantry did not use the income from farming to invest in the upkeep of a landless clientele. In this changed social setting, the caste-class of agricultural labour was commodified and converted into a rural proletariat. The dominant landowners also gave expression to their capitalist rationale when they switched to crops that were less labour intensive and/or required less farm management. In the late-colonial decades, the Anavil Brahmans had already started planting mango orchards, which enabled them to fulfil their desire for a lifestyle as landlords but on the basis of a distinct capitalist mode of production (Breman 1974a). The Kanbi Patidars, with a modest background as peasant cultivators in their immediate past[3] achieved the same objective by switching to sugar-cane in the 1950s. The crop schedule was much more labour-intensive than the earlier ones for millet and cotton had been but the organization of production put an end to self-cultivation and self-management. The farmers set up co-operatives and agro-industrial enterprises (first for ginning cotton, half a century later for sugar-cane crushing and processing) that took over supervision of field operations and recruited a vast army of seasonal migrants for the duration of the harvest campaign (Breman 1978–9 and 1985).

In my perception colonial policies had contributed to the emergence of a dominant class-caste of landowners in most parts of India, a background that explains why this landowning elite at the local level was also the main beneficiary of the land reforms carried out around Independence. Having established themselves in the colonial era in hegemonic control at the apex of the village, Anavil Brahmins and Kanbi Patidars in Gujarat, and Jats, Reddys, etc. elsewhere, spearheaded the transition to agrarian capitalism. The blinding poverty at the lower end of the agrarian hierarchy that Thorner witnessed in his travels around the states persisted because this local oligarchy refused to provide the land-poor and landless with adequate income and opportunities of employment that would safeguard their existence and protect them against adversities that put their social reproduction at risk. The already dispossessed and

---

[3] With their domicile in Central Gujarat, the Kanbis had been a rough and vulgar class but slowly gained in respectability, David Hardiman noticed. 'They had worked the fields with their own hands. As their position improved in the late nineteenth century, they hired labourers for dirty work and improved their standing within the caste by becoming vegetarian and forbidding widow remarriage' (Hardiman 1977: 54). Still in their low caste status in Charotar many Kanbis used to be engaged as sharecroppers by the higher-ranking Patidars whom they emulated. David Pocock hinted at their even more humble background as landless labourers employed by the low-caste Bareiyas of Rajput stock. The latter claimed to have lost their holdings to the upwardly mobile Kanbis who, accordingly, also overtook them in the caste ranking (Pocock 1973: 75–6).

marginal owners had no other choice than to try and obtain credit from moneylenders to hang on and make do as best as they could. Forced to mortgage their smallholdings in return for usurious cash loans, many self-cultivating but land-poor peasants slid down to the level of tenants or sharecroppers of their own fields. Below them the landless were forced to hypothecate their labour power as security for the contracted debt. Surplus value was squeezed out of the agrarian workforce in a strategy of exploitation aimed at accumulation. However, it was not the brand of capitalism that Thorner was eagerly looking for: a maximal rate of profit as the outcome of investment in production and productivity. In his argument this had been the pathway of urban-industrial modernization that transformed the imperial countries in achieving growth and development. The labour intensity of the production transition from agrarian-rural to industrial-urban in the Global North had been high. However, after an initial period of immiserization caused by the commodification of labour (Polanyi 1944), this model of industrial capitalism started to improve the bargaining position of the working class, facilitated schooling and skilling and brought many other gains. The problem of social inequality was tackled with state mediation and a fair deal agreed upon by all stakeholders. The turning tide found expression in a standard labour contract that boiled down to a compromise between the interests of labour and capital and found its climax in the emerging welfare state. It was this trajectory that the founding fathers of the Indian nation had in mind as the blueprint for the future. However, there were striking dissimilarities between the colonizing and colonized countries at the start of the process: any idea that a parallel development, a follow-in-your-footsteps kind of restructuring, would enable the latecomers held back in stagnation to catch up with the transforming frontrunners was misconceived from the very beginning. Capitalism came to India in a colonial incarnation and this extraterritorial control over the forces of production contributed to the reification of economy and society in an appropriation of surplus-value mode of production that culminated in the exploitation and oppression of the peasantry in the lower ranks. While intensifying the long-standing process of dispossession, it did not result in an agrarian proletariat that became double free in the orthodox Marxist sense – free from means of production as well as free to sell it labour power at the best possible price in the labour market.

The Agricultural Mode of Production Debate

How should we characterize the merciless extraction that was the focus of Thorner's concern? The views he expressed were contributions to a sequence of debates in the 1960s–70s on the nature of the prevailing mode of production. It was the Indian version of the seminal debate in Europe around the turn of the twentieth century on the role of agriculture and its producers in the progressive transition to industrial capitalism. Economists from different schools of thought took part in the discussion and their contrasting perceptions were mostly published in the pages of *Economic and Political Weekly*.[4] Amit Bhaduri attributed the backwardness prevailing in Indian agriculture to semi-feudalism, a condition that had more in common with the classic master-serf relationship than with industrial capitalism. Its features were roughly the same ones that Thorner distinguished: sharecropping, perpetual indebtedness of the land-poor peasantry and the main landowners as lenders of consumption loans (Bhaduri 1973: 120–1). But Thorner had explicitly and quite appropriately rejected the idea that changes in India's agricultural order could be compared to the European evolution from feudalism to capitalism.[5] So if it were not a stage in the transition between these two production regimes, what was the character of India's post-colonial peasant economy?

A decade after the publication of his five lectures on land reform Thorner seemed to have changed his opinion. On his return to India for a second stint he again travelled far and wide to see the rural lay of the land. In his tour notes of 1966–7 he reported capitalist stirrings in the countryside.[6] In a brief note, comments provoked by an article which Ashok Rudra et al. had published on big farmers in Punjab, Thorner reported that he had found capitalism spreading from the cities across the surrounding countryside. 'Gentlemen farmers' was his label for an assortment of industrialists, professionals, military officers, civil servants – all high-caste, well-to-do and urban-based people eager to invest money subject to taxation in non-taxable agrarian ventures (Thorner 1978: 223–38). It was not a very plausible follow-up to his quest, and Amiya Bagchi gently took him to task for it in an otherwise warm appraisal (Bagchi 1981). Although having second thoughts about the absence of capitalism in the agrarian economy and now highlighting its appearance on an all-India scale – Thorner ended his note on his latest tour by concluding that capitalistic farmers seemed to be the most rapidly growing formation in rural India and already the most powerful element

---

[4] The essays were never brought together in an edited volume in India. The ones referred to are from a pirated edition published anonymously in Lahore in 1978.

[5] 'I would suggest that the idea of feudalism in rural society in India be relegated to the same quiet corner as the terms "Asiatic" or "Oriental" society' (Thorner, A. & D. 1962: 11).

[6] 'Capitalist Stirrings in Rural India: Tour Notes', republished in *The Shaping of Modern India* (Thorner, D. 1980: 223–38).

where they materialized– Thorner was wary about the prospects for the multitude of land-poor peasants for whom the new and path-breaking mode of production would remain a forlorn option (Thorner 1980: 253). And if indeed the depressor had been lifted, what did it mean for the largest working class in the country, that of agricultural labour? A mixed bag was his short answer. Thorner's stocktaking did not differ from the received wisdom that claimed bondage and capitalism to be incompatible. This was a major reason for him to deny that capitalism was of late-colonial vintage and, the other way round, led him to recognize in the first stirrings of capitalism the end of labour bondage. His pertinent observation in *Land and Labour in India* was that 'to speak of capitalism in the nineteenth century, when the agricultural labourers were largely unfree, may be quite misleading' (Thorner, A. & D. 1962: 11–12). In an unpublished conference paper (included in Thorner 1980),[7] his verdict was that apart from in a few specified pockets landless servitude no longer existed:

... the various forms of bondage and unfree labour services, which were formerly rampant in many parts of India, have now virtually disappeared, except in States still notorious for this, as parts of Bihar and adjacent areas. (Thorner 1980: 246)

Nevertheless, Thorner remained ambiguous over his reconsidered opinion that 'in every major region of India today there is a boom in capitalist agriculture' (Thorner 1980: 238). It was a scepticism he did not hesitate to express and which was also emphatically endorsed by other scholars participating in the mode of production debate. His final conclusion writing on the subject was clear. Holding on his ambivalence, he now stressed the bewildering complexity of the situation. The heated debate over agricultural modes of production led him to argue that to do justice to the complexity and diversity, it would be better to suggest that there might be more than one capitalist mode of production:

... it is quite possible that "capitalism" is such an overloaded term that it may have to be broken up into four or six or even eight sub-categories; possible into several modes of production. (Thorner 1980: 387)

My dissenting point of view is that the built-in depressor that Thorner correctly identified does not concern an outdated and reified mode of production. It was a regime that did not fade away, for a variety of reasons, and should be regarded as the manifestation of a modality of capitalism that had already begun to penetrate India's agrarian economy

---

[7] The Emergence of Capitalist Agriculture in India. Unpublished paper presented at the Conference of European Scholars on South Asia, Cambridge 1968.

in the second half of the nineteenth century. The classical maxim that 'land was to rule' , as discussed by Walter Neale (1962), no longer applied under late-colonial authority. Land waited to be cultivated, however, not by investment in growth of production and productivity but by keeping the subaltern *kisans* and *mazdur log* weighed down in unfreedom. The depressor did not obstruct the arrival of capitalism; it was rather the form in which capitalism manifested in the peasant landscape of colonial India.

Taking his cue from a set of articles in which Terry Byres restated the agrarian question in the rural economy of what became labelled poor countries, Henry Bernstein persuasively argued that:

There are no longer any pre-capitalist agrarian classes to be the carriers of a transformation; pre-capitalist peasant and landlord classes have, by now, been almost universally transformed into capitalist farmers, petty commodity producers and 'classes of labour', all existing within capitalist social relations (Bernstein 1996: 42–3);

… 'generalized commodity production' already ruled in agriculture across the globe at the end of colonialism and, concurrently, so did capitalist relations of production and reproduction. (Bernstein 2006: 454)

I agree with both Bernstein and Jens Lerche (Lerche 2013) in their conclusion that the agrarian question as originally framed has lost the substantive meaning it once had.[8] In the region of my fieldwork commercialization and monetization strengthened the hold traders and moneylenders of the Baniya-Brahman upper-caste cluster had over the cultivation and marketing of the new cash crops. Landlordism of the *ancien régime* went into decline but, spurred on by colonial policies, a new class-caste of landowners, imbued with the spirit of capitalism, emerged to take control of the social relations of production. Their increasing dominance at the grassroots was part of a strategy of accumulation that should be defined not only in economic but also in political, social and cultural terms. Concentration of property, power and status at the top of the village hierarchy was reinforced by the ongoing dispossession of the subjugated echelons of the peasantry who were the actual tillers of the land. The leverage exercised by the dominating caste-class of farmers in the countryside steadily widened the gap between winners and losers in the restructured agrarian economy. An ingrained ideology of inequality became embedded in a new mode of production that resulted not in a fair

---

[8] For a further discussion on the specific nature of the agrarian question in the setting of India, see also Bosale in Kumar 2016: 277–311.

deal for peasant labour but an outcome in which the poorest were both excluded and exploited.

This dynamic of change, which ran counter to emancipatory progress, was legitimized by the land reform operation in the aftermath of Independence. Reflecting on how the appropriation of land above the fixed ceiling took place and why its promised redistribution to the dispossessed peasantry failed to be achieved, brought Thorner to reiterate a conclusion he had already drawn with his wife Alice in 1962:

... to the extent that government policies in India were promoting anything in the countryside, it was not socialism but the growth of capitalism. (Thorner 1976: 2; Thorner, A. & D. 1962: 12)

In my reading of the political economy during the subsequent decades the in-built depressor that exploited and oppressed the lower castes-classes was not phased out. It spread wider and became distinct in what was initially called an urban informal sector. Squeezing labour as a routine and accepted practice also infiltrated into the formalized economic activity that had sprung up in the late-colonial centres of growth. The earlier policy trend from informal to formal employment was turned around to deregulation, even to the extent that by the end of the twentieth century informality had become the organizing principle of the whole economy (Breman 2004, 2013a). Growth and accumulation were promoted but in a mode of production more detrimental than beneficial to the bottom ranks of the workforce. This was definitely not the industrial type of capitalism envisaged as the model to follow in the long-awaited pathway to development. The capitalism that I have observed operating over half a century in my rural and urban sites of fieldwork in Gujarat is of a different brand that I tend to classify as being grounded in mercantile-cum-financial interest, property and power. It has no concern for the plight of the masses of men, women and children who are overworked and paid a pittance when employed but ruthlessly laid off on the spur of the moment when declared redundant to demand. If capital accumulation is considered to be better served by other means than the extraction of surplus value from agrarian labour, the presence of this swelling and footloose reserve army is experienced as a nuisance. The in-built depressor did not let up and has in its further trajectory resulted in prolonging the existent large-scale impoverishment.

Before further elaborating on this outcome I would first like to put forward the thesis that the agrarian question should not be regarded as having withered away. On the contrary, looked at from a somewhat different perspective one could argue that its relevance and urgency has increased. This point of view is at variance with the current wisdom as discussed above but I shall briefly substantiate why revisiting the agrarian question does not necessarily involve a rerun of the debate as it has been waged in the past. It was previously taken for granted that the transformation going on in Europe implied a major change in the fabric of economy and society, broadly understood as a shift from an agrarian-rural to and industrial-urban order. The grand metamorphosis awaited would not merely irreversibly reshape society as it had done in the Global North but was also scheduled to become the pathway to follow for the still stagnating underdeveloped Global South. With the regime of capitalism slowly spreading worldwide, increasing the pace of change after decolonization in the mid-twentieth century, industry and industrial workers were going to dominate the overall structure of the global economy. The rising trend in living standards, leading to a general state of improved well-being and welfare, would enable the mass of mankind who had been left behind to escape their rural habitat and settle down in urban localities to partake with their much higher income levels in the comfort of modernity and indulge in consumerism. Another half a century later the realization set in that this changeover trajectory from imposed backwardness and scarcity to emancipation and welfare had failed to materialize. The promised march forward of the workforce from field to factory, facilitated by schooling and skilling, did not take place at the expected scale. For a variety of reasons – such as the tenacious market hegemony of the early industrializers and the fact that innovation in technology led to a rapid decline in the absorption of labour in industrial production – the predicted massive change in employment did not happen. However, due to the already high and still rising man-to-land ratio large segments of the agrarian population, the land-poor and landless in particular, are being driven out of agriculture and for lack of other steady work opportunities also out of the countryside. The urban economy is flooded with masses of newcomers who hope to find better prospects for a partly decent livelihood, at least. While the agrarian-industrial transition has failed to materialize, the impoverished segment of the working population has become footloose – the rate of urbanization is much higher than in the past. But this conclusion needs to be critically examined. The absence of proper jobs and of sufficient pay for the erratically available waged work has resulted in a deeply problematic type of urban living. This is seen in a preponderance of slums, which have come to dominate city and town life (Davis 2006). A marked presence of incomplete households both at the site of departure and at arrival indicates the tendency of workers to pass through as transients rather than settle down in regulated residences. Even the urban zones in which the non-poor dwell, in conditions of much greater stability, face increasing habitat problems caused by traffic congestion and pollution. Environmental degradation is aggravated by the absence of a public domain – parks, squares, greenery, playgrounds, lanes to walk and cycle along – destroyed in the commodification of space and the marketization of public provisions. Life in the mega-cities, with their polluted environments, is increasingly unsustainable, even unlivable – especially in congested metropolitan areas with their lack of amenities and degraded levels of maintenance. Underlying the spurt in urban growth is the incapacity and unwillingness of neoliberal capitalism to generate enough decent jobs for India's growing workforce both at home (in the village) and away from it (in the city). It is against this ominous background that I think the time has come to take a fresh look at the agrarian question. Let me clarify that it should be part of a much wider political and policy framework, in an effort to try and find a way out of the conundrum of jobless growth, the dire lack of social security and, as a direct consequence, a stark rise in ineqality between deepening poverty and staggering wealth. The search for inclusive progress should be based on a sense of bonding in togetherness, a commonality prioritizing solidarity rather than allowing for boundless accumulation, on a spirit of moderation restraining the urge to satisfy unlimited wants, on sharing in solidarity instead of giving in to the urge for rank competition. It is an agenda that implies the imperative need to defeat the ethos and praxis of neoliberal capitalism.

To elaborate on the broader canvas for such an ambitious design is beyond the scope of this treatise but rurality and a reinvigorated peasant economy should figure in a major way in the reappraisal of planned development. In the exploration of this route to a better future several schools of thought can be distinguished. Ela Bhatt, the famed founder of the Self-Employed Women's Association in Ahmedabad, which has branched out to become the biggest trade union in the informal economy, has in the venerable Gandhian tradition designed a model for small-scale rural reconstruction (Bhatt 2015). From an agronomic point of view, some have argued that the crisis of primary production looming not only in India but also worldwide requires a fundamentally different approach to the business of farming. One can be sceptical of the manner in which Jan Douwe van der Ploeg (Ploeg 2009) has made the case for boosting the trend he discerns in favour of re-peasantization. However, there can be no denying that from a political economy perspective a reversal from urban to rural living as well as from industry to agriculture would make eminent sense. This would be justified not only for reasons of ecology and demography but also for coping with waged worklessness and to bring under societal control the balance between capital and labour, which has run haywire – escalating in relentless inequality. Of course, such a turnaround would not be feasible without a thorough overhaul of the social relations of production, which requires a major redistribution of land and other capital assets as well as an infrastructural and institutional reconstruction of the countryside. In the present political configuration such a fundamental reversal of today's order in the face of the powers that be at both global and national levels seems a pipe dream. But the top-down obstruction to finding an alternative pathway to the future – there is an alternative - should not restrain us, while in taking stock of the ravages of untamed capitalism, to express our support for attempts to redirect development politics and policies to the welfare of nature and humanity.

Dealing with Insolvency

What was the size of the debt the commodified *hali* used to run up? In my first round of fieldwork in 1962–3 I tried to calculate the budget available to a sample of landless households over intervals of a few weeks in different seasons in order to figure out the flow of income and expenditure. The survey failed to result in the set of concrete and reliable data I was looking for. The condition of indigence in which most Halpatis live does not easily lend itself to the collection of such numerical evidence. Respondents reacted haphazardly, vaguely and dismissively to my concrete and pointed questions. In their reluctant reactions I detected a mixture of ignorance, indifference and suspicion. Farm servants were no less evasive in responding when I asked them when, how and at what price they became attached to their master: the contract had been made with their father or elder brother; in other cases it was the cumulation of a series of petty advances for services to render later on, which slowly came to a much higher amount, that made the transition from casual wage earner (*chhuta*) to farm servant (*kayem*) inevitable. The daily ration of food grains (*bhata*) that had been converted into a monetized equivalence was the major wage item (eight *annas* for farm servants, twelve *annas* for casual earners) and should hypothetically have allowed me to 'guesstimate' the annual income for agricultural workers. In addition, that calculation resulted in ambiguous data. Variation in days of employment and fluctuation in the going wage rate between peak and slack seasons for casual work could only be found out by continuous and meticulous registration, a task beyond the scope of a single-handed fieldworker. To gather information on hidden income e.g. from theft of crops or the substantial expenditure on illegally distilled alcohol was even more difficult. More quantification was certainly possible but would have required a different method of investigation to the one I used. Of course, I also checked with employers how much they spent on fixing a *hali* with loans and tying down *chhuta majoor* with small cash advances to claim their labour power on busy days. The landowners turned out to be equally unable or unwilling to provide this information with any degree of reliability. Farm servants, when not employed, did claim the daily food ration but if the master was willing to oblige and paid out in kind this non-worked wage, it was added to the accrued debt given in kind but written up as a cash amount. However, details of the 'loans' given were withheld from the receivers. My attempt to gauge the magnitude of indebtedness was not the only one made in vain. The Hali Enquiry Committee earlier discussed reported that:

> It was not possible to collect information about indebtedness of the Hali families examined, because the illiterate Halis have no idea about the extent of their borrowings from the Dhaniyama. Besides, not all Dhaniyama even maintain accounts which can be useful for finding out the amounts borrowed and returned by the Halis from time to time . . . A scrutiny of the purposes of the debts from the Dhaniyama's books of accounts showed that the borrowed money was utilised in the purchase of necessities like food, clothes, shoes, sickles, materials for repair of the hut, to meet expenses on sickness and maternity and ceremonies following the death of relatives. (Report of the Hali Labour Enquiry Committee 1948: 20)

The findings of the Minimum Wages Advisory Committee of 1966 showed that not much had changed in the interlude of nearly two decades. Pointing out that borrowings against future wages and default in repayment of loans were rampant, the report surmised that most of the debts of agricultural labourers would be incurred for consumption purposes and implied their perpetual bondage and exploitation (Government of Gujarat 1966: 39–43). Behind this façade of opaqueness I discerned that both parties to the labour contract vehemently disagreed on what they owed each other. This is in my regard the main reason for the lack of clarity on the size and record of indebtedness, rather than feigned ignorance or failure to register on both sides. While landowners tended to exaggerate the claim they had on labour services in lieu of advance payments made, *halis* were inclined to consider these 'loans' as postponed wage components due to them to compensate for the deficit in the daily household budget they needed for sheer survival. They steadfastly refused to surrender their tenacious claim to livelihood.

How does my micro-level perception of indebtedness of the rural proletariat in south Gujarat accord with the macro-level and large-scale accounts on this issue? I have extensively referred in the first part of this study to the two Agricultural Labour Enquiries, which also included information on the budget deficit of this huge workforce. An intensive survey conducted in the first round in 1950–1 found that nearly half of the families investigated were indebted, a percentage that rose to nearly two-thirds of all households in the second round held in 1956–7; the average amount of debt had doubled from Rs. 47 to Rs. 88 in the six years that had passed. These were very pertinent figures and precisely for this reason quite disputable. The first volume, published in 1954, included the warning that the data collected during the survey should not be taken at face value:

The agricultural labourers mostly did not maintain any proper accounts of their assets and liabilities and often put too much reliance on their creditors in regard to their debt position. This was more so in the case of attached workers, the bulk of whose borrowings was from their employers. Besides, being illiterate, the agricultural labour families were also incapable of giving precise information on their debt position, and it was therefore difficult to get at the exact figure of debt, rate of interest, source and purpose of debt, etc. (Government of India. Ministry of Labour, vol. I (All India) 1955: 155)

In light of the reservations expressed one wonders how the estimates and the stated increase over time were worked out with a fair degree of reliability. In their scathing review of the first Agricultural Labour Enquiry, Alice and Daniel Thorner (Thorner, A. & D. 1962: 173–88) foregrounded the distinction made between attached and casual as the most fundamental one. They criticized the directors of the nationwide investigation for not having properly investigated the implications of this categorical divide and blamed them for understating the unfreedom inherent in the notion of attachment and for underestimating the size of the workforce held captive. The definition the Thorners gave of labour bondage was crystal clear and remains today as astute and valid as it was when written:

An unfree, or bond, labourer . . . is one whose bargaining power is virtually non-existent, or has been surrendered. Such a labourer does not possess the right, or has yielded the right, to refuse to work under the terms set by his master. Through custom, compulsion, or specific obligation, the bond labourer is tied to his master's needs. He can neither quit nor take up work for another master without first receiving permission. (Thorner, A. & D. 1962: 21)

I could not agree more, but this succinct appraisal is in my view difficult to reconcile with Daniel Thorner's claim in his later writings that with the further spread of 'capitalist stirrings', as he termed it, and the widening of the labour market labour bondage would also disappear from the last pockets where it was still holding out (Thorner 1980: 246). Debt was indeed the instrument with which segments of the working classes at the bottom of the economy were chained in unfreedom in the past as well as the present.

The dominant class-caste of farmers became increasingly reluctant to disburse loans. While they had little choice other than to give in to the persistent pressure to provide credit, they tried to keep the scale and frequency of 'advances' to a minimum. After all, the chances of repayment either in work or in cash were minimal in case of default since there were no legal provisions that held labourers accountable for the debt they had run up with employers. Landowners could no longer rely on the government's unconditional support in their attempt to subjugate labour by attaching them in debt. Even if officials rarely took action against employers who transgressed the few and inffective labour laws, the landless knew all too well that attempts to manipulate them through indebtedness were not backed up by penal sanctions. To reclaim the outstanding loans from the debtor was useless because they had been instantly spent when given. Trying to retrieve the money from the assets of the *hali* household also made no sense since the average value of possessions was estimated at Rs. 11, while one-third of the families investigated had no valuables at all (Report of the Hali Labour Enquiry Committee 1948: 19). The average property found added up to an amount equal to around two weeks' earnings. Relations between the labour contract's two stakeholders were continually strained and easily erupted into serious conflict.

Not many other macro-sets of data are available that assess in detail the indebtedness burdening the dispossessed classes in the rural economy. However, recognizing the need for sound data, the Government of India followed up on the first and second Agricultural Labour Enquiries by broadening the scope to include all rural labour households, instead of restricting the survey to agricultural labour households alone. Hence, the third enquiry in the series – with the changed name, the first Rural Labour Enquiry (RLE) – was conducted in 1963–5. This was followed by the second in 1974–5, the third in 1977–8, the fourth in 1983, the fifth in 1987–8, the sixth in 1993–4, the seventh in 1999–2000 and the eighth in 2004–5. The ninth enquiry in the series was conducted during the sixty-sixth round (2009–10) of the NSS (National Sample Survey). Households deriving half or more of their total income from wage-paid manual labour in agricultural activity were classified as agricultural labour. A clear indication of the proletarianization of the peasantry between the first and the most recent round of these large-scale investigations is that, clubbed together, the proportion of rural and agricultural labour households to all rural households increased from 47.2 per cent in 1963–5 to 66 per cent in 2009–10. More than 4 out of 5 belonged to the depressed segments of Scheduled Castes, Scheduled Tribes and Other Backward Castes. Information on indebtedness in this series of reports is not only scant but also questionable. In view of the trend towards progressive dispossession, the steady decline in the percentage of indebted households from 60.6 in the first round to 36.2 in the last one is difficult to accept at face value – and more so because the average debt per indebted household went up from Rs. 244 in 1963–5 to Rs. 13,090 in 2009–10. The striking contrast in these figures remains unexplained. Cost of food (cereals mainly) had come down from more than 70 per cent to just under 60 per cent of all expenses but to interpret this shift as a clear sign of improvement is contentious. Over time expenditure has become thoroughly monetized and a larger part of the household income has to be set aside for other urgent needs that require cash such as clothing, housing and health. There is no good evidence to suggest that a large majority of land-poor and landless households manage to run a lower budget deficit than they had in the past, or even run no deficit at all. To bridge the gap between inadequate income and rising expend-iture, advance wage payment, loans, credit or whatever other term is deemed suitable, going into debt is the only way for the impoverished masses to cope to some extent with their insolvency.

My surmise is that the liability of debtors to work off the cash amounts they received remained beneath the radar of the Rural Labour Enquiries (RLE). But their obligation to pay off what they owed with labour was duly picked up by the National Commission on Rural Labour (NCRL). This panel commented on the RLE findings and argued that wages below subsistence needs forced the labouring families to contract 'con-sumption loans' for sheer survival. The NCRL called this the most important aspect of the indebtedness of rural labour and added that the budgetary deficiency was inextricably linked to the extremely high degree of dispossession among rural labour families:

.... because they have little to offer by way of collateral, institutional credit is not easily available to them, and they have to borrow from rich landowners, professional moneylenders, shopkeepers, and the like, especially for consumption purposes. Such credit not only involves a very high rate of interest (which may even be 100 per cent per annum or more), but also tends to be linked with other economic and non-economic transactions. A borrower may be forced to work for the provider of credit at a very low wage rate or without payment of wages, he may have to surrender a part or whole of his output to a moneylender at an exploitative price, and so on. (Government of India, Ministry of Labour 1991 vol. I: 49)

The Labour Bureau is responsible for processing and disseminating data collected by the RLE. Fieldwork for the eighth survey in the series was undertaken by the NSSO in 2004–5 and one of the reports published as the outcome of this round concerned indebtedness of rural labour households. Agricultural and rural labour households taken together constituted two-thirds of all rural households. The incidence of indebtedness had increased to nearly half of these households, twice as much as the percentage found in the previous survey in 1999–2000. This doubling in a period of five years, mentioned without further explanation, contributes to my scepticism as to the reliability and verifiability of the data presented in the RLE series. The incidence of indebtedness was higher among the somewhat lesser deprived, which again indicated that dispossession goes at the cost of creditworthiness and tends to spiral poverty into pauperism. Spelling out the purpose of debt shows that more than half was spent on household consumption and life-cycle events (marriage, in particular). The percentage was actually higher because house construction and repair should also have been included as part of this calculation. In the case of tribal communities such as the Halpatis, the total in these categories would constitute more than two-third of the debt amount. It adds up to a total that in my view demonstrates that in the long transition from a subsistent to a market and monetized economy, the rural poor have refused to forfeit their claim to a livelihood that goes beyond mere survival. No doubt, avoiding starvation is their overriding priority. But the basic-needs strategy to which they are attuned impels them to aspire for a lot more than food security alone. Their claim is *social* reproduction, the attainment of a life standard that provides a fair measure of decency and dignity. Hoping to realize this deeply felt urge to gain in (self-) respect they are willing to land themselves in debt. The paradox is evident because it is an entrapment that for the time being restricts their maneuverability and bargaining power until they have worked off the burden that keeps them attached.

Moneylenders were identified as the major source of debt while friends/relatives as well as shopkeepers provided micro-credit. Indeed, I witnessed in the course of my fieldwork the arrival of shopkeepers in the landless colonies. In my first village research the *hali* household used to get almost all of what they consumed from the master's household in kind. Without a single shop in their neighbourhood, the main cash expense was on alcohol bought from illegal distillers in their own midst. Already then much more of the landless budget used to be spent on this item alone than was registered in all official enquiries, which could not report expense prohibited by law even though the amounts owed to the local drink sellers were not insignificant. In the course of time shopkeepers have become important figures in the working-class habitat willing, albeit perforce and selectively, to allow labouring households known to them to run up a tab on days or weeks of unemployment. Institutional credit has by and large remained beyond the reach of the land-poor and landless classes. The RLE report 2004–05 classified employers as lenders of rural labour households with a negligible 5–6 per cent near the bottom of the source list, while they actually should have been ranked with a much higher proportion close to the top. Jobbers, foremen and (sub-) contractors, but also big farmers, traders, shopkeepers, etc., engage in moneylending as very profitable sidebusiness. These suppliers of informal credit, who chain labour to capital at a usurious rate of interest that may run up to 120 per cent per year, remain totally absent from official surveys filed in the annals of the state. This is in contrast to local-level case studies on the impact made by the Mahatma Gandhi National Rural Employment Guarantee Scheme (MNRGS, colloquially abbreviated to *narega*), reporting that of wages earned one-fifth to one-third had to be spent on repayment of debt (Sahu 2017: 250). The conclusion I derive from this ongoing failure of registration is that the NSSO, the agency commissioned to report on what is going on in the rural economy, has wilfully neglected to take account of debt bondage. It means that this series of macro-investigations have from beginning to end missed out on the crucial role indebtedness plays as an instrument of capital to hold labour captive in (neo-) bondage. I have already documented when and how this transpires in circular short-term migration, a type of mobility in which a huge army of land-poor and landless labour is involved because of their redundancy at home, temporarily or chronically. In the next and last section of this chapter I shall elaborate on how other contingents of the rural as well as urban workforce are contracted in a similar condition of immobility.

A state of acute crisis affects not only agriculture but the rural economy at large. Although this is an undeniable conclusion shared by all stakeholders, politicians and policymakers have so far failed to address let alone redress the problem, which imperils the life and work prospects of a major part of the country's population. Malcolm Darling's famous dictum that the Indian peasant is born in debt, lives in debt and dies in debt has been often quoted. To the extent that it appears to have become normalized as a natural condition, indebtedness must be endured stoically and with resilience. But in recent years many thousands of farmers, the overwhelming majority of them owners of small or marginal holdings, have committed suicide to get out of an ordeal of default and bankruptcy they were no longer able and willing to face. The media have reported widely on these signs of ultimate despair, as well as on the self-serving comments of senior politicians who refused to be held accountable for the drama that unfolded. What I find striking is that such tragic cases are also quite common among the totally dispossessed, the members of landless castes-classes who have lost the vitality any longer to endure sliding down a slope to the condition of being treated as less than human. I have come across such instances of alienation leading to suicide in sites at home or at work in the course of my fieldwork. It seems that many occurrences of suicide among the down and out fail to be put on public record. Having spent their life at the margins of society they also leave unnoticed, usually alone although sometimes with wife and children. While loan waivers are meant to rehabilitate farmers burdened by indebtedness, the dire conditions into which the agrarian proletariat has sunk is consistently unaddressed. The presence of landless labour as a major segment of the agrarian workforce is not mentioned at all in official reports on how to cope with the agrarian crisis, as for instance in the one drafted by an Expert Group on Agricultural Indebtedness (Government of India, Ministry of Finance, Department of Economic Affairs 2007). In their dispossessed condition these tillers of the land qualify neither for free cash handouts nor for formal credit and often, due to lack of collateral to back up a loan request, are also turned down for informal credit. The survival strategy on which they are forced to fall back is to sell the labour power of one or more members of their household in advance, in debt bondage.

The Absence of a Regular Payday

A standard labour contract is a goal in the working-class fight for progress all over the world. Its main feature is regularity, and this can take many forms. The contract offers continuity and stability in employment. Once this level of security has been achieved, many other gains are possible – in the form of labour rights bargained for through collective action. Past struggles yielded a higher wage; restrictions in the length of the workday and working life; and protection against adversity (Breman & van der Linden 2014). In terms of wage payment modalities the standard labour contract was associated with the shift from wages given in kind to payment in cash – and, subsequently, the change from earnings being settled by piece rate to payment on a specified time rate. A third but much less frequently noted dimension of regularity was the conversion from erratic to steady wage settlement, captured in the notion of the payday. The transition from haphazard to fixed and full payment of wages earned in a regular schedule enabled the working classes in the advanced economies to structure the household budget in a less uneven rhythm and allowed them to better adjust expenditure to income. It was a practice long denied India's workforce even in the formal economy. The

Payment of Wages Act 1936 was reluctantly granted by employers and did no more than concede payment of wages in the middle of the month after the one worked for; it was used as a weapon against insubordination and desertion. The system of wage-arrears meant that regular mill workers remained dependent on usurious moneylenders for their sustenance (Breman 2004: chapters 1 and 2; Sarkar 2018: 98, 259–71). The fast drift away from a formal back to an informal regime has put paid to many of the gains made in the realm of work and employment. My comment on this reversal has to start by pointing out that the earlier trend towards formalization was not only short but remained largely absent in the vast landscape of my investigations, among the labouring classes at the bottom of the rural and urban economy in Gujarat.

While in my fieldwork villages the contract binding the labourer used to be an oral one, in other parts of India it was written up in a stamped document to suggest that it had legal standing. The first Agricultural Labour Enquiry report included a true copy of such a labour contract executed in Madhya Pradesh in 1949, which spelled out the details:

We hereby agree that I (the executor of the document) shall daily perform all the agricultural work in connection with your cultivation in the village according to the orders passed by you or your representative and shall, after the harvesting of paddy, attend your fields and watch the harvested crop till it is threshed. If on any day your work suffers on account of my negligence I agree that no payment may be made to me for that day. If I am absent for one to three days, I agree to compensate you for the loss caused to you from our wages. I hereby agree to perform your service on these terms and have in lieu of the agreement received an advance of Rs. 300 being the amount of principal, at *Sawai* interest (25 per cent per annum), which comes to Rs. 75, the total thus being Rs. 375. This amount has been received as follows: Rs. 200 cash, Rs. 100 being the price of grain advanced. Total Rs. 300.

I agree to serve on Rs. 18 per month in lieu of the advance mentioned above and agree that this remuneration of Rs. 18 may be adjusted towards the repayment of the debt mentioned above. It is further agreed that for the days on which I shall remain absent no payment may be made to me. I shall continue to serve you until the debt mentioned above is repaid in full and if I leave your service before such full payment it is agreed that we shall, without any objection, pay amount equal to twice the amount of the balance of such debt. This *Nauka Nama* (service bond) is executed by me voluntarily and I hereby agree that it will be a charge on my estate and shall be binding on my heirs. (Government of India. Ministry of Labour 1952 vol. I: 33–4)

The agreement had to be witnessed by a third party who stood security for proper completion of the contract and was held accountable for full repayment of the debt. As can be derived from the calculated interest the expected duration of the contract, duly thumb-printed by the debtor, was for three years. Drawing attention to this attempt at formalizing a relationship that was informally executed from beginning to end, the Thorners noted that the amount of the principal debt plus interest (Rs. 375) was considerably higher than the annual earnings of the worker (Rs. 216). They pointed out that a loan of this magnitude was not likely ever to be repaid, and that repayment was not really expected (Thorner, A. & D. 1962: 33).

The commodified *halis* I encountered in my first round of fieldwork were commonly debt-contracted on a perpetual basis and were supposed to receive their customary wage at the end of each and every workday. While in the past their stipulated wage used to come in kind from the master's household, they now had to buy their daily allowance in the village shop at the higher retail price. The terms of exchange from kind to cash were to their disadvantage and barely kept up with the rate of inflation in subsequent years. On days when there was no work the farm servant could no longer claim the daily wage. The master expected him first to try to find work with another farmer; only in a period of continuing and complete lack of employment, notably during the monsoon, did his boss feel obliged to yield to the *hali's* repeated pleading and give him some coins to buy his daily food. For the same reason the landlords were not prepared to comply with requests a servant deferentially made to defray a high incidental cost – for instance, expenses in case of injury or bouts of illness, a birth or death at home, the collapse of his hut in the monsoon rains, etc. At the same time the master knew that in the end he would have to help out – if he wanted to keep the relationship intact. The farm servant had at least a possible source of credit, even though laboriously obtained. The drawback, however, was profound dependency, since the employer manipulated the debt as a means to compel obedience. The remuneration paid to a servant was determined by the work he had delivered and was likely to deliver. It was a kind of bargaining in which both sides tried to figure out the cost-benefit involved. The time had gone when wages were based on the master's moral obligation to maintain his *hali*. An 'insolent' servant was sometimes not given work for days on end to teach him a lesson. The boss knew how to demonstrate his authority in numerous ways and highhandedly refused to shell out the wage at the end of the workday, sending off his servants saying that he was short of cash and would give them what he owed next day or next week. Their show of adroit and deferential begging for at least part payment could capriciously be granted or denied. In the latter case a child in the servant's household (usually a girl) was sent to the local shop to ask the storekeeper to provide a measure of the staple food, at least enough for the evening meal. Frequently witnessing such a scene during

my first round of fieldwork made me aware of the hand-to-mouth existence that was the normal routine in the landless milieu.

When employed at all, casual labourers were also paid off at the end
of the workday and their precarious budget was run on the same
capricious footing as the much-reduced number of farm servants. For
this growing majority of the agrarian workforce it was of crucial importance to have more than one wage provider in their household in order
to cope with the sharp fluctuations in income versus expenditure. In
comparison to the new brand of *halis* this much larger contingent faced
great difficulty in qualifying even for day-to-day credit, let alone managing to contract loans they needed to pay for more costly outlay on
health care, life-cycle events or housebuilding/repair. Frequent bouts of
unemployment and the extremely low wage rate did not allow them to
save up for such recurrent eventualities. These were dire problems in
particular for the senior age-cohorts among them who did not have the
staying power to work for many hours. The younger ones, if able-
bodied and not much older than 30 years of age, assembled in small
groups and were contracted for building wells, cutting wood and constructing access roads or for a variety of agricultural operations, such as
harvesting paddy, picking fruits, etc. *Udhad* (contract) was a rapidly
spreading employment modality, but not altogether a new one. It was
mentioned as a standing arrangement in the first Agricultural Labour
Enquiry:

There was an annual exodus of about 1,000 workers from Uttar Pradesh and
Vindhya Pradesh into the wheat zone of Madhya Pradesh during the month of
Falgun (February–March). These workers moved and worked in gangs consisting
of men, women and children. Usually two or three families moved together. This
imported labour was engaged on piece rates. The unit for determining the wage
was 20 bundles of approximately a uniform size. An average worker who
harvested 20 bundles of wheat or gram in a day received one bundle as wages;
. . . Members of the entire gang worked together and its leader received the total
remuneration for the work done by all members of the gang. There was no
complaint about the distribution of wages between the members. These
workers earned more than the local employers but were more proficient than
local labour. In certain parts of the rice zone, especially in the Bhandara and
Balaghat districts, the operation of first ploughing, locally known as *Chirata*, and
transplanting were entrusted to a group of workers, the whole field being given on
hunda or contract, to a group for a specific amount. (Government of India.
Ministry of Labour 1952 vol. I : 99–100)

As discussed earlier, in Chapter 6, I also came across such circular
migrants roaming around the region of my research during the high tide
of the agricultural cycle; but the local landless also teamed up in small
gangs to do this type of work. Their frenzied pace at work enabled them

to earn in a couple of weeks much more than casual labour would fetch them outside this peak period. The fluctuating up-and-down remuneration made it difficult to streamline their budget. The total income of these labouring households showed a striking diversity impossible to explain only by the different ratio between earning and dependent members. In addition to this variable I noticed other individualized factors. The leaders of teams or gangs came around in advance to collect a prepayment from big farmers for undertaking to turn up at the proper time and in sufficient strength for the operation contracted. They might or might not hand out part of the advance to recruit hands and also distributed the received earnings at the end, not in equal shares but in accordance with the nature of their relationship to members of the team or gang brought along. Relatives qualified for a higher share than non-relatives but more crucial was whether they belonged to the (constant) core or the (fluid) periphery of the gang that joined them to go around. In the course of time the direct connection between employer and worker had been replaced by linkmen such as jobbers or (sub-) contractors. This trend facilitated the management of labour and indicated the desire of the propertied castes-classes to distance themselves from the dispossessed. Being the linkman between capital and labour had gradually become a professional role. Those taking this mediating role stand out as important figures among the land-poor and landless.

While payday is supposed to be a feature of standard labour contracts, as a regulated fixed point it is alien to the working practices described above. Payment for labour services rendered tends to take place intermittently as the outcome of continuous haggling in what has the character of an ongoing debtor-creditor relationship. In an earlier publication I portrayed this footloose army of labour as wage hunters and gatherers (Breman 1994). Although in their mode of employment traces of bondage can still be discerned, this workforce at the bottom of the economy appears to be engaged in a free-floating drift. It is a state of flux that should also be understood as a strategy to avoid being caught in labour-tying arrangements such as that of the farm servants. However, many among the casualized contingents are not able to escape practices of neo-bondage as documented in Chapter 7. In these manifold instances pre-payment of wages – earnest money handed out at the time of recruitment, at the low tide of the agrarian cycle – is combined with postponed settlement of wages earned in both non-agrarian and agrarian industries, such as brickworks, sugar-cane harvesting, salt-pans, stone quarries, cotton picking, tobacco curing, etc.

The price at which labour is attached for the season depends on workers' productive capacity on a sliding scale for men, women and children. When this debt is worked off neo-bondage perpetuates because wages are only settled on dismissal and the workers go home. They are paid the piece rate but are told what this amounts to no earlier than at the very end of their attachment. They receive their net balance from the jobber who deducts not only their cost of maintenance but also his unspecified commission from the earnings made. Even the cost of maintenance paid out in kind – a grain ration in two-weekly instalments – is provided on the basis of output produced. Those who have missed work due to illness or injury, a trip home on family business or sheer fatigue do not get the full quantity, which means that they will be short of food in the subsequent fortnight and will have to stock up out of their own pocket. In the report on her fieldwork among cane-cutters in the region of my research, Gauri Raje included an entry from her diary that tells of the tension building up while the allowance is being distributed and partly taken back again:

Each sack is slowly filled with the *jowar* (millet) one after another. But no one leaves. As Divli aunt's sack is filled, she snorts to herself, 'eh-he. It's all going to go away. Why do this.' 'Why, where is it going to go?', I ask. Divli is quiet. Her sack is one of the last to be filled. By now I am really puzzled, as everyone is still standing with their filled sacks in front of them, suddenly the silence is palpable. Even the kids are quietly holding on to their mother, aunts or elder siblings . . . By now, and all of this takes no more than a few minutes, Urmilayahaki's brother-in-law, followed by Naru, are back at the beginning of the circle, and emptying some jowar from the. sacks just filled. At each of the sacks, Vechiyabhai calls out the number of turns missed, and Naru spoons out the jowar from the particular sack an equal number of times. Most sacks have at least one turn of jowar emptied. The husband from jungle Amalpada has nearly half his grain gone, and questions the number called by Vechiyabhai. The latter asks him to talk to the *mukaddam* (jobber), since the figures have been given him by the mukaddam. Then a few women break in – 'Well, the mukaddam is not here. And he is fat enough, he won't even know.' 'Tell him you are illiterate anyway.' (Raje 2005)

I encountered similar precarity among the rural migrants who come to Ahmedabad to sell their labour power in one of the early-morning labour markets (*nakas*) that daily operate at intersections and junctions around the city. They are hired for construction work by jobbers, foremen or other agents of the building trade who have come to fetch them for the day or the job. Standing there in a crowd men and women hope to close a deal that fits their unskilled to semi-skilled experience at the going wage rate; bargaining is not much more than saying yes or no to the offer made. The younger and more experienced ones manage to get hired for about twenty days a month, all those among them older than forty years of age are happy if they are picked up on twelve to fifteen days a month.

Work does not always end in pay because being sent off at the end of the day or after a longer bout of engagement without receipt of the full wage is not a rare occurrence. Workers are blamed for whatever goes wrong at the construction site and are docked for lacking performance:

Paliben Dhayabhai Rathod of Navsari Bazar narrated how the behaviour of the contractor changes after the work is completed. When the work is about to be finished, the contractor begins making false complaints. He would say that they have not done the work properly. They have spoiled the work, etc. and then he would withhold part of their wages. 'That is their usual trick and we know this very well', she said. (S. P. Punalekar and A. Patel, quoted in Breman 1996: 149)

The standard excuse of the jobber or contractor for not shelling out is that the builder has not yet settled accounts. But it may also be a ploy to press the workers to continue to be available the next day and week in the hope of full compensation at the end. When further checking on this prevalent abuse I found that on average roughly 20 per cent of the wage sum claimed gets never paid. My final round of fieldwork in 2013–15 was spent in the company of these land-poor and landless people at drift between country-side and city. Pushed out of their village in search of work, they are pushed back again when building comes to a halt with the onset of monsoon. After work and on days of no work they hide away in an illegal *basti*, a camp on the outskirts of the city, a makeshift shelter built of waste material lying around. They are bonded but in a more intricate way than the sugar-cane harvesters or brick-kiln workers I investigated in my earlier fieldwork. These footloose labourers hang around the city's outskirts because indebt-edness at home forces them to migrate in search of work. They try to sell their labour power in order to pay back the money borrowed from big farmers or traders and needed to afford life-cycle events (mainly marriage) or housebuilding or to cope with adversities such as illness, disability and old age in the family. These debts can run up to one *lakh* (100,000) rupees, a liability that is a heavy burden because of the extremely high rate of interest – which may lead to the doubling of the debt for the least credit-worthy ones within a year. Failure to comply with payment of regular instalments is a slippery slope that ends in complete bankruptcy. It comes as no surprise that such mishaps result in breaking away from the village and moving the whole household on a more permanent footing to the illegal camp at the city's periphery (Breman 2016: 186–7).

Wage Theft

In her fieldwork on wage practices at construction sites in Kerala, Mythri Prasad-Aleyamma found an astounding diversity of wage practices.

Koolipani or wage work is the apt label for the thoroughly commodified transaction between buyer and seller. In the city's street-corner markets trade unions keep a watchful eye on hiring and the bargaining over wages – though none of their members may be around. As one female Tamil worker told her:

There are union people here. They are Malayalis. Beyond that car over there. If some worker who stands here goes to work for less than 350 rupees, the fellow workers report to them. They call us and tell us that you cannot go for less than rupees 350. If you are going to work for less, then you need not stand here. They tell us: 'If you are so unhappy, then go back to your places'. It is the head load workers' union of Malayalis who decide this. They then communicate the decision to us. (Prasad-Aleyamma 2017: 15)

Migrants are paid a lower wage and/or work longer hours than local labourers. Trade union officials, supposed to facilitate workers' agency, are in collusion with the building contractors to get a share of the wage differential for the preferential employment of the much cheaper outsiders. She quotes from sources arguing that labour can be defined as unskilled because it is understood to belong to the category of 'inferior' workers or to ensure that 'undesirable' tasks are performed by 'undesirable' people, regardless of their abilities or experience. Non-payment of wages at the sites of her investigations is a widely prevalent practice and the faint efforts of workers to trace their defaulters remain fruitless:

The disparity between 'the going wage rate' and the actually paid wages can be substantial depending on the arrears and the extent of non-payment. This questions our notions of a single wage rate which apply across the board for a certain set of workers and skill level. Breach of contract and cheating are outside the parameters of capitalist rationality. Yet, they are very much central to the accumulation process in capitalism. (Prasad-Aleyamma 2017: 23)

Her resolute conclusion is that wage theft in South Asia is intimately related to histories of unfree labour and debt bondage. Neo-bondage tends to be identified as a form of attachment to which a vast army of labour is subjected, prised out of their habitat for sorties of a shorter or longer span of time but sent away when the activity for which they have been recruited comes to a halt. This workforce, which keeps on circulating between 'home' and 'work' for years on end, is indeed a very substantial segment of men, women and children mobilized for employment in a state of immobility. No reliable statistics are available to work out the size of this footloose multitude and estimates for the last decade vary from 40 million up to 140 million. The size of the proportion among them contracted in debt and unable to leave before they are allowed or even forced to go away again when their labouring presence is no longer required is anybody's guess. Extrapolating from my stock of rural and urban fieldwork findings my own estimate would be close to half of the huge number engaged in one-season to working-lifetime labour nomadism.

In addition, there are several occupational profiles in the informal economy that are quite susceptible to becoming waged or self-reliant in some mode of neo-bondage even though they stay put wherever they have come to. A clear example of postponed payment of wages earned is the *sumangali* system in the textile industry of South India. Factory scouts visit low-income homes to recruit adolescent girls for three years. For the period of employment these girls remain under the close scrutiny of the management. Accommodated in dormitories, they receive in addition to meals only a maintenance allowance in cash while working long shifts in the sweatshops. The main part of the earnings is withheld until the end of the contracted period. Paid out in a lump sum these compulsory 'savings' are meant to take care of the dowry that has to be spent on marriage. But the end balance often turns out to be a smaller amount than earlier promised (Kompier 2015). Forms of attachment are rampant in the textile industry and prevent this workforce, which includes men as well as women, from engaging in collective action. They also are unable to adjust their household expenditure in tune with the erratic flow of wage pay. Geert de Neve has studied how power-loom operators in Tamilnad are contracted in debt and are supposed to work off the amount (*baki*) they have received. But do the workers feel bound, entrapped in a 'voluntary' contract they are obliged to honour indefinitely? Compliance in dependency is exactly what their employers are willing to pay for. The loom operators are aware of this and portray themselves as being bonded in the same way as the permanent farm servants (*pannaiyals*) were in the past. But is bondage the correct term for their labour status? The politics of immobilization happen to be an outright failure. The telling comment of de Neve is that the loom operators did not strike him as being unduly bothered by their attachment. This is because they have devised their own strategy to escape from bondage. For sure, saving up from the wages received to get out of debt and be free from all bonds is, for most of them, next to impossible. Much more prevalent is finding another workshop owner willing to settle accounts with the current boss. Notwithstanding *baki*, labour is indeed footloose. The rotation of this proletariat from one power-loom shed to another undermines the strategies of the employers to control and discipline their workforce (de Neve 2005). In the presentation of her research findings on the sweatshop regime in different parts of the country, Alessandra Mezzadri documents how the piece-rate system, subterfuge modes of wage payment and a myriad of middlemen keep the workforce shackled to their sites of toil in factories, workshops or at home (Mezzadri 2017) – as long as they last, because their working bodies are not up to the relentless pace and the debilitating conditions of the labour process. When these worn-out commodities fail to produce the required output, they have reached the end of their working life, at anywhere between thirty and forty years of age, and are replaced by a fresh cache of victims. Mezzadri concludes that neo-bondage is the operative principle that holds this huge army of footsoldiers captive in multiple forms of unfreedom at the bottom of the global value chain. Wage theft comes in many forms and a common one is to default on the piece-rated tariff. When payment is shelled out for quantity-based production – moulding bricks, cutting stones, manufacture of bidis and incense sticks, sewing garments, etc. – either the boss, jobber or subcontractor take a cut of the wage sum earned, claiming that part of the commodity produced is not up to the quality mark. Discount on 'rejects' often add up to 10 per cent or more of what they think they have earned with their toil.

In the diamond-cutting and -polishing business that I investigated in Surat city, payment of wages is irregular and frequently has to wait until the boss receives payment from the dealers to whom the processed stones

Figure 8.1 Diamond-cutting and polishing – the wage paid is marginal to the value added

are returned. The *kharkanedar* has varying degrees of success in persuading the traders to pay an advance when complying with their orders. On the other hand, the cutters are often unable to wait so long for their earnings, and they ask their patron for an advance, called *baki*. This is not only done to get hold of their wage arrears, but also to meet some items of expenditure that have to be made at various times of the year. The custom is so large-scale and widespread that most experienced diamond-cutters need to continue working to pay off the amount they have taken from their employer, who keeps the worker tied to him. In case of default they are forcefully called to order, as happened in the instance described below:

One morning I observed a stranger walk into the premises of a diamond factory and call out one of the workers. The stranger was talking most of the time and the worker did little more than mumble a few words. After a couple of minutes of this one-sided dialogue a small crowd gathered around the two. The spectators consisted mostly of the worker's colleagues who had come out of the factory. The stranger then started slapping the hapless worker. The worker did not resist; he only tried to protect his face with his hands. The worker's colleagues who had been following the dialogue did not disapprove of this assault. The stranger was a *kharkanedar*. The worker who had been in his employment had taken a loan from him but had left the factory without repaying the loan, or even informing his creditor that he was changing his job. The *kharkanedar* had traced the missing debtor and demanded instant payment. The worker and the *kharkanedar* worked out a compromise whereby the former agreed to return to his old employer and work for him until his debt was fully repaid. The workers and *kharkanedars* are agreed that a worker may leave his employment only after clearing his debt. (M. Kalathil, quoted in Breman 1996: 164)

I could go on listing other occupational profiles in the informal economy ridden with debt bondage. What passes for self-employment is often a disguised form of waged labour. Examples that come to mind are street vendors and home-based workers written up as self-employed but tied to their suppliers in a debt-credit relationship that does not allow them to work and live in freedom. Next there are the domestic servants, minors and adults, both males and females, who spend many years in better-off households taking care of children; do the regular chores of washing, cooking and cleaning; and finally become caretakers of their aging employers. Even if the services rendered do not begin with advance payment, the terms of waged employment tend to be converted into a bonding between a greedy debtor and a reluctant creditor when engagement is full-time and of a perpetual nature. In a narrative on a conflict between a house maid and her madam, Maya John commented on the practice of domestic employers releasing only part of the wage owed to the servant:

Neither do they abide by a fixed day of the month for release of payment. As a consequence, domestic workers are often not paid up to a month to three months. When backlog wages are released, a part of the wages is always withheld to supposedly ensure the commitment of the worker to the (unwritten, implied) contract. Such 'staggered' wages very often violate the initial understanding of the amount fixed between the employer and the worker, especially since the quantity of work extracted far exceeds the remuneration. (John 2018: 24)

The old type of male or female menial with a long-standing, sometimes intergenerational attachment to the family that retained them had features that are comparable to the *hali-dhaniyamo* nexus as it existed in the past. Also in this occupation an increasing sense of instrumentality and loss of familial types of relationship may be noticed. The part-time maids who run between three or four households to wash, cook or clean on a job-specific tariff insist on monthly payment on the dot and are not eager to build up a lasting relationship with their part-time bosses.

It will be clear from the occupational profiles outlined above that debt bondage is a burden that has to be graded in degrees of rigidity. Skilled workers such as power-loom operators and diamond cutters-cum-polishers who operate machines seem to have more agency, which enables them to withstand the economic and extra-economic pressure exercised by the jobber or employer. Their greater assertiveness tends to coincide with an identity that ranks them a little bit higher up in the class configuration – they come from a background with at least some means of production. This is in contrast to the footloose mass fixed at the bottom of the scale, a thoroughly dispossessed multitude that has neither the means to invest in acquiring skills nor the contacts required to make a better deal and work towards a somewhat stable existence. Recurrent or chronic insolvency is the added penalty to their subordination. My contention is that not less than 15 per cent of the country's total workforce, amounting to 50–75 million men, women and children in the informal economy are unable to sell their labour power when, where, to whom and at what price they would want to claim for their livelihood. They are made to work under a regime of duress that varies from moderate to stark severity. More than 80 per cent of them hail from the residual categories of Scheduled Tribes, Scheduled Castes, the lower chunks of the Other Backward Castes and the dispossessed among the Muslim minority.

Part IV

Conclusion

9   Capitalism, Labour Bondage and the Social Question

The High Price of Indebtedness

India's informal economy is capitalist in nature and capitalism has consequently also become the dominant feature of the labour regime in which the country's workforce is engaged. In an earlier publication I elaborated on how the shift to this political economy occurred (Breman 2013a). In this follow-up treatise I have described the character of informal employment within and outside agriculture, in rural and urban settings and for local as well as migrant labourers. Underlying my analysis are the findings of my rounds of fieldwork from 1962 to 2015, all in Gujarat. The focus of my investigations at the grassroots of the economy and of society has been on the castes-classes that are to a large extent or even totally without the means of production and therefore face many difficulties in providing for their livelihood. The main or only capital they possess is their labour power, which they have to sell in order to make a meagre living. Quite a substantial number are dispossessed to the extent that they are unable to freely dispose of the physical force they have and find out how to get the highest possible price and best terms of employment. Tracing the ordeal of this unfree workforce back over time, I have documented how colonial legislation fabricated the idea of a contract to classify as crime what had been custom in order to justify the practice of agrarian bondage all over the country after the abolition of slavery. Being 'liberated' from resources required for production and subsistence did not mean being double-free in the classical Marxist sense. The operative principle of capitalism is the extraction of labour surplus, but there is variety in the manner in which appropriation takes place. As Jairus Banaji has argued, capitalism has insistently tried to draw on and exploit a mix of 'free' and 'unfree' labour (Banaji 2003, Banaji 2010).

Capitalism and bondage are not interdependent. They can and do exist without each other, but neither are they mutually exclusive. The process of labour commodification monitored in this study is distinct from the pre-capitalist type of agrarian bondage that was the subject of my initial fieldwork research. The capitalist nexus that I call neo-bondage is today a major feature of labour exploitation in India's informal economy at large. It is a mode of short-term or long-term employment practised wherever people are recruited for work at sites near to or far away from home. Coming to the end of my village-based investigations a decade ago, I wrote up the predicament of the land-poor and landless castes-classes made footloose in the landscape I had observed for over half a century:

A reserve army of labour has accumulated in rural south Gujarat that can be deployed according to the demands of the moment, in and outside agriculture, in factories and workshops, in construction and the service sector, or to transport goods and people. These working men, women and children are sometimes needed in the towns and sometimes in the countryside. Sometimes they are put to work in the obscure and degraded landscape in between these two extremes: alongside the highways and railway lines, in agro-industrial enclaves, brick-kilns, quarries and saltpans, gathered together in temporary camps that arise where rivers are dammed, where earth has to be moved to dig canals or lay pipelines, where roads have to be laid or bridges and viaducts built, and so on. They live and work at these sites as long as the job lasts. The rest of the time they are confined in slum-like, sprawling settlements on the fringes of villages, squatting with no legal title, waiting until the call comes for them to leave again. If the work is relatively close to home they commute back and forth each day, if it is farther afield they stay away longer, sometimes for whole seasons. But sooner or later the work is completed again and they return to their waiting room that lies beyond the purview of politicians and policy-makers. Yet the fact that these people are hidden away from mainstream society in colonies and transit camps is no reason to label them as marginal and peripheral. They are an army of reserve labour that is at the heart of the predatory capitalism that emerged so violently on the subcontinent of South Asia in the second half of the twentieth century. (Breman 2007a: 409)

I have documented in the earlier chapters of this book how a substantial segment of this intermittently employed workforce is contracted for work under duress by employers or their agents. Driven out of their habitat in search of gainful work, a major chunk of this huge army of labour is recruited in neo-bondage. Informalization and circulation of labour have risen sharply in tandem; immobilization of the reserve workforce, which is hired on and off, is another feature of this configuration. Overemployment, when the engaged workforce is required to work day and night with no let-up, alternates with being laid off for shorter or longer spells in an erratic rhythm that makes official figures and statistical data on unemployment – according to the International Labour Organization, 3.5 per cent were unemployed in India in 2018 – a figment of wishful thinking. By means of advance wage payment, the large numbers or people temporarily or chronically out of work are mobilized in a labour-tying employment that often lacks an exit option – other than running away and the possible forfeiture of back pay. In my analysis exploitation and exclusion are successive stages in the misuse versus disuse of labour. In response to my account on the prevalence of widespread pauperization, Alpa Shah and Jens Lerche argue that because of continual employment pauperism has only diagnostic relevance (Shah & Lerche et al., 2018: 11). In this assessment they fail to take account of the fact that for many of the footloose labouring poor spells of work in bondage interspaced with bouts of unemployment alternate and reinforce each other. The plight of these people is summed up in the combination of being overworked and underpaid when employed and bereft of any means of survival when laid off, a condition that drives them back again into a new round of debt bondage. As demonstrated in Chapter 8, neo-bondage is a mode of engagement for waged work that varies both in length of time and intensity of constraint. Similarly, the free-unfree divide plays out as a continuum ranging from greater to lesser ability to choose when, where and for whom to work (see e.g. Lerche 2007, 2012). More to less free or unfree is how Banaji (Banaji 2003) has labelled these bottom ranks of the workforce. The most thoroughly dispossessed are also at risk of being the most hampered in their labour-market manoeuvrings – without any bargaining power and also socially marginalized.

In the post-colonial era 'the development paradigm', postulated as a transitional route ahead, promised promised to duplicate in a globalized world order the achievements of the advanced economies of the Northern hemisphere. The idea that the countries lagging behind would eventually catch up with the frontrunners has from the very beginning met with severe criticism. Over time the promise of matching prosperity, welfare and social justice across the world has been watered down to Millennium Development Goals that vow to bring down rising levels of poverty. I have argued in the preceding chapters that this pledge has remained unfulfilled for a huge mass of people in India stuck at the bottom of economy and of society. The aim of levelling down inequality has been surrendered and replaced with the aim of merely reducing the vast and rising levels of deprivation. More documentation is required to highlight the divergent tracks between the Global North and South. There is an urgent need for studies that transcend the level of the nation-state (Nayyar 2013). While I am greatly in favour of a wider-ranging analytical approach (Breman 2017; see also Breman et al. 2019), elaboration of a comparative perspective is beyond the scope of this book.

The Rationale of Bondage in a Labour-Redundant Economy

Why is it, when labour is abundantly available and can be fetched from all over the country readily and free of mobility cost, that employers and their agents are willing to shell out large sums of money to contract and tie down the workforce they need? The question arises because the arrangement to pay labour in advance for work to be done later carries the risk of wasting the money invested. Today's employers cannot pursue their defaulting debt-bonded workers in the same way the old type of master used to deal with a trespassing *hali*. Gone are the days when colonial legislation saw to it that farm servants who ran away stood accused of breach of contract and were brought back to work out their attachment – which they had after all, in legalistic jargon, 'voluntarily' entered. As argued in the first part of this study, government can be blamed for having done precious little in the wake of Independence to put an end to the system of labour bondage. The saving grace is that at least workers can no longer be prosecuted and punished for not paying off their debt. The creditors, of course, try to cover themselves against this liability. They hold their recruiting agent, the jobber or labour contractor, accountable for tracking down deserters or replacing them with substitutes at no extra cost. If that remedy fails to fully recover the amount lost, the solution is to deduct it from the jobber's commission at the end of the season. In their turn these labour brokers also have ways of protecting themselves if members of the gang they have recruited do not turn up at the time fixed for departure or if they run away from the work site. In the course of my fieldwork I came to know that the jobbers had parcelled out the terrain of recruitment. They kept in touch on what and how much had been advanced when and to whom in order to blacklist workers who entered into a deal with more than one jobber. But irrespective of such fail-safe attempts to prevent breach of contract, labourers attached in debt bondage are not at all shy of absconding from employment that taxes them beyond tolerance level or – and this is by no means exceptional – because they get a better offer somewhere else.

Employers whom I asked why they continued to fix workers in debt bondage, used to reply indignantly that they were the ones who were bonded. According to them the initial 'loan' as well as subsequent ones had to be given because they would be short of hands if they refused to pay up in advance. This wily retort makes sense only if you disregard their persistent unwillingness to raise the labour price and offer fair conditions of employment. They compete with each other on the size of loans required to tie down their workforce and do not hesitate to outbid a competitor. Ruthlessly driving down the labour cost enables them to run their business at the highest possible profit. I characterize the attachment of labour to the site of their temporary or indefinite employment as commodity fetishism. Debt bondage is designed to keep workers in a state of subjugation that often brings with it practices such as extending the day shift into the night, working on piece and not time rate, involving the worker's wife and children in the labour process as unpaid 'helpers', putting up with industrial hazards and risk of injury, haphazard and stalled payment, docking of wages earned and depriving captives of benefits that would guarantee a measure of financial security and of protection against adversity. The contract they enter into deprives them of the right to representation, other than as individuals, and effectively prevents forms of collective bargaining for a better deal.

Why do labourers in the informalized economy cede control over the use of their labour power and allow themselves to become entrapped in extreme exploitation and oppression? Because in the terrain of hire-and-fire employment in which these masses have to survive there are no other and better prospects than debt bondage. For seasonal migrants this engagement brings the security of waged work for the next six months or so. In the case of unwritten contracts entered into for an indefinite period – in power-loom workshops or diamond ateliers, for instance; among 'self-employed' home-based workers; among street vendors; or in engagement as domestic servants – acceptance of the meagre offer made may be fuelled by the hope for a somewhat better deal as the relationship with the provider of work becomes longer-lasting. The sale of labour power in advance and the apparent willingness to be attached is, last but not least, inspired by the need to pay for life-cycle events, housing, health care and the cost of looking after the old, young or otherwise dependent members of the household and family.

In Chapter 8 I substantiated how indebtedness has continued to cast a heavy shadow over the life of the working poor. The subaltern classes in the rural economy include categories that have a little land or other means of production, but not enough to make do. In the past the government extended *taccavi* loans to alleviate the difficulties of the agrarian workforce when affected by crises. But this financial relief for the vulnerable segments among the peasantry only targeted landowners and the credit supplied tended to be written off again shortly before elections were due. The landless were never bailed out by such support schemes although they have been documented to be in even direr straits than the peasants above them, who have at least some means of production. Their crisis of improvidence does not occur only once in a while, but is a chronic one. The first round of the countrywide Agricultural

Labour Enquiry in 1950–1 reported that close to half of the landless had to spend more than they earned in order to somehow make do and in the second round held in 1956–7 this percentage had increased to roughly two-thirds. They did not have enough to survive, and made up the shortfall by going into debt. Significantly, the proportion of indebted agricultural labourers working as daily wage earners was not much lower than that of farm servants classified as attached. In the subsequent decades my fieldwork findings in south Gujarat confirmed that, despite hunting for wages far and wide, the land-poor and landless households in the villages of my research did not collect enough to support themselves in their frugal existence. Debt and more debt had become the motor driving them on and off out of their habitat in a state of neo-bonded mobility. The migrant workers from the hinterland I found standing in 2013–15 in a *naka* (labour market) on the outskirts of Ahmedabad told me that borrowers have to guarantee their solvency with collateral such as land, cattle, ornaments and other valuables. Redemption is a first-order priority because of the high interest rates, dependent on their economic condition, of 5–10 per cent per month. Such a usurious rate means that without full repayment in time, the outstanding amount doubles within one year. The more dispossessed the workers are, the lower their credit rating. They are actually beyond redemption and exposed to pauperization (Breman 2016; Sengupta & Vijay 2017).

The Rural Labour Enquiry 2004–5 reported that close to half of all rural labour households were indebted and that the average amount of loans extended to them had risen to a little over Rs. 10,000. I expressed my doubts earlier about the reliability of the data provided. In view of the very low incomes and lack of regular employment, indebtedness among the rural proletariat is, in my view, greatly underestimated in the NSSO tabulation. However, even more questionable is the information that fewer than 3 per cent of contracted loans were set aside for repayment of debt. It is an astounding finding that should not be accepted at face value. As a matter of fact, new loans are made and on receipt have to be instantly handed over to creditors of earlier liabilities. In my last and final fieldwork round I noticed a trend in the contractualization of ties between members of the labouring household at the bottom of the economy. It goes together with the splitting up of this core social unit into longer or shorter spells of multi-locational separation, with the male providers heading off to search for wages while women have to stay back with the small children waiting for much-needed remittances. The disruption of bonds of cohabitation and affinity seems to give an instrumental slant instead of feature even to close interpersonal relationships. The household has once more become a workshop and the ethos of capitalism has penetrated deeply into the milieu of the labouring poor, expressed in pronounced individuation. It is in this respect that the multiple and quite often conflicting roles of working women in running the household while simultaneously engaged in production, reproduction and care needs to be articulated.

Compliance and Resistance

The *halipratha* system as it existed in the pre-capitalist setting of peasant society was portrayed, in ideal terms, as a mutually beneficial relationship between a generous landowning master and a landless servant grateful for the security and protection bestowed on him and his dependents. Within the frame of the subsistence-oriented economy the claims of the one were held to be the obligations of the other and vice versa. The need for food security, at least the promise of it, was the prime motive for the Dublas (as the Halpatis were then still called) to enter into a relationship of bondage and to defer to the master as a benevolent patron. They did so because there were no other, better alternatives available. But what prevented them from working and living as free labourers? Colonial reports pointed out that not all Dublas were bonded – a statement made all the more intriguing because the records do not contain further details on the size of this minority or how they made a living. Were they independent in the sense that they did not have a permanent employer? Were they 'free' because they chose to avoid servitude or were they unable to find a master able and willing to attach them? I draw my conclusions from the repeatedly reported claim that they were worse off than the *halis* and that this unattached status was not their own preference – in other words, their 'freedom' was not a wilful decision on their part, but a result of the main landowners' reluctance to take responsibility for them. This might have been because supply of labour exceeded demand, or because the segment that was denied entrance into servitude lacked the qualities expected of *halis*: willingness to work at all hours, obedience and loyalty to the master accompanied by a display of servility. However, the declining prosperity of the landowners was also a decisive factor. Servants taken on in good times were released again when harvests failed. Famine conditions at the end of the nineteenth century prompted farmers in Chikhli to send their *halis* away. Such fluctuations indicate that the farm servants were part of a broader community of tribals who were made landless and included a segment who did not qualify for being attached to a landlord. The colonial chronicles considered the dismal poverty of the *halis* to be the reason why they fell into servitude but did not fail to attribute their indigence to their own shortcomings. In response to a survey on the incidence of slavery, the collector of the Surat District described the Dublas as drunkards, blamed them for their immoral behaviour and incapacity to make ends meet and, in short, declared them an inferior species (Lumsden 1826: 8 August 1825). This view had not changed by the end of the colonial era. The etymological meaning of the word Dubla was weak, according to the Census of 1931 (Census of India 1931, vol. XIX: 460).

The superiority of the master was validated by the subordinate behaviour he imposed on his *halis*. Having no possessions of their own, they were the recipients of gifts from their benefactor, 'riches' barely enough for survival. The great divide between them in status was however mitigated by a way of life marked by how much they shared despite their separate identities. The master ate the same food he gave to his *halis* and allowed them, with wife and children, into the intimacy of his household. For their part, the servants could expect generosity or at least to receive sufficient means to survive if they adhered strictly to the servile code of conduct. The presentation of the *hali-dhaniyamo* relationship in this imagery concurs with the ideology of patronage, which highlights the desirable behaviour of both parties and their mutual affection. Writing up the *halipratha* system in these terms implies that the servants internalized their dependency and subjugation. No doubt, such testimonies of allegiance in inferiority came from landlords and were communicated to colonial officials who had no unmediated interaction with the dispossessed landless – and also eschewed such contact. Ongoing servility had supposedly robbed the Dublas of all vitality and reduced them to creatures lacking even the strength to stand on their own feet. This portrait confirmed the colonial view that the *halis* had only themselves to blame for the regime of bondage under which they had entered. Having lived from generation to generation in the shadow of Hindus who had raised their own status in the caste-class hierarchy by subordinating the Dublas, the latter were classified in the colonial records as semi-Hindus. It was a 'half-way' label that left unclear what they were before and what they had not become.

Having neglected in my first spell of village-based fieldwork in south Gujarat to draw out memories of past struggles from my landless subjects, I made up for this oversight in a later publication when I set out to relate how the Gujarat branch of the Kisan Sabha union dared to oppose the Congress leadership in launching a campaign in the 1930s to end the system of agrarian bondage as practised in south Gujarat. As narrated in my account of this struggle in Chapter 4, the frontmen of this movement gave voice to the exploitation and oppression of the lower ranks of the peasantry. While the agitation was started by the leaders of the union, it was instigated from below by activists at the grassroots. The frontmen among the landless Dublas/Halpatis remained unidentified but reacted instantly and with fervour to the initiative from outside. The protest was widespread and only fizzled out because Congress stalwarts saw to it that the Gandhian subterfuge of caste-class harmony was played up to safe-guard the domination of the substantial farmers. We were already at the stage of the fully commodified *hali*, the farm servant who in the transition to agrarian capitalism remained bonded as before but was shorn of the features of patronage that were supposed to have been practised in the past. The main landowners had become wary of extending subsistence loans. In the end they would have to give in to the persistent pressure, but they tried to keep the scale and frequency of these advances as low as possible. The chances of repayment were minimal and the borrower might also refuse to work when he was asked to do so. For their part, the labourers tended to see the credit they acquired with difficulty as an irregular supplement to a wage that did not provide enough for them to live. They therefore felt no obligation to repay. In the eyes of each party the other one refused to act reasonably and, consequently, there was a complete lack of trust on both sides. Quite probably, relations were not much better as prescribed under the *ancien régime*, but in the changed setting the farm servant no longer displayed the obedience and humility expected of a *hali* employed by a master who shrugged off his customary obligations.

Poverty clearly perpetuated the dependence of the landless Halpatis but they now openly refused to subordinate themselves to the higher-caste farmers or recognize their claim to allegiance. Bonded labour came to an end not because of proactive government intervention but because employers and employees in agricultural production for different reasons wanted it that way. Freedom did not come overnight and was by no means complete, with one side fighting to achieve it and the other granting it only with great reluctance in a process that slowly unfolded throughout the first half of the twentieth century. Just as the existence of unfree labour cannot be explained in purely economic terms, its disappearance must also be related to the changing social and political climate. When all is said and done, the disintegration of the *halipratha* system cannot be understood without taking into account the resistance of the landless underclass to the ingrained ideology and praxis of inequality. Daniel Thorner also picked up the growing mood of assertion at the fag-end of the agrarian hierarchy in one of his tours around the country during the 1960s:

. . . close to the heart of the problem lies the embittered, indeed poisoned, relations among the Tanjore mirasdars (landlords), their tenants, and their pannaiyals (permanent farm servants). When I asked in Tanjore recently about the importance of the agrarian problem here, it was no less a person than the most scientific cultivator in the district who passed on to me the unforgettable remark of another's mirasdar's pannaiyal: seeing the bejeweled wife of his landlord-employer walking proudly down the village street, the pannaiyal called out: "Madame, your ears are adorned with my blood." (Thorner 1980: 236)

Over time and exacerbated by the pressure on cultivable land due to population growth and the subsequent splitting up of holdings, the absence of sufficient employment has forced the land-poor and landless underclasses to give up their mainstay in agriculture and vie for additional work and wage opportunities in the rural or urban economy. Dispossession in combination with displacement and dislocation takes shape in the context of a regime of informality that keeps the expanding reserve army of labour footloose but tied down in neo-bondage. Sometimes this new form of attachment is a matrix that stretches over long periods or even the whole working life (e.g. in power-loom sheds or diamond-cutting ateliers) or remains restricted to bouts of shorter duration (as in the case of seasonal migration to brick-kilns and sugar-cane fields). The commodified arrangement of bondage differs from the pre-capitalist type, but both prevent labour from depressed castes-classes exercising their free will and making their own choices. As with the former *hali* debt is the device of employers or their agents to appropriate labour power in an advance deal without an exit option, one that lowers the price paid in the open market, imposes abominable conditions of employment, drives the labourers to ruthless self-exploitation and prevents the workforce thus contracted from resorting to collective action. (Neo-) bondage has to be endured for lack of alternatives in making a living freely and fairly.

In the fragmented terrain of the informalized economy trade union activity is extremely rare – even more so among the vulnerable labour force held captive in recurrent indebtedness. The members of the proletariat are unable to team up to bargain with their exploiters for higher wages, tenured jobs, social security and a modicum of protection when out of work. Can no assembling in solidarity be forged at all? Wildcat strikes do occur, in a flash of anger and resentment, although such occasional protests go largely unreported. These once-in-a-while outbursts are usually disorganized and of short duration and tend to remain highly localized, not only because the bosses deliver instant, harsh repression but also due to lack of wherewithal to maintain the struggle for longer than a few days. Does it mean that debt-bonded labour abstains from challenging the terms of the contract to which they fall prey? With few exceptions all of them endeavour to get more out of their employers or contractors than the providers of waged work are inclined to give, but

Figure 9.1 Diamond workers on a wildcat strike protest against a wage cut

do so in their individual capacity: asking for a little higher piece rate, taking overtime work when some among the next shift do not turn up, requesting a new loan before the earlier one is worked off, seeking a lower penalty for not complying with the production quota stipulated, wanting a contract extension when the time has run out, bringing along a relative or neighbour to the site of work, etc. Resistance to what they feel is an abuse of power by the boss, too strenuous a workload or not enough pay for their toil takes the form of what James Scott has labelled the everyday weapons of the weak. This is a rich arsenal ranging from feigned ignorance, foot-dragging, shirking, evasion, subterfuge and sabotage to outright desertion and I have come across all of these acts of intransigence in the milieu of the labouring poor. They know how to bargain tacitly and without risking an open confrontation that would inevitably end in defeat. Ishita Mehrotra reports in her fieldwork account on the tactics used by both sides (Mehrotra 2017: 256). She narrates how local farmers justify paying less to Dalit women who with or without permission use their fields to graze livestock, for defecation and to gather fodder or firewood and occasionally turn to the farmers for help with food and credit. As part of the impressive weaponry of the strong, employers routinely delay wage settlement or make only part-payments in order to ensure the continued availability of Dalit female workers. Mehrotra rightly adds that having repeatedly to ask for one's wages is humiliating and a cause for holding a grudge. It comes as no surprise to read that landowners on their part lament the 'disrespectful' attitude of Dalit women workers who have to be called to work two or three times before they actually come and who then leave in between to attend to domestic chores. The story shows how interaction between domination and subordination is the battlefield on which the class struggle is daily although covertly waged.

Footloose workers often meet meet with hostility in the places to which they migrate for employment, as Mythri Prasad-Aleyamma observed during her fieldwork, conducted on the early morning labour market in a Kerala town:

Migrant workers were rounded up and chased away routinely where they stood in the square even when they possessed electoral identity cards. In September 2008, the local police issued a notice to all factory owners in Perumbavoor that their employees must carry a police clearance card that should certify them as Indian citizens and should provide proof of residence. Besides this, the card was to be signed by the district magistrate after a certification from the local police station in the migrant's place of origin stating that he/she has no criminal record. (Prasad-Aleyamma 2018)

Her findings show that labour gangs in large-scale construction projects commissioned by corporate business are subject to surveillance by national or transnational capital itself. Closely monitored, restricted in their movements, the members of this huge workforce recruited from far and wide rarely dare to venture outside their assigned quarters on site. Meanwhile, workers employed by small-scale enterprises with locally raised capital who frequent the labour market in the town square are often subjected to police harassment. Commenting that the interests of local labour and migrants tend to be at odds with each other, she points out that migrant workers and their employers find common ground against police, the government and local trade unions. The latter act as agents and mercenaries of the municipal authorities and behave at times as if they are an arm of the state. In a similar vein the city police of Chennai tend to accuse interstate migrants of being prone to criminal behaviour and insist that these 'outsiders' provide proof of identity and regularly submit their names and whereabouts for verification:

This kind of policing often restricted the free movement of the migrant workers. They lived in constant fear. Sometimes, the police circulated stories that owing to a slowdown in the economy, many migrant workers were temporarily unemployed and since they did not have any system to fall back on, they took to crime. And to prevent such crimes, the police needed to know them and hence the order to provide information on migrants. (Jeyaranjan 2017: 299)

Displacement and dislocation driven by lack of wherewithal does not fit well with an agenda of governance that for reasons of discipline and control insists on citizens staying put where they 'belong' in their habitat of origin.

Dispossession and Accumulation

In the course of my fieldwork at th grassroots I have observed the deep inroads capitalism has made in the terrain of impoverishment. The high cost of coping with disabilities or medical treatment in cases of serious ailments cannot be avoided. Spending lavishly on marriage celebrations and annual festivals must be a heavy burden on the household budget of the land-poor and landless. Itinerant vendors of consumer durables find a ready market in their neighbourhoods and make a round every fortnight to collect the instalments with which wares such as second-hand TV sets, plastic chairs, household appliances, mobiles, transistors, ready-made garments etc. are paid off. Should all this be seen as signifying an insatiable indulgence in consumerism? The loans advanced amount to figures unheard of in the past: up to Rs. 40,000 or Rs. 60,000 for a male worker and more than 1 *lakh* if wife and working children of the male head of household also come along to the sugar-cane fields, brick-kilns or *nakas* on the city's outskirts. Employers and informants hailing from the higher-up classes in general never tire of discussing the improvidence of people at the bottom of the economy who refuse to live within their means, spending what they do not have and then, to cover the deficit, asking for another loan to work off – with the labour power of their whole household as collateral. Such stories fit all too easily the age-old stereotype of the feckless lower classes. The suggestion is that the poor are to blame for not 'economizing' and not sticking to the most minimal of needs – food, shelter and the little that is required to enable their bare survival.

The economic, social and cultural setting in which they live is thoroughly monetized and cannot be ignored either in their search for income or the way in which they spend it. Clarinda Still explains concern about female respectability in terms of the desire to gain in honour: Dalit parents are eager to get their daughters educated in order to marry them up. Payment of a higher dowry to settle them in a suitable match in their community is part of a strategy of upward mobility: it liberates the girls from shamefully toiling in the fields alongside men – together with all that this might entail. The price that has to be paid for civil inclusion is high. This aspiration, which drives increasing indebtedness, bears witness to the growing power of patriarchy among the Dalits (Still 2017: 198–207). My guess is that such a pathway to progress strikes the landless Halpati household as a futile dream. Grace Carswell and Geert de Neve have aptly phrased the dilemma between family claims that need to be met and the burden of indebtedness that then becomes inevitable:

When power-loom workers take on a debt (*kadan*) – and when they ask for further advances over time – they are in fact prioritizing their obligations (*kadamai*) to family and kin (e.g. organizing a wedding, paying a dowry or attending to ill health) over and above anything else. Such obligations to kin cannot easily be neglected as they are a key to the long-term reproduction of honour, status and networks of social protection. In prioritizing such obligations, workers are willing to suffer the condemnation of employers, including accusations of being lazy and untrustworthy, as debts to employers (located in the sphere of the market) are seen as less pressing than duties to kin (located in the sphere of reproduction). Nevertheless, cash advances can rapidly accumulate beyond what is repayable, and while initially many hope that one day they will be able to settle their advances – and thus meet both types of obligations – in reality few of them manage to do so. The result is more likely to be a deepening of financial debts over time and a gradual realization of being trapped in debt bondage. (Carswell & de Neve 2013: 447)

Making a similar argument, Isabelle Guérin points out how the growing pursuit of consumerism has led to a higher percentage of neo-bonded migrants going back at the end of the season still indebted, which forces them return the following year (Guérin 2013: 419–20; Breman 2016: 183–8). This view sees investment in prestigious social and ritual events as an attempt by caste-class underdogs to qualify for access to mainstream society. But paradoxically, Guérin adds, 'increasing aspirations for equality and integration are helping to reproduce the very harsh conditions of capitalist exploitation and extraction of surplus value' (Guérin 2013: 421). How to achieve merit and dignity if you are time and again caught up in bondage? Workers are well aware that employers use debt to keep them entrapped and avoid taking loans if other and better paid work is available and accessible, as Carswell and de Neve note (Carswell & de Neve 2013: 451). The growing insight that getting into debt does not solve the problem of deficient existence but adds to it is a change for the better. It would give hope for the future when the attempt to cut loose from dependency by not selling one's labour power in advance can be confirmed as part of a more general trend. Is that indeed the case?

While my investigations into the plight of circular migrants hired for construction work in Ahmedabad are based on my last adn final round of fieldwork (2013–15), my research on footloose labourers employed in the power-loom sheds or diamond ateliers in Gujarat took place more than two decades ago. Has there been a turn for the better in the labour contract of the workforce in these branches of industry since then? Indira Hirway carried out a survey among labour migrants who have come to the cities of Ahmedabad and Surat to find work in construction, power-loom or diamond businesses. But her up-to-date findings on collective bargaining are as bleak as my accounts of these industries going back to the 1990s:

> . . . no worker from the sample [my note: 317 in total] has joined any union. As was revealed during discussions, this is because they are likely to be thrown out of their job if they joined a union. Employers clearly do not like workers forming or joining unions. It appears that migrant workers are here to earn some income for survival or to diversify their risks to address their vulnerability. They are totally at the receiving end and accept whatever is available to them. They are not in a position to demand their rights from employers. (Hirway & Singh 2017: 28)

Her conclusion is that the insolvency that pushes the land-poor and landless to leave their rural habitat persists throughout their short- or long-term engagement with the urban economy. To the extent they succeed in finding employment at all, the price paid for their labour is reduced to the lowest possible level. It is a scenario that explains why the majority of the Halpati households in the villages of my fieldwork in south Gujarat remain stuck in dire poverty while a portion among them slide even further down in pauperization. In both Chikhligam and Gandevigam I used to meet a few resilient young men who tirelessly tried to find a better niche than the one into which they were born. Having passed matriculation, they were admitted to an Industrial Training Institute to qualify for a skilled job as craftsman. Paying the maintenance costs of these adolescent boys meant hardship for the households to which they belonged. On completion of their one-year coursework, they failed to generate the money to pay for their apprenticeship, let alone to be able thereafter to buy a proper job. Not yet giving up their dream of a better future, they turned to a member of the village elite, one of the substantial farmers from the dominant caste-class who are the gatekeepers for giving or refusing access to sources beyond the locality and contacts in the bureaucracy without which 'you cannot get your work done' as the saying goes. Daniel Thorner commented on the crucial role the village oligarchy plays in the management of local affairs and the settling of scores with those who behave or misbehave:

> . . . a small group of people are used to running the village, economically, socially and politically. The members of this group have both a sense of power and the

means of exercising it. They have devised a thousand ways of getting around the land reforms. (Thorner 1980: 161)

My young interlocutors were well aware that in order to get the support needed to realize their ambition to become craftsmen they depended on the benevolence of people whose family had held their parents and grandparents captive in the not so remote past. 'Where else can we go?' was their matter of fact reaction. Pointing out what is at stake, Stuart Corbridge et al. have argued that the patronage networks that enabled India to establish itself as a formal democracy 'are precisely those that impede substantive democratization'(Corbridge et al. 2013: 157). This apt observation brought Jonathan Parry to conclude that the way democracy operates in India may be as big a part of the problem as it is of the solution (Gooptu & Parry 2014: 3).

What has the role of government been in this sordid tale of exploitation and oppression? In mild-toned criticism Hirway points out in the write-up of the survey of workers in Ahmedabad and Surat cited above that labour is not a priority area for the central government and even less so for the government of Gujarat. The Bonded Labour System (Abolition) Act 1976 is one of several laws still on the statute list that are not enforced – and openly flouted by the official inspection agency. She vividly describes how migrant workers, often hired in debt by employers or contractors, are exploited and treated as captive labour, forced to toil without rest days and at low rates of pay for ten to twelve hours at a time, or even longer. Other labour rights and legal ordinances are violated with impunity and the workers also face abuses, insults, violence and in the case of women (as also of young children) sexual harassment that is often overlooked. Her damning conclusion is that the government has no accurate data on the size of the footloose workforce in the three industries she investigated and is thoroughly uninformed as well as unconcerned about their predicament:

Our discussions with the government officials revealed that the state government does not have any systematic approach to help migrant workers, who add to the prosperity of the state. No efforts are made to create awareness among them about the laws, their enforcement and their welfare schemes. A few ad hoc scattered acts/rules for the welfare of these workers have not made much impact on the life of these workers. Frequent complaints were made . . . against the unholy nexus between government officers and employers/unit owners. (Hirway & Singh 2017: 33)

Is the labour regime in Gujarat exceptionally brutal to the footloose workforce held in neo-bondage? In the preceding chapters I have contextualized my fieldwork findings in India's informalized economy and referred to research carried out elsewhere in the subcontinent and by other authors. In 2012 Siddarth Kara published a study mapping the frequency and diversity of ongoing human servitude in the subcontinent of South Asia. He wrote that there were 18–20.5 million bonded labourers in the global economy at the end of 2011, of whom more than four-fifths were in India. Because India excels in what Kara labels modern slavery, he travelled widely around the country over the course of eleven years to investigate the condition of servitude in agriculture and industries such as brick-kilns, carpet looms, bidi manufacture and stone quarries but also in shrimp processing, domestic service, tea gardens and eighteen more classified as 'other'. This broad sweep revealed 504 cases of bondage. But this data set was not broken down in any detail – neither in age and gender, nor according to the nuances in grades and shapes of attachment, the role of labour brokers, the why and how of bondage, action taken or not by the state machinery, etc., etc. In a critical review essay, I elaborated on my differences of opinion with him (Breman 2014a). Indeed, the setting of bondage within an ideology of inequality makes dispossessed communities in particular susceptible to discrimination and denigration. The author correctly blames the civilizational heritage of the region for keeping servile labour alive but does not discuss the political economy of a financialized and mercantile capitalism that not merely condones but actively promotes 'the exploitation of an immense underclass of systematically impoverished and vulnerable people' (Kara 2012: 37–8). Why blame the state alone and not capitalism itself, which should be addressed as the prime culprit? Moreover, Kara portrays the indebted workers as docilely accepting their ordeal and in his argument raises the bogey of an internalized servility:

In speaking with numerous *dalit* bonded labourers, many told me that bondage and servility were their divinely ordained fates, which they must perform dutifully if they hoped to accrue a positive karmic balance that may elevate them upward in the next life. The sedimented and centuries-old fatalism inherent to the caste system of ancient India is a deplorable anachronism in modern times. (Kara 2012: 20)

I reject this assessment as being derived from a method of investigation that remained at a distance and failed to gain the confidence of the workers. Kara commiserates with them, but without having come close enough for long enough to comprehend their world-view and consciousness. My fieldwork findings over half a century in the milieu of the down and out resonate with the argument in critical social science literature that the superiority-inferiority binary pertains to a view imposed from above without having been internalized down below. The notion of social hierarchy ranked in a neat top-down fit and approved of by all stakeholders as a natural and justified order of inequality – embodied in the Louis Dumont's idea of the homo hierarchicus – has since long been contested. To the extent that such articulate apprehension has ever existed, it has lost its appeal and backing – other than in biased upper-caste lore. Of course, the Hindu order of caste has not faded away. However, what struck me in the changes apparent at the grass-roots level was the shift from vertical to horizontal ranking, the growth of a consciousness that emphasizes a parallel, a next-to-each-other segmentation rather than a high-to-low stratification. A recurrent finding in my fieldwork encounters among the down-and-out was the unwillingness to abide by the strictures and commands of those who dominate dispossessed communities. Instead of outright subjection I found defiant though unstated assertiveness challenging the idea of natural inequality. The identity politics that mobilize ties of loyalty depends on a sense of togetherness in caste, ethnicity or creed. Dalits and adivasis are exhorted to identify themselves within these parameters and join the movement to which they belong. In the current political climate of Hindutva intolerance Muslims are unable to lift their voices and raise their profile in this way.[1] But mobilization from below on the basis of primordial identities has a parochial streak since it is built on separateness instead of creating a common platform and fighting collectively for emancipation. The fault lines drawn make for compartmentalization and keep fragmented what should be united.

The deepened spread of capitalism in India has impacted on a workforce with composite social identities. These identities are partly class-based but in addition co-constituted by caste, tribe and religion. Such loyalties did not fade away with the gradual intrusion of capitalism and were instrumental in keeping wage labour in the lower echelons of the socio-economic ranking segmented and divided. This blend of class and non-class forms of identification has obstructed the development of a class-in-itself consciousness and collective action in solidarity. As a consequence, exploitation is driven by class-directed domination in combination with the appropriation of surplus value extracted through pre-existent forms of subordination. Lerche & Shah (2018) have aptly addressed the multidimensional outcome as conjugated oppression. While accepting the label they have attached to this syncretic configuration, I disagree with them that the resulting fusion of identities would disallow us from branding these highly diverse working masses – at drift in the informal economy, working off and on in or outside agriculture

---

[1] See on this issue Harsh Mander's February 2018 column published in *The Indian Express* and the debate to which this gave rise.

Figure 9.2 Office of a trade union organizing Dalit workers in the informal economy

and for stints of variable length in rural or urban locations – as a proletariat. The fact that these prime victims of capitalist exploitation do not constitute a class-in-itself, let alone for itself, in my opinion does not invalidate their proletarian condition and habitus.

Back to the question – whether Gujarat is exceptional in its denial of social justice and labour rights and its lack of commitment to catering for the welfare of labour in the informal economy and more particularly for that of the people Mahatma Gandhi cared for as the lowest-ranking in the social hierarchy. The answer: no, it is not. But this state, which boasts of a higher growth rate than elsewhere in India, tolerates more brazenly what should be obliterated. Gujarat is a test case *par excellence* to keep track of the growing divide between the opulence enjoyed in the comfort zone higher up and the absence of decent work and a dignified life for the masses down below – who are forced to trek around in their search for casual employment and income. The trend towards increasing well-being in the higher echelons does not mean that the majority of the workforce stuck in the lower echelons is getting more deprived than they were before. This is not how the prosperity-precarity opposition takes shape. No doubt, a substantial segment at the tail end is pauperized and I have elaborated on this residuum in another publication (Breman

2016). However, impoverishment should not only or even mainly be understood as a further progression in absolute destitution. That may happen – and explains why and how chronic illness, disability and old age or coollase of the whole household collapse due to the premature death or desertion of its main provider are major causes of pauperism. The labouring poor without sufficient or any means of production who are able to work but do not succeed in finding a minimum of waged employment and income are at risk of sliding down into immiserization. When all is said and done, poverty means being unable to satisfy your basic needs. What constitutes a minimum is not fixed but relative and relational in nature, as Thorner pointed out in *The Shaping of Modern India*:

> I do not mean that the poor are getting absolutely poorer. I would be the last to deny, or to try to minimize, the hardships of life of the bottom one-third of the rural population – India's millions of small cultivators and rural labourers who do not earn enough to eat three square meals a day. My contention, nonetheless, is that even they have been affected by the prosperity of their neighbours, and by the changed conditions of life generally since 1947. Their actual level of living may still be miserable, but the level to which they aspire has risen. (Thorner 1980: 233)

The quotation shows that Thorner was alert to the concept of relative deprivation, a notion economists tend to disregard in their analysis of poverty. In my village investigations I used to ask Halpatis with whom I was more familiar to compare their predicament to what their parents and grandparents had been forced to endure. Their steadfast retort was that talking about those days could not help them to deal with the kind of deprivation they faced today, pointing out how they lagged behind in the progress made. What is basic now is more than what was considered basic then but the gap that sets them so visibly apart from those higher up the social scale has widened a great deal. The unhappy outcome of the growth trajectory squarely contradicts the gospel of capitalist development as a steady trickle-down of welfare.

The part of the country in which I carried out my research is exemplary not merely for highlighting the stark contrast between the better-off and wdespread indigence but also for demonstrating how accumulation and dispossession should be seen as interdependent. This dismal record in the failure to redistribute the fruits of growth is by no means of recent standing. Right from the state's formation in 1960 Gujarat has been avidly pro-business and its political management tried for decades to lure capital with the promise that, in addition to liberal licensing, subsidies and tax exemption, industrialists would have a free hand in dealing with labour. Congress supremo Madhavsinh Solanki was already dreaming in the mid-1980s of turning the state into a mini-Japan (Shah 2014:

521). Why then was the regime change in 1995 from Congress to BJP the beginning of a trajectory far worse than the one preceding it – and even more so since Narendra Modi took over BJP leadership in 2001? On his nomination as chief minister this high-profile driver of the neoliberal credo went out of his way to placate India's big business with favours and easy access to land, credit and infrastructure. His mission was to make Gujarat the most attractive destination for investments in the world. Modi ushered in a reign of crony capitalism, much admired by the vocal lobby of free and unfettered market enterprise. The huge state outlay on tax breaks and other freebies was made at the cost of public funding for all social sectors – education, health care, family welfare and social security – which explains why on this expenditure Gujarat's ranking on the development index is much lower than most other states. On his watch the balance between capital and labour balance was further distorted, while the rural-urban incongruity intensified. The ongoing shift towards urbanity is pushed by a capital-intensive development paradigm resulting in slum demolitions and deportation of the working poor to the municipal outskirts. A total disregard for the plight of labour explains the excessive underpayment of men and women: the state with the proudly declared highest growth rate stands close to the bottom of the national wage table.

'The Gujarat Model of Growth and Development' has in Newspeak rhetoric been ceaselessly propagated as an astounding success. It was the slogan with which the man who proclaimed this charade fought and won the national elections in 2014. Mandated by the hard core of the BJP as their one and only hero, the populist leader promised his jubilant party that the design that had been the manual for bringing *vikas* to Gujarat would now be the agenda for leading the nation to its vainglorious destiny. In line with the Hindutva mindset and its majoritarian bias, secularism, tolerance of dissent and praise for cultural diversity stand condemned. In 2002 a pogrom was carried out against Muslims – with state complicity. It should therefore not come as a surprise that events with a *Nacht and Nebel* taint are now widely documented in the country. There is equal cause for alarm in the way in which the rule of law has been subverted by arbitrary procedures that bypass or corrupt the judiciary and empower the high command to decide who and what is subversive and needs to be 'excluded'. In retrospect it is remarkable that what happened in this state under authoritarian rule in 2001–14 was duly reported by dissenting activists but remained largely uncriticized in public opinion outside its territory. When I discussed my anxieties and worries with friends or colleagues elsewhere in India, their usual comment was that the country's citizenry would never allow such a regime, which divided the included from the excluded, to come to power – let alone to last. Branding the religious minority as 'the enemy within' has torn up the fabric of mainstream society and a vicious policy of ghettoization taken shape in a setting of blatant apartheid. The sizeable Muslim minority has been drive out of mainstream society, and they have complied with their eviction, if only to seek safety together. But in my view poverty-stricken citizens are also ghettoized if they are forced to live apart in urban slums or colonies on the village outskirts. Underlying the economic policies is a belief in the trickle-down gospel of neoliberal capitalism. Is this a genuine belief, grounded in goodwill? Looking back it could also be characterized as a ploy to stem protest from below by setting the excluded out of public sight, locking them up in marginality at a safe distance. In evaluating the prime minister's record so far, commentators have mainly focused on the social-cultural ramifications and repercussions of his Hindutva politics – for good reason, no doubt, since this seems to be the most disconcerting side of his plan for the nation. Still, I would argue that his side-tracking of the social question and his attempt to deal with it by simply denying that it exists is of no lesser significance.

In Denial of the Social Question

The dismantling of existing labour legislation has not yet reached its nadir. To remove whatever rigidities in the labour market have not yet been dealt with, a last round of flexibilization is due to give capital a free hand in its exploitation of the workforce. Modi considers himself a man of many talents who intuitively knows when and how to make the decisions that are best for the country and the people in all domains of politics and governance. Out of the blue he announced in November 2016 a demonetization drive with the stated objective of getting hold of the black money he imagined to be stashed away as an immense hoard of cash waiting to be raided.[2] The ordinance to declare illegal high-value banknotes of Rs. 500 and Rs. 1000, which were being used in an overwhelming proportion of transactions, created havoc in the cash-dependent informalized economy. It led to dismissal on the spot of a casualized workforce in all sectors of waged activity. All over the country labour migrants were forced to go back home without having received their backpay. For months the concomitant cash crunch badly affected the purchasing power of working-class households. A year later, with much evidence available that the demonetization drive had been a

---

[2] For a discussion of more ulterior motives to digitalize financial transactions, Ghosh, Chandrasekhar & Patnaik 2017; Chandrasekhar & Ghosh 2018: 420–36.

complete failure, the prime minister went on to insist that the action had borne out his wisdom and that he has outsmarted all his critics. The Goods and Services Tax (GST) enacted in mid-2017 has harmed business in the informal economy equally badly and the resulting rise in the price of commodities and services has been another major setback for workers and consumers in the lower scales of the economy. Both monetary interventions have been criticized for bringing about an abrupt breakdown of cash flow in the informal economy that was accompanied by instant dismissal of large segments of the rural and urban workforce – quite rightly so, but these misconceived policy ruptures also seem to signal the slowing down of casualized and unregulated employability all around. Local-level case studies carried out in different parts of the country attest to a marked fall in the volume of migrants moving out of the countryside in search of waged work. Savings from income earned away from the village to maintain the household in the village are on the decline, while finding sufficient employment at home is next to impossible. The result, growing indebtedness and indigence, seems to illustrate that the informal economy does not have an infinite capacity to absorb manpower. The cherished assumption that jobs would always be found for all those able and willing to search around for them now stands exposed as a myth.

The turning economic tide has sullied the political appeal of the prime minister and his party. What will happen next is anybody's guess but a change to a more labour-friendly direction and a reprieve for the beaten - down workforce is unlikely to be on the cards. The policy script that has unfolded should be seen as an attempt to formalize capital in the informal economy while at the same time leaving labour throughout informalized, caught up in a casualized, insecure and unprotected work regime. The capital that remains untaxed in the informal economy is huge and a sizeable part of it finds its way higher up, creamed off by corporate business, bureaucracy and politics. In this lofty circuit of the so-called formal economy the loot of black money resulting from the rigorous exploitation and repression of labour is laundered in fraudulent transactions and stored safely away. It has been reported that of 73 per cent of national wealth generated in 2017 accrued to the richest 1 per cent of the population. Although such figures of wealth and income concentration remain disputable for lack of transparency, the economic inequality is obscenely stark and has become more lopsided in recent decades. The dissolved Planning Commission of India, not known for overreporting on the magnitude of poverty, estimated in 2011–12 that 363 million people or about one-third of the country's population were stuck in poverty (Government of India, Planning Commission 2014). The size of this figure – the estimate should be even higher than officially conceded – is a telling comment on the government's dismal policy record in catering to the needs of the labouring classes, who are kept locked up in the lower echelons of the economy.

In all this gloom there is a single ray of hope: the growing assertiveness of the down-and-out castes-classes in South India. The plight of these social formations in Kerala and Tamilnad in particular appears to be less severe than in most states in the northern part of the subcontinent. The regional contrasts are stark and tend to be ascribed to populist programs that have brought down the price of food and cost of health care, to the acknowledgement of claims for access to public education – generally to conceding that the down-and-outs have a right to be included in mainstream society. Such a climate of populism helps to alleviate the deprivation to which the labouring poor are exposed. It would be misconceived, however, to relate these compromises to a more even-handed style of political leadership. The benevolence is in reaction to mounting pressure from below for at least a share in the spoils of growth. The urge for emancipation seems to be more manifest in these quarters than among the underprivileged contingent in Gujarat who have been the focus of my empirical investigations. Careful monitoring is required to develop a nuanced and comparative perspective over time and space in order to create agency in transforming processes of exclusion to those of inclusion. But it would be premature to conclude that the prime minister will be able to execute the policy design in the country at large that he claims to have successfully implemented in Gujarat. At the same time, it is disheartening to note that the Hindutva ideology and its embodiment in a wide range of front organizations with their reiteration of deep-seated inequality have started to make inroads in the southern parts of the country. Does it mean that this upsurge of caste-cum-class-based supremacy is going to find a sizable berth there as well? The feeling of dismay is deepened on taking note of what the Congress Party has in store when it will be – rather unlikely in the short term – voted back in power. Its soft Hindutva agenda has remained unaltered and its economic programme, proclaimed in March 2018, is a rehash of worn-out ideas and shows it to be still unreservedly committed to the tenets of neoliberal capitalism.

What are the further prospects? In earlier chapters I have analyzed the informal economy as a landscape in which the accumulation-by-dispossession mechanism is pushed ahead with a vengeance (see also Harvey 2003, 2005). In my final rounds of fieldwork I noticed a new and very alarming trend for labour to be displaced by capital in all branches of employment. This occurred in agriculture and industry to begin with, as I observed in the sites of my earlier fieldwork, the plantations of Bardoli and industries in Surat. The managers of the cooperative agro-industry have plans to get the cane cut by combine harvesters which would do away with the recruitment of a huge army of migrants deployed for the duration of the campaign.

In an interview with the managing director of the Bardoli sugar mill in 2013 I was told that the replacement of labour by machinery was under consideration and that tests with combine harvesters had already been successfully carried out. It was a veiled threat, actually, in an oblique answer to my question as to why the cost of labour had stagnated for decades at an extremely low level and why a huge army of migrants was annually recruited for the duration of the campaign while an abundant supply of local labour remained unused. A repeat survey in 2017 of my earlier study confirmed that, in contrast to the farmers who have grown rich on the crop, today's harvesting hordes of migrants are as badly treated and exploited as they were half a century ago (Prayas 2017).

In the textile workshops of Surat more power looms are being installed and handled at a higher speed by a single worker. Embroidery production is being computerized and dyeing-and-printing manufacture similarly mechanized. In transport and construction, as well, a great deal of manual labour has been rapidly made redundant. The manufacture of hand-moulded bricks from mud is being phased out and substituted by machine-made cement bricks while building roads and flyovers has become a high-tech industry. The story is not different for trade and services. Shop chains take over distribution from the multitude of small kirana (grocery) stores at the corner; household appliances for cooking, washing and cleaning reduce the need to employ day-long domestic servants; electronic devices cordon off property and replace surveillance by security guards. Having travelled the painful path to dispossession labour at the tail end of the economy now has to face the problem of increasing disuse. What strikes me in reflecting on the meaning and consequences of this major turnaround is that the substitution of capital for labour does not always seem to be driven by an urge for greater cost effectiveness. It is as if the owners and managers of capital consider labour to be a nuisance, a commodity they want to do away with. They find equipment easier and also much more prestigious to handle than labour. In the financialized, mercantile brand of state-boosted capitalism that has come to dominate in the globalized economy the procurement of capital is easy and cheap since, contrary to the usury to which labour bonded by indebtedness is exposed, no or hardly any interest has to be paid.

When industrial capitalism transformed Europe's peasant economy in the nineteenth century, the growing mass of vagrants torn loose from their rural habitat were viewed as a *classe dangereuse*. Drifting around in search of regular jobs and better employment, they were deemed to be a threat to the established order. This looming risk persuaded the vested interests to allow for collective action by the working poor and to facilitate their inclusion in mainstream society. It seems as if the kind of financialized and mercantile capitalism that has come to dominate the global economy – and not least so in India – revels in downgrading labour. In today's India the dispossessed, footloose and fragmented masses at the bottom of the urban and rural economy are denied the ability to rise in revolt and fight in concerted action for incorporation in mainstream society on a par with others. They rather stand condemned to remain where they are, beyond the barriers thrown up to citizenship because of defects detected in their way of life.

Stigmatized and ranked as 'the undeserving poor' such dispossessed and footloose people are blamed for lacking the mettle required for inclusion. In the early days of colonial rule the *halis* were already branded as incapable of becoming civilized. Commenting on bondage in the wake of Independence, the Hali Labour Enquiry Committee argued that this practice still existed because the Dublas/Halpatis refused to give up their daily grain ration whether they had worked or not. In a similar vein, employers indignantly deny that indebtedness is the lever they use to keep labour responsive to their exploitative demands. In this rhetoric the condition of extreme poverty is explained as improvidence, an obnoxious refusal by the down-and-out to save up as the accumulating citizenry does, choosing instead to spend instantly whatever they earn. This appraisal blames the bonded workforce for their bondage and the poor for their poverty. The Surat District development officer answered me along these lines in 2013 when I asked him why the workfare programme *narega* was not operating in the villages of my fieldwork. His pat reply was that the Halpatis are congenitally defective. When their labour power remains unused, it is because they have no value to make use of (Breman 2016). Those in control of today's political economy remain resolutely unwilling to pose and solve the social question, which should be on the agenda of the powers behind neoliberalism instead of being callously ignored. As before, the poor are blamed for their poverty, as the World Bank argued in its 2015 Development Report, suggesting that such people lack the propensity to accumulate since they refuse to defer immediate gratification of their needs for future gains. Their improvidence is explained as unwillingness to save and discipline themselves to behave as 'economic man' does.

Does it mean that the working classes have no choice other than accept the fate meted out to them? From start to finish in my fieldwork rounds

I encountered men, women and even children who obstinately refused to bow down in subordination. To remain footloose can also be understood as an escape from stifling economic, social and or political subordination in sedentary existence (Breman 2018). It is the kind of behaviour portrayed in *A Free Man* by Aman Sethi. The main figure in his narrative is the archetypal tramp or hobo whose perambulations in work and life keep him on the road. He is footloose not because he is driven out but because his waywardness enables him to avoid getting on the treadmill and become commodified. He succinctly sums up the need to do *kamai* (waged work) without surrendering his freedom (*azadi*):

'Kamai is what makes work work. Without kamai, it is not work, it is a hobby. Some call it charity, others may call it exercise – but it certainly isn't a job. A job is something a man is paid to do – and his pay is his kamai. Many of us ....' Ashraf paused to stand up and take in the tea-sipping mazdoors, the gossiping mistrys, and the lazing beldaars in a smooth arc of his arm, 'many of us choose jobs only on the basis of their kamai. Six thousand rupees a month! A man could get rich with that kind of money! But they forget a crucial thing. What is that crucial thing? Azadi, Aman bhai, azadi', he continued without waiting for an answer. 'Azadi is the freedom to tell the maalik to fuck off when you want to. The maalik owns our work. He does not own us.' (Sethi 2011: 19)

With due respect for this show of self-assertiveness, his bravado is one of the weapons of the weak, the sort of coping behaviour that keeps self-respect intact. One admires such a courageous stance, the resilience to escape from becoming bogged down in defeat. Nevertheless, it is not the spirit that fuels the class struggle and builds up to collective action in a consciousness of solidarity.

Is India unique in combining capitalism with labour bondage? Not at all. The subject has attracted renewed attention, a firm refutation of the idea that unfree labour is no longer of significance (Brass & van der Linden 1997). Contextualizing my findings in a comparative setting is beyond the scope of this treatise but the study by M. L. Bush (Bush 2000) on servitude in modern times, which has a separate chapter on debt bondage, contributes to the wider debate. The International Labour Organization (ILO) estimated in 2005 that 12.3 million people worldwide were victims of forced labour or bondage. This figure was updated in *The Cost of Coercion* (International Labour Organization 2009), which discussed the nature of the problem and documented its main pattern and geographical spread. The persistence of bonded labour in South Asia, although nominally prohibited, was mentioned as a matter of particular concern (International Labour Organization 2009: 17). Together with a private Australian foundation and the International Organization for Migration, the ILO brought out a new report in

2017 that attests that 40.3 million people in the world are victims of 'modern slavery'. Under this unfortunate heading an odd mixture of human trafficking, state-imposed forced labour, forced marriage and debt bondage is clubbed together. The tally for the latter category is said to amount to 8 million men and women. The survey-based data set, which covers a five-year reference period (2012–16), is guesswork at best and also questionable in many definitional and methodological respects. The root causes need to be identified: the document attempts this by relating debt bondage to the informal economy and condemning the exploitation of labour. However, from beginning to end the report refrains from holding capitalism culpable for the practice. Although figures are not laid out by country, the sparse factual evidence made available suggests that as far as bonded labour is concerned, India ranks at the top of the list. The country's government stands exposed as a chief perpetrator in not abiding by the convention that explicitly prohibits forced labour. In an instant rebuttal the Ministry of Labour and Employment contested the findings in a strongly worded letter.[3] This flat-out rejection is not surprising since, as pointed out in the first part of this study, the government of India has consistently either ignored or covered up the widespread existence of labour bondage as substantiated not only in the social science literature but also in officially commissioned reports. Indeed, the figures mentioned by the ILO should not be taken at face value. As stated in Chapter 2, my own estimate of men, women and children caught up in the worst forms of debt bondage amounts to at least 10 and possibly 15 per cent of India's workforce, a multitude of about 50–75 million men, women and children. This is for India alone, which means that the ILO number of people working in unfreedom in the world at large should be fixed at more than ten times the size guessed at in its latest publication on the issue.

To conclude, in this study I have substantiated the contention that capitalism and bondage are not mutually incompatible but coexist. India's depressed castes-classes are forced to pay the price for this fearsome interdependence. Identified as an operational trigger the depressor has not lost its leverage. It is kept activated to promote capitalism in a predatory format and to resist the increasing pressure for inclusion from below. The situation seems to bear witness to a

---

[3] 'We would like to know the basis on which the data has been verified for credibility when apparently it has been neither verified with any official data source, including that of the ILO nor any national governments have been consulted regarding the survey methodology' (datelined 4 October 2017). The letter was published in *The Hindu* and placed on the daily newspaper's website on October 6, 2017: www.thehindu.com/news/national/india-disputes-ilos-slavery-report/article19803909.ece

progressive imbalance between well-being and impoverishment and reflects an abysmal failure to address the insistent claim for decent work and a dignified life for the masses without voice and visibility, victims of misdirected development. In a society bent on the maintenance of steep inequality as the organizing principle of social order, it comes at no surprise that the most vulnerable segment of its huge workforce is not allowed to move around freely in the labour market and to engage in collective action that would release them from bondage and enable them, no longer debt-shackled, to strike a better deal.

References

Colonial Accounts

All India Congress Committee Papers, G6-KW, Manuscript Section of the Nehru Memorial Museum and Library, Delhi.

Banaji, D. R. (1933). *Slavery in British India*. Bombay: D. B. Taraporevala Sons & Co.

Broomfield, R. S. and R. M. Maxwell (1929). *Report of the Special Enquiry into the Second Revision Settlement of the Bardoli and Chorasi talukas*. Bombay.

Bukhari, J. (1938). *National Front*, 6 March: 8–11.

Census of India 1901 (1902). *Baroda*, vol. XVIII, part 1. Bombay.

Census of India 1921 (1922). *Bombay*, vol. VIII, part 1. Bombay.

Census of India 1931 (1932). *Baroda*, vol. XIX, part 1. Bombay.

Darling, M. L. (1928). *The Punjab Peasant in Prosperity and Debt*. Bombay/New York: Oxford University Press.

Dave, J. (1946). *Halpati-mukit;halipratha ane mukitadanni hilachal*. Ahmedabad.

Desai, D. (1942). 'Agrarian Serfdom in India', *Indian Sociologist*, July–August, 14.

Desai, I. I. (1971). *Raniparajna Jagruti*. Swatantra Ithihas Samiti, no.3. Surat.

Desai, M. (1929). *The Story of Bardoli*. Ahmedabad: Navjivan.

Enthoven, R. E. (1920–2). *Tribes and Castes of the Bombay Presidency*, 3 vols. Bombay: Government Central Press.

Gandhi, M.K. (1927a). 'Face to Face with the Pauper', *Young India*, 31 March. (1927b). *Navajivan*, 15 June.

Gazetteer of the Bombay Presidency (1877). *Gujarat: Surat and Broach*, vol. II. Bombay.

Government of Bombay (1938–40). Home (Special Department, Maharashtra State Archives, S. D. 718, first half March 1938, first half of June 1938; S. D. 115, first half of January 1939; S. D. 340, first half of February 139;S. D. 440, first half of February 1939; S. D. 2867, first half of August 1939; file no.1019, 6 March 1940.

Keatinge, G. (1921). *Agricultural Progress in Northern India*. London: Longmans, Green & Co.

Kishore, J. (1924). 'The Village Labourer in Western India', *Hindustan Review*: 425 ff.

Lorenzo, A. M. (1943). *Agricultural Labour Conditions in Northern India*. Bombay: New Book Company.

Lumsden, W. J. (1826). Collector of Surat, letter of 9 August 1825 to David Greenhill, Acting Secretary to the Government of Bombay. Consultation 108 of 1825, Judicial Department 1826, vol. 25–126. Bombay Record Department.

Maconochie, E. (1897). *Revised Survey and Settlement Report on Chikhli taluk, Surat district.* Bombay: Selections of Records from the Bombay Government, New Series 381.

Malkani, N. R. (1926). 'The Agricultural Condition of Bardoli', *Young India,* vol. 8, no. 29: 263–5, no. 30: 266–7, no. 32: 286–7, no. 33: 290–1 and no. 34: 302–3.

Mehta, D. (1975). Oral history interview with Shri Dinkar Mehta, Ahmedabad, 27 July 1975, by Dr Hari Dev Sharma for the Nehru Memorial Museum and Library.

Mehta, J. M. (1930). *A Study of the Rural Economy of Gujarat.* Baroda: Baroda State Press.

Mehta, S. B. (1923–4). 'Kaliparaj ke Raniparaj', *Yugdharma 3.*

(n.d.). *Atmakata (Autobiography).* Bhogilal Gandhi (ed.) Ahmedabad: Maha-kavish Nananlal Smarak Trust.

Mukhtyar, G. C. (1930). *Life and Labour in a South Gujarat Village.* Bombay, Longmans, Green & Co.

Notes Regarding Kisan Movement (1940–1). Report by the Superintendent of Police, Surat 21 March 1940 Government of Bombay, Home (Special) Department, file no. 1019, of 1940–1. Bombay: Maharashtra State Archives.

Parikh, N. D. (1926). 'Bardoli kheduta', *Navajivan,* vol. 7–8, August–October.

Report from the India Law Commissioners and Papers Relating to Slavery in the East Indies (1841). *Session 1841.* Irish University Press.

Report from the Select Committee of the House of Lords appointed to inquire into the present state of the affairs of the East India Committee, together with the Minutes of Evidence and Appendix (1830). London.

Report of the Baroda Economic Development Committee, 1918–19 (1920). Bombay.

Report of the Revision Survey Settlement of the Jalalpur Taluka (1900). Bombay.

Royal Commission on Agriculture (1928). Report, vol. II, part 2. Evidence taken in the Bombay Presidency. Bombay: Central Government Press.

Settlement Report on Bardoli Taluk, Surat District (1895). Selections from the Records of the Bombay Government, no. 359, New Series. Bombay.

(1925). Selections from the Records of the Bombay Government, no. 647. M. S. Jayakar, 25 June.

Shukla, J. B. (1937). *Life and Labour in a Gujarat Taluka.* Calcutta: Longmans, Green and Co.

Slavery. Accounts and Papers (1837–8). *Vol 16. Session 15 November 1837–16 August 1838. 697 Correspondence between the Directors of the East India Company and the Company's Government in India, on the subject of Slavery; - Orders and Regulations issued, and Proceedings taken thereon; also, Copies or Extracts of all Communications relating to Slavery in the Island of Ceylon.* Deposited in the library of the University of Minnesota: class 326.9548, book fEa77.

Slavery (East Indies) (1841). *Copy of the Despatch from the Governor General of India in Council to the Court of Directors of the East India Company, dated the 8th day of February 1841 (No. 3) with the Report for the Indian Law Commissioners and its Appendix Enclosed in that Despatch, on the subject of Slavery in the East Indies. Ordered by The House of Commons to be printed 26th April 1841.*

Yagnik, I. (1938a). 'Lavet Makes a Little History', *National Front*, 19 June.

(1938b). 'Agrarian Unrest in South Gujarat', *National Front*, 24 July.

(1938c). 'The Raniparaj Are Stirring', *National Front*, 25 December.

(1943). *Gandhi as I Know Him.* (Revised and enlarged edition). Delhi: Zaehner RC.

Post-Colonial Accounts

Official Publications

Government of Gujarat (1966). *Report of the Minimum Wages Advisory Committee for Employment in Agriculture.* Ahmedabad: Education and Labour Department.

(1972). *Report of the Committee on Unprotected and Unorganized Labour.* Gandhinagar: Education and Labour Department.

Government of India (1948). *Report of the Committee on Fair Wages 1948.* New Delhi.

(2011). *Socio-Economic Caste Census 2011.* https://secc.gov.in/welcome

Government of India, Labour Bureau, Ministry of Labour and Employment. Agricultural Labour in India (1960). *Report on the Second Agricultural Labour Enquiry, 1956–57,* vol. I (All India) and vol. V (West India). Delhi.

Government of India, Ministry of Finance, Department of Economic Affairs (2007). *Report of the Expert Group on Agricultural Indebtedness.* July. New Delhi.

Government of India, Ministry of Finance (2018). *Economic Survey 2016–17.* Accessed October 15, 2018. http//Indiabudget.nic.in/es2016–17/echapter.pdf.

Government of India, Ministry of Labour (1952). Agricultural Labour Enquiry: *Agricultural Wages in India,* vol. I. Delhi.

(1954a). Agricultural Labour Enquiry: *Rural Man-Power and Occupational Structure.* Delhi.

(1954b). *Agricultural Labour: How They Work and Live.* Delhi: B. Ramamurti.

(1955). *Agricultural Labour Enquiry: Report on Intensive Survey of Agricultural Labour, 1951–52,* vol. I (All India) and vol. V (West India). Delhi.

(1956). *Summary of the Report on Forced Labour by Shri P. S. Dhamne.* Government of India Press.

Government of India, Ministry of Labour, Employment and Rehabilitation (1969). *Report of the National Commission on Labour.* Delhi.

(1991). *Report of the National Commission on Rural Labour.* 2 vols. New Delhi.

(2002). *Report of the (Second) National Commission on Labour.* 2 vols. New Delhi.

Government of India, Ministry of Labour and Employment. (2010). Labour Bureau – Rural Labour Enquiry *Report on Indebtedness among Rural Labour Households* (Round of N. S. S. 2004–05). Shimla/Chandigarh.

Government of India, Ministry of Labour and Employment. Labour Bureau. Rural Labour Enquiry (2016). *Report on Consumption Expenditure of Rural Labour Households* (66th Round of NSS, 2009–10). Shimla/Chandigarh.

Government of India, National Statistical Commission (2012). *Report of the Committee on Unorganised Sector Statistics*. February.

Government of India, Planning Commission (2014). *Report of the Expert Group to Review the Methodology of Measurement of Poverty*. June.

International Labour Organization (2009). *The Cost of Coercion*. Global Report on the Follow-Up to the ILO Declaration on Fundamental Principles and Rights at Work. Geneva.

International Labour Organization, Walk Free Foundation and International Organization for Migration (2017). *Global Estimates of Modern Slavery. Forced Labour and Forced Marriage*. Geneva.

National Commission for Enterprises in the Unorganised Sector (2006). *Report on Social Security for Unorganised Workers*. New Delhi.

(2008). *Report on Conditions of Work and Promotion of Livelihoods in the Unorganised Sector*. New Delhi: Academic Foundation.

NCEUS (2009). NCEUS Working Paper No.3 *Definitional and Statistical Issues Relating to Workers in Informal Employment*. New Delhi.

Report of the Hali Labour Enquiry Committee (1948). M. L. Dantwala and M. B. Desai. Unpublished. Bombay.

Report of the National Commission for Enterprises in the Unorganised Sector, Government of India (2009). *The Challenge of Employment in India: An Informal Sector Perspective*, vol. I, Main Report. Government of India. New Delhi: Academic Foundation.

Report of the Scheduled Areas and Scheduled Tribes Commission, 1960–61 (1961). Delhi.

United Nations Supplementary Convention on the Abolition of Slavery, the Slave Trade, and Institutions and Practices Similar to Slavery (1956).

World Development Report 1995 (1995). *Workers in an Integrating World*. Washington, D.C.: The World Bank/New York: Oxford University Press.

World Development Report 2015 (2015). *Mind, Society and Behavior*. Washington D.C.: The World Bank/ New York: Oxford University Press.

Books and Articles

Abraham, V. (2009). 'Employment Growth in Rural India: Distress-Driven?' *Economic and Political Weekly*, vol. 44/16:97–104.

Amin, S. (1988). 'Agrarian Bases of Nationalist Agitations in India: A Historiographical Survey', in Low (1988).

Anandhi, S. (2017). 'Gendered Negotiations of Caste Identity; Dalit Women's Activism in Rural Tamil Nadu', in Anandhi & Kapadia (eds.) (2017): 97–130.

Anandhi, S. & K. Kapadia (eds.) (2017). *Dalit Women: Vanguard of Alternative Politics in India*. London/New York: Routledge, South Asian edition.

Anonymous (1954). 'Editorial', *The Farmer*, vol. 5/1, January: 49.

Anonymous (ed.) (1978). *Studies in the Development of Capitalism in India*. Essays by A. Rudra, D. Thorner, U. Patnaik and others. Lahore: Vanguard Books Limited.

Bagchi, A. K. (1981). 'Daniel Thorner's India', *Economic and Political Weekly*, vol. 16/13: 572–8.

Banaji, J. (2003). 'The Fictions of Free Labour: Contract, Coercion, and So-Called Unfree Labour', *Historical Materialism*, vol. 11/3: 69–95.

(2010). *Theory as History: Essays on Modes of Production and Exploitation*. Leiden/Boston: Brill Academic Publishers.

Bernstein, H. (1996). 'Agrarian Questions Then and Now' *Journal of Peasant Studies*, vol. 24/1: 22–59.

(2006). 'Is There an Agrarian Question in the 21st Century?', *Canadian Journal of Development Studies*, vol. 27/4: 449–60.

(2008). 'Agrarian Change in a Globalising World: (Final) Farewells to the Peasantry?' Paper presented at the Journal of Agrarian Change Workshop, SOAS, 1–2 May.

Bhaduri, A. (1973). 'Agricultural Backwardness under Semi-Feudalism', *The Economic Journal*, vol. 83/329: 120–37.

Bhatt, E. R. (2015). *Anuhandh: Building Hundred-Mile Communities*. Ahmedabad: Navajivan Trust.

Bhukuth, A., J. Ballet and I. Guérin (2007). 'Social Capital and the Brokerage System: The Formation of Debt Bondage in South India', *Journal of Economic Studies*, vol. 34/4: 311–23.

Bhukuth, A., J. Ballet and N. Sirven (2016). 'Bonded Labour or What Else? A Case Study in Tamil Nadu, India', *Journal of International Development*. 21 October, DOI: 10.1002/jid.3261.

Bosale, A. 2016. 'The Agrarian Question in India', in Kumar, R. (ed.) (2016): 277–311.

Bosma, U. and K. Hofmeester (eds.) (2018). *The Lifework of a Labor Historian: Essays in Honor of Marcel van der Linden*. Leiden: Brill Academic Publishers.

Brass, T. & M. van der Linden (eds.) (1997). *Free and Unfree Labour: The Debate Continues*. Bern: Peter Lang.

Breman, J. (1974a) *Patronage and Exploitation: Changing Agrarian Relations in South Gujarat, India*. Berkeley: University of California Press, 1974/Delhi: Manohar, 1979.

(1974b) 'Mobilisation of Landless Labourers; Halpatis of South Gujarat', *Economic and Political Weekly*, vol. 9/12: 489–96.

(1978–9). 'Seasonal Migration and Cooperative Capitalism: Crushing of Cane and of Labour by Sugar Factories of Bardoli', *The Journal of Peasant Studies*, vol. 7:41–70 and 168–209.

(1985). *Of Peasants, Migrants and Paupers: Rural Labour Circulation and Capitalist Production in West India*. Delhi/Oxford: Oxford University Press/Clarendon Press.

(1989). *Taming the Coolie Beast: Plantation Society and the Colonial Order in Southeast Asia*. Delhi: Oxford University Press.

(1993). *Beyond Patronage and Exploitation*. Delhi: Oxford University Press.

(1994). *Wage Hunters and Gatherers: Search for Work in the Rural and Urban Economy of South Gujarat*. Delhi: Oxford University Press.

(1996). *Footloose Labour: Working in India's Informal Economy*. Cambridge: Cambridge University Press.

(1999a) 'The Study of Industrial Labour in Post-Colonial India – The Formal Sector: An Introductory Review', in Parry et. al. (1999): 1–41.

(1999b) 'The Study of Industrial Labour in Post-Colonial India – The Informal Sector: A Concluding Review', in Parry et. al. (1999): 407–31.

(2003). *The Labouring Poor in India: Patterns of Exploitation, Subordination and Exclusion*. New Delhi: Oxford University Press.

(2004). *The Making and Unmaking of an Industrial Working Class: Sliding Down the Labour Hierarchy in Ahmedabad, India*. New Delhi: Oxford University Press.

(2007a). *The Poverty Regime in Village India: Half a Century of Work and Life at the Bottom of the Rural Economy in South Gujarat*. New Delhi: Oxford University Press.

(2007b). *Labour Bondage in West India: From Past to Present*. New Delhi: Oxford University Press.

(2010a). 'Neo-Bondage: A Fieldwork-Based Account', *International Labor and Working-Class History*, No. 78, Fall: 48–62.

(2010b). 'India's Social Question in a State of Denial', *Economic and Political Weekly*, vol. 45/23: 42–6.

(2010/2012). *Outcast Labour in Asia: Circulation and Informalization of the Workforce at the Bottom of the Economy*. New Delhi: Oxford University Press (paperback).

(2013a). *At Work in the Informal Economy of India: A Perspective from the Bottom Up*. New Delhi, Oxford University Press.

(2013b). 'The Practice of Poor Relief in Rural South Gujarat', in Kannan & Breman (2013): 293–334.

(2014a). 'On Labour Bondage', *Contributions to Indian Sociology*, vol. 48/1: 133–41.

(2014b). 'The Gujarat Model of Growth, Development and Governance', *Economic and Political Weekly*, vol. 49/39: 27–9.

(2016). *On Pauperism in Past and Present*. New Delhi: Oxford University Press.

(2017). *The End of Social Welfarism?* Paper contributed to Herrenhaeuser Symposium *Workers of the World*. Hannover 28–30 June.

(2018). 'Driving Out the Undeserving Poor', in Bosma & Hofmeester (eds.) (2018): 136–55.

Breman, J., & A. Das (text), R. Agarwal (photographs) and B. Datta (design) (2000). *Down and Out: Labouring under Global Capitalism*. New Delhi: Oxford University Press/Amsterdam: Amsterdam University Press.

Breman, J., I. Guerin & A. Prakash (eds.) (2009). *India's Unfree Workforce: Of Bondage Old and New*. New Delhi: Oxford University Press.

Breman, J. & P. Kloos & E. A. Saith (eds.) (1997). *The Village in Asia Revisited.* New Delhi: Oxford University Press.

Breman, J., C. K. Lee, K. Harris & M. van der Linden (eds.) (2019). *The Social Question in the Twenty-First Century: A Global View.* Berkeley: University of California Press.

Breman, J. & S. Mundle (eds.) (1991). *Rural Transformation in Asia.* New Delhi: Oxford University Press.

Breman, J. & M. van der Linden (2014). 'Informalizing the Economy: The Return of the Social Question at the Global Level', *Development and Change,* vol. 45/5: 920–40.

Bush, M. L. (2000). *Servitude in Modern Times* (Themes in History). Cambridge: Polity Press/Blackwell Publishers.

Byres, T. J. (1991). 'The Agrarian Question and Differing Forms of Capitalist Agrarian Transition: An Essay with Reference to Asia', in Breman, J. & S. Mundle (eds.) (1991): 3–76.

Carswell, G. and G. de Neve (2013). 'From Field to Factory: Tracing Transformations in Bonded Labour in the Tiruppur Region, Tamil Nadu', *Economy and Society,* vol. 42/3: 430–54.

Chakravarti, U. (1985). 'Of Dasas and Karmakaras: Servile Labour in Ancient India', in Patnaik & Dingwaney (1985): 35–75.

Chandrasekhar, C. P. & J. Ghosh (2018). 'The Financialization of Finance? Demonetization and the Dubious Push to Cashlessness in India', Forum 2018, *Development and Change,* vol. 49/2: 420–36.

Chopra, P. N. (ed.) (1991). *The Collected Works of Sardar Vallabhbhai Patel,* vol. II, 1926–9. Delhi: Konark Publishers.

Chopra, P. N. and P. Chopra (eds.) (1996). *The Collected Works of Sardar Vallabhbhai Patel,* vol. VII (1 July 1937–31 December 1938) and vol. VIII (1 January 1939–31 March 1939). Delhi: Konark Publishers.

Corbridge, S., J. Harriss & C. Jeffrey (2013). *India Today: Economy, Politics and Society.* Cambridge: Polity Press.

Davis, M. (2006). *Planet of Slums.* London/New York: Verso.

Desai, I. P. (1964). *The Patterns of Migration and Occupation in a South Gujarat Village.* Poona: Deccan College Postgraduate and Research Institute.

(1969). *The Vedcchi Movement.* Manuscript. Surat: Centre for Regional Development Studies.

Desai, M. (1972). *Marun Jivan Vrutant* (My Life History). Ahmedabad: Navajivan Trust.

Desai, N. (1990). *Women's Work and Family Struggles in a Rural Community in South Gujurat.* Delhi: Indian Council of Social Science Research.

Deshingkar, P. & J. Farrington (eds.) (2009). *Circular Migration and Multilocational Livelihood Strategies in Rural India.* Delhi: Oxford University Press.

Dhanagare, D. N. (1983). 'Peasant Organizations and the Left Wing in India, 1925–47', in *Peasant Movements in India, 1920–1950.* Delhi: Oxford University Press: 119–54.

Drèze, J. & R. Khera (2009). 'The Battle for Employment Guarantee', *Frontline,* vol. 26/1, January.

Editorial note (2010). 'Jobless Growth', *Economic and Political Weekly,* vol. 45/39: 7–8.

Geertz, C. (1963). *Agricultural Involution: The Processes of Ecological Change in Indonesia*. Berkeley: University of California Press.

Ghosh, J., C.P. Chandrasekhar & P. Patnaik (2017). *Demonetization Decoded: A Critique of India's Currency Experiment*. Delhi: Routledge Focus.

Gooptu, N. & J. Parry (eds.) (2014). *Persistence of Poverty in India*. New Delhi: Orient Blackswan.

Guérin, I. (2013). 'Bonded Labour, Agrarian Change and Capitalism: Emerging Patterns in South India', *Journal of Agrarian Change*, vol. 13/3: 405–23.

Gupta, A. K. (1996). *The Agrarian Drama: The Leftists and the Rural Poor in India, 1934–1951*. Delhi: Manohar.

Gupte, D. B. and A. S. Charan (1978). *Report on Bonded Labour in Valsad District*. Manuscript. Surat: South Gujarat University.

Hardiman, D. (1977). 'The Crisis of the Lesser Patidars: Peasant Agitations in Kheda District, 1917–34', in Low (ed.) (1977): 47–75.

(1988). 'The Quit India Movement in Gujarat', in G. Pandey (ed.) (1988): 77–104.

(2003). *Gandhi in His Times and Ours*. Delhi: Permanent Black.

Harriss, J. (1992). 'Does the Depressor Still Work? Agrarian Structure and Development in India: A Review of Evidence and Argument', *The Journal of Peasant Studies*, vol. 19/2: 189–227.

Harvey, D. (2003). *The New Imperialism*. Oxford: Oxford University Press.

(2005). *A Brief History of Neoliberalism*. Oxford: Oxford University Press.

Hauser, W. (1994). *Sahajanand on Agricultural Labour and the Rural Poor*. Delhi: Manohar.

Hensman, R. (2014). 'The Gujarat Model of Development', *Economic and Political Weekly*, vol. 49/11, 15 March, 14.

Hirway, I., A. Shah & G. Shah (eds.) (2014). *Growth or Development: Which Way is Gujarat Going?* New Delhi: Oxford University Press.

Hirway, I. & U. B. Singh (2017). 'Migration and Development: Rural-to-Urban Temporary Migration to Gujarat: A Study in Migration and Development', in Reddy & Sarap (eds.) (2017): 269–98.

Jeyaranjan, J. (2017). 'The Life and Time of Migrant Workers in Chennai', in Reddy & Sarap (eds.) (2017): 299–326.

John, M. (2018). 'One Day in the Life of Johra Bibi: Unveiling the New Technologies of Employer's Power in the Delhi-NCR Domestic Service Industry'. Paper presented at the xiith International Conference on Labour History, V. V. Giri National Labour Institute, Noida, 26–28 March.

Kalathil, M. (1978). 'Industrial Relations in a Small Scale Industry', in Ramaswamy (1978): 89–107.

Kannan, K. P. (2014). *Interrogating Inclusive Growth: Poverty and Inequality in India*. New Delhi: Routledge.

Kannan, K. P. & J. Breman (eds.) (2013). *The Long Road to Social Security: Assessing the Implementation of National Social Security Initiatives for the Working Poor in India*. New Delhi: Oxford University Press.

Kannan, K. P. & V. Jain (2013). 'Historic Initiative, Limited by Design and Implementation: A National Overview of the Implementation of NREGA', in Kannan & Breman (2013): 33–80.

Kara, S. (2012). *Bonded Labour: Tackling the System of Slavery in South Asia*. New York: Columbia University Press.

Kompier, C. (2015). *The Strange and Persisting Case of Sumangali*. New Delhi: ILO paper, www.indianet.nl/pdf/TheStrangeAndPersistingCaseOfSumangali.pdf.

Kosambi, D. D. ([1956] 1976). *An Introduction to the Study of Indian History*. Bombay: Popular Prakashan.

Kothari, U. (1990). *Women's Work and Rural Transformation in India: A Study from Gujarat*. Ph.D. Thesis. University of Edinburgh.

Kumar, R. (ed.) (2016). *Contemporary Readings in Marxism; A Critical Introduction*. Delhi: Aakar Books.

Lal, R. B. (1977). *Bonded Labour in Gujarat (Does It Exist in Gujarat?)*. Manuscript. Ahmedabad: Tribal Research and Training Institute, Gujarat Vidyapith.

Lerche, J. (2007). 'A Global Alliance against Forced Labour? Unfree Labour, Neo-liberal Globalisation and the International Labour Organization', *Journal of Agrarian Change*, vol. 7/4: 425–55.

(2012). 'Labour Regulations and Labour Standards in India: Decent Work?', *Global Labour Journal*, vol. 3/1: 16–39.

(2013). 'The Agrarian Question in Neoliberal India: Agrarian Transition Bypassed? *Journal of Agrarian Change*, vol. 13/3: 382–404.

Lerche, J. and A. Shah (2018). 'Conjugated Oppression within Contemporary Capitalism: Class, Caste, Tribe and Agrarian Change in India', *The Journal of Peasant Studies*, vol. 45/5–6: 927–49.

Low, D. A.(ed.) (1977). *Congress and the Raj: Facets of the Indian Struggle, 1917–47*. London: Arnold Heinemann.

(ed.) (1988). *The Indian National Congress: Centenary Hindsights*. Delhi: Oxford University Press.

Mander, H. (ed.) (2014). *India Exclusion Report, 2013–2014*. New Delhi: Centre for Equity Studies/New Delhi: Books for Change.

(ed.) (2018). 'Sonia, Sadly', *The Indian Express*, 17 March, and a subsequent series of columns published on the paper's editorial page 20–26 March.

Marla, S. (1981). *Bonded Labour in India: National Survey on the Incidence of Bonded Labour*. New Delhi: Gandhi Peace Foundation. Biblia Impex.

Mehrotra, I.(2017). 'Subsidising Capitalism and Male Labour: The Scandal of Unfree Dalit Female Labour Relations', in Anandhi & Kapadia (2017): 246–75.

Mehta, S. (1984). *The Peasantry and Nationalism: A Study of the Bardoli Satyagraha*. Delhi: Manohar.

Mezzadri, A. (2017). *The Sweatshop Regime: Labouring Bodies, Exploitation and Garments Made in India*. Cambridge: Cambridge University Press.

Mohapatra, P. P. (2009). 'From Contract to Status? Or How Law Shaped Labour Relations in Colonial India, 1780–1880', in Breman, Guerin & Prakash (2009): 96–125.

Mundle, S. (1979). *Backwardness and Bondage: Agrarian Relations in South Bihar*. Delhi: Indian Institute of Public Administration.

Nayyar, D. (2013). *Catch Up: Developing Countries in the World Economy*. New Delhi: Oxford University Press.

Neale, W. C. (1962). *Economic Change in Rural India: Land Tenure and Reform in Uttar Pradesh, 1800–1955.* New Haven: Yale University Press.

Neve, G. de (2005). *The Everyday Politics of Labour: Working Lives in India's Informal Economy.* New Delhi: Social Science Press.

(2019) 'The Sociology of Labour in India', in Srivastava, Abraham & Arif.

Nieboer, H. J. (1910). *Slavery as an Industrial System: Ethnological Researches.* The Hague: M. Nijhoff.

Ornati, O. A. (1955). *Jobs and Workers in India.* Institute of International Industrial and Labour Relations. Ithaca: Cornell University Press.

Padovani, Fl. (ed.) (2016). *Development-Induced Displacement and Migration in India and China: A Comparative Look at the Burdens of Growth.* New York/ London: Lexington Books.

Pandey, G. (ed.) (1988). *The Indian Nation in 1942: Writings on the Quit India Movement.* Calcutta: K. B. Bagchi and Co.

Papola, T. S. & K. P. Kannan (2017). *Towards an India Wage Report.* ILO Asia– Pacific Working Paper Series. October.

Parry, J. P., J. Breman & K. Kapadia (eds.) (1999). *The Worlds of Indian Industrial Labour.* Contributions to Indian Sociology, Occasional Studies 9. New Delhi: Sage Publications.

Patel, R. D. (1981). *Class Structure and Agricultural Resources of a Village of Bardoli Taluka.* Unpublished M.A. thesis. Surat: South Gujarat University.

Patnaik, U. & M. Dingwaney (eds.) (1985). *Chains of Servitude, Bondage and Slavery in India.* Madras: Sangam Books.

Picherit, D. (2009). '"Workers, Trust Us!" Labour Middlemen and the Rise of the Lower Castes in Andhra Pradesh', in Breman, Guerin & Prakash (2009): 259–83.

(2018) 'Rural Youth and Circulating Labour in South India: The Tortuous Paths Towards Respect For Madigas', *Journal of Agrarian Change*, vol. 18/1: 178–95.

Ploeg, J. D. van der (2009). *The New Peasantries: Struggles for Autonomy and Sustainability in an Era of Empire and Globalization.* London, Taylor & Francis.

Pocock, D. (1973). *Mind, Body and Wealth: A Study of Belief and Practice in an Indian Village.* Oxford: Basil Blackwell.

Polanyi, K. (1944). *The Great Transformation: The Political and Economic Origins of Our Times.* Boston: Beacon Press.

Prakash, G. (1990). *Bonded Histories: Genealogies of Labor Servitude in Colonial India.* Cambridge/New York: Cambridge University Press.

Prasad-Aleyamma, M. (2017). 'The Cultural Politics of Wages: Ethnography of Construction Work in Kochi, India', *Contributions to Indian Sociology*, vol. 51/2: 1–31.

(2018). Cards and Carriers. Migration, Identification and Surveillance in Kerala, South India. Paper presented at the xiith International Conference on Labour History, V. V. Giri National Labour Institute, Noida, 26–28 March.

Prayas (2017). *Bitter Harvest: Study of Migrant Sugarcane Harvesters of South Gujarat.* Ahmedabad: Prayas Centre for Labour Research and Action.

Q&A (2011). 'Q&A: Saji Narayanan, President Bharatiya Mazdoor Sangh', *Business Standard*, 25 February.

Raje, G. (2005). *Remembering Displacement: Hunger and Displacement in Three Resettled Villages of South Gujarat*. Ph.D. Thesis. University of Warwick.

Ramaswamy, E. A. (1978). *Industrial Relations in India: A Sociological Perspective*. Delhi: Macmillan.

Reddy, D. N. & Sarap, K. (eds.) (2017). *Rural Labour Mobility in Times of Structural Change: Dynamics and Perspectives of Asian Economies*. Delhi: Springer.

Report of the Congress Agrarian Reforms Committee (1951). Delhi.

Sahu, B. K. (2017). 'Migration and Household Labour Use for Adopting Climatic Stress: A Study of Drought-Affected Areas in Odisha', in Reddy & Sarap (eds.) 2017: 237–68.

Sankaran, K. (2009). 'Bonded Labour and the Courts', in Breman, Guerin & Prakash (2009): 335–51.

Sarkar, A. (2018). *Trouble at the Mill: Factory Law and the Emergence of the Labour Question in Late Nineteenth-Century Bombay*. New Delhi: Oxford University Press.

Sarkar, T. (1985). 'Bondage in the Colonial Context', in Patnaik & Dingwaney (1985): 97–126.

Saxena, N. C. (2015). 'Socio-Economic Caste Census: Has It Ignored Too Many Poor Households?', *Economic and Political Weekly*, vol. 50/30, 25 July: 14–17.

Sen, P. (n. d.). *Challenges of Using Administrative Data for Statistical Purposes: India Country Paper*. Undated and Unpublished.

Sengupta, T. & G. Vijay (2017). 'The Uncivil and De-institutionalizing Labour Relations of Accumulation through Disuse: The Case of Brick Kiln Industry in Telangana', in Reddy & Sarap (eds.) (2017): 327–45.

Sethi, A. (2011/2012). *A Free Man*. Noida: Random House India (paperback edition).

Sethia, S. (2014). 'Bonded Labourers', in *India Exclusion Report 2013–14*: 203–20.

Shah, A. (2006). The Labour of Love: Seasonal Migration from Jharkhand to the Brick Kilns of Other States in India', *Contributions to Indian Sociology*, vol. 40/1: 91–118.

Shah, C. H. (1952). *Effects of World War II on Agriculture in India (With Special Reference to Gujarat)*. Ph.D. Thesis. University of Bombay.

Shah, G. (1974). 'Traditional Society and Political Mobilization: The Experience of Bardoli Satygraha (1920–1928)', *Contributions to Indian Sociology* (NS), no. 8: 89–107.

  (1978). *Agricultural Labourers: Are They Bonded?* Manuscript. Surat: Centre for Social Studies.

  (2014). 'Governance of Gujarat; Good Governance for Whom and for What?', in Hirway, Shah & Shah (eds.) (2014): 516–55.

Shah, A., J. Lerche, R. Axelby, D. Benbabaali, B. Donegan, J. Raj and V. Thakur (2018). *Ground Down by Growth: Tribe, Caste, Class and Inequality in Twenty-First Century India*. London: Pluto Press.

Shah, G. & D. C. Sah (2002). *Land Reforms in India,* vol. VIII, *Performances and Challenges in Gujarat and Maharashtra.* Delhi: Sage Publications.

Shah, M., R. Rao and P. S. Vijay Shankar (2007). 'Rural Credit in 20th Century India: Overview of History and Perspectives', *Economic and Political Weekly,* vol. 42/15, 14 April: 1351–64.

Shah, P. G. (1958). *The Dublas of Gujarat.* Delhi: Bharatiya Adimjati Seva Sangh.

(1959). 'A Serf Tribe', *Journal of the Gujarat Research Society,* vol. 21, no.1/81, January: 42–58.

Shankardass, R. D. (1988). 'Provincial Consolidation: 1928', in *Vallabhbhai Patel: Power and Organisation in Indian Politics.* Delhi: Orient Longman: 60–91.

Singh, J. & A. Mitra (2018). 'Counting Jobs in India': A Detailed Review of Labour Database', *Economic and Political Weekly,* vol. 53/10: 28–31.

Sivaswamy, K. G. (1948). 'Serf Labour among the Aboriginals', *Indian Journal of Social Work,* vol. 8/4.

Soto, H. de (1989). *The Other Path: The Invisible Revolution in the Third World.* New York: Harper & Row.

(2000). *The Mystery of Capital: Why Capitalism Triumphs in the West and Fails Everywhere Else.* London: Bantam Press.

Srivastava, R. S. (2009). 'Conceptualizing Continuity and Change in Emerging Forms of Labour Bondage', in Breman, Guerin & Prakash (2009): 129–46.

(2011a). 'Labour Migration, Inequality and Development Dynamics in India: An Introduction', *Indian Journal of Labour Economics,* vol. 54/3: 373–85.

(2011b). 'Migration in India: Recent Trends, Problems and Policy Issues', *The Indian Journal of Labour Economics* vol. 54/3: 411–40.

Srivastava, R. S. & S. K. Sasikumar (2003). *An Overview of Migration, Its Impact and Key Issues. Paper no. 2, Migration and Development and Pro-Poor Policy Choices in Asia.* London: DFID.

Srivastava, S., J. Abraham & Y. Arif (eds.) (2019). *Critical Themes in Indian Sociology.* New Delhi: Sage Publications.

Still, C. (2017). 'Dalit Women, Rape and the Revitalisation of Patriarchy', in Anandhi & Kapadia (2017): 189–217.

Thorner, A. & D. (1962). *Land and Labour in India.* London: Asia Publishing House.

Thorner, D. (1957). 'Employer-Labour Relations in Agriculture', *Indian Journal of Agricultural Economics,* vol. XII (April-June).

(1976). *The Agrarian Prospect in India: Five Lectures on Land Reform Delivered in 1955 at the Delhi School of Economics.* Bombay: Allied Publishers (2nd edition).

(1978). 'Capitalist Farming in India', *Studies in the Development of Capitalism in India:* 37–42.

Thorner, D. (ed. Alice Thorner) (1980). *The Shaping of Modern India.* New Delhi: Allied Publishers.

Tiwari, R. (2014). *The Pariah Problem; Caste, Religion and the Social in India.* New York: Columbia University Press.

Vishwanath, L. S. (1985). 'Gujarat Kisan Sabha, 1936–56', *Economic and Political Weekly,* vol. 20/28: 1197–1200.

Weber, M. (1922). 'Wirtschaft und Gesellschaft', in *Grundriss der Sozialoekono-mik*, III Abteiling, Tuebingen: Verlag J. C. B. Mohr (Paul Siebeck).

   (1984). *Die Lage der Landarbeiter im ostelbischem Deutschland.* [The Condition of Agricultural Labour in Eastern Germany 1892], republished and edited by. M. Riesebrodt. J. C. B. Mohr. Tuebingen: Halbb.2, (Paul Siebeck).

World Inequality Report 2018 (2018). Written and coordinated by Alvaredo, F., L. Chancel, Th. Piketty, E. Saez & G. Zucman. The World Inequality Lab, WID. World. Cambridge, MA: Harvard University Press.

Yagnik, I. *Atmakatha* (1956). Autobiography, translated from Gujarati, vol. III Mehmedabad, 1956 and vol. V Ahmedabad, 1971. (The English translation of the manuscript is deposited in the Nehru Memorial Museum and Library, New Delhi, where I accessed it. The book entitled *The Autobiography of Indulal Yagnik* came out under the auspices of Gujarat Vidyapith, translated and edited by I. K. Yagnik, D. N.Pathak, H. Spodek and G. Wood, and was published by Manohar Publishers, New Delhi, in 2011).

Index